THE
MIND MAP® BOOK

THE
MIND MAP® *BOOK*

by Tony Buzan
with Barry Buzan

BBC ACTIVE

® Mind Map is a registered trademark of the Buzan Organisation 1990

We dedicate this book to all those Warriors of the Mind fighting, in the Century of the Brain and Millennium of the Mind, for the expansion and freedom of Human Intelligence.

BBC Active, an imprint of Educational Publishers LLP, part of the Pearson Education Group
Edinburgh Gate, Harlow, Essex CM20 2JE, England

BBC logo © BBC 1996. BBC and BBC ACTIVE are trademarks of the British Broadcasting Corporation

First published in 1993
Revised and updated 2000, 2003
This edition published in 2006

ISBN-10: 1-4066-1279-0
ISBN-13 978-1-4066-1279-0

Designed by Sara Kidd
Artwork by Julian Bingley
Computer Mind Maps by Vanda North

Commissioning Editor: Emma Shackleton
Project Editors: Sarah Lavelle and Julia Charles

The Publisher's policy is to use paper manufactured from sustainable forests.

Printed and bound in (SWTC/01)

Photograph, page 2: *Natural Architecture Plate 1*

ACKNOWLEDGEMENTS

BBC Worldwide would like to thank the following for providing photographs and for permission to reproduce copyright material. While every effort has been made to trace and acknowledge all copyright holders, we would like to apologise should there have been any errors or omissions.

Bell Telephone Laboratories, New Jersey page 310 (*top*); **Bettmann Archive** pages 307 (*top right*) and 310 (*bottom*); **British Museum** page 309 (*top*); **Edison National Historic Site** page 304 (*bottom*); **Gemeentemusea van Amsterdam** page 308 (*top*); **Max–Planck–Institut**, Dortmund, Germany: Mario Markus and Benno Hess, pages 47 and 82, Mario Markus and Hans Schepers page 195; **Museu Picasso, Barcelona,** © DACS, 1993 page 41 (*top*); **NHPA** pages 19 (A. Bannister), 58 (J. Carmichael), 122, 167 (both, B. Jones and M. Shimlock), 187 and 222 (both, N. A. Callow); **Dr D. E. Nicholson/Sigma Chemical Co.** page 134; **Northwestern University Library,** Evanston, Illinois, USA – Special Collections Dept. page 307 (*bottom*); **Oxford Scientific Films** pages 62 (Okapia/K. G. Vock), 70 (Animals Animals/ T. Rock), 78 (H. Taylor), 95 (Animals Animals/ J. Lemker), 118 (T. Tilford), 142 (R. Jackman), 151 (P. Henry), 179 (T. Heathcote), 247 (S. Hauser) and 254 (J. Watts); **Royal Collection** © 1993 **Her Majesty the Queen** pages 41 (*bottom*) and 301 (*bottom*); **Royal Observatory Edinburgh and Anglo-Australian Telescope Board** (D. F. Malin) pages 2–3; **Science Museum, London** page 305; **Science Photo Library** pages 30 (K. Kent), 42 (J. C. Revy), 55 (A. Smith), 135, 155 (S. Moulds), 203 (NASA), 218 (J. Burgess), 234 (K. Kent), 263 (Aeroservice), 283 (J. Burgess) and 290 (M. Kage); **Dr M. Stanley/Boeing** page 171; **Syndics of Cambridge University Library** pages 303, 306 and 312; **Tate Gallery,** London page 311 (*top*); **UPI/Bettmann** pages 304 (*top*) and 311 (*bottom*); **Witt Library, Courtauld Institute of Art/Moravcké Galerie, Brno** pages 307 (*top left*).

For technical reasons all but six of the Mind Maps in this book have been copied (these are named in the following list as 'original'). All other artworks, except the sketches by Tony Buzan on page 73, have been redrawn by Julian Bingley. The Mind Maps, however, remain the copyright of their owners as listed below.

Sean Adam, page 143; **Tony Bigonia, Richard Kohler, Matthew Puk, John Ragsdale, Chris Slabach, Thomas Spinola, Thomas Sullivan, Lorita Williams,** page 171 (*top*); **Claudius Borer** (original), page 119; **Douglas Brand,** page 227; **Mark Brown,** page 106; **Barry Buzan,** page 226; **Tony Buzan** (sketches) page 73, Mind Maps pages 75 (original), 194 (original), 198 (original), 258, 259 (*top*); **Pan Collins,** page 146; **Lynn Collins** and **Caro Ayre,** page 207; **Kathy De Stefano,** page 120 (*top*); **Ulf Ekberg,** page 118 (*top*) (original); **Thomas Enskog,** page 215 (*top*); **Dr John Geesink,** page 120 (*bottom*); **Lorraine Gill,** pages 158–159; **Denny Harris,** page 150; **Brian Heller,** page 243; **IBM,** page 219; **Lana Israel,** page 242; **Jean-Luc Kastner,** page 271; **Raymond Keene OBE,** page 259; **Donna Kim and family,** page 202; **Charles La Fond,** page 230; **B. H. Lee,** page 270; **James Lee,** page 215 (*bottom*); **Jim Messerschmitt** and **Tony Messina,** pages 266 and 268; **Jonathan Montagu,** page 298; **Katarina Naiman,** page 214 (*bottom*); **Vanda North,** pages 75, 126 and 239; **Karen Schmidt,** page 214 (*top*); **Jan Pieter Six,** page 262; **Lars Soderberg,** page 231; **Norma Sweeney,** page 162; **Sheikh Talib** (*original*), page 299; **Nigel Temple,** page 263; **Tessa Tok-Hart,** page 186; **Lady Mary Tovey,** page 246; **Graham Wheeler,** page 227; **Benjamin Zander,** page 163.
The authors of the Mind Maps on pages 178 and 251 prefer not to be named.

The authors would also like to offer their special thanks to Dr Stanley and Boeing for allowing the reproduction of Dr Stanley in front of his Mind Map masterpiece! (See page 171.)

APPRECIATION

We would like to express once again our great appreciation and enormous thanks to: our parents, Gordon and Jean Buzan, for launching us on this incredible journey, and especially to Mum for the depth of caring and days of work she has contributed to the preparation of this manuscript; Vanda North, our External Editor, who put in as much work in helping us with *The Mind Map Book* as most authors do in writing their own creations; Lorraine Gill, the artist, for her profound insights into the importance and nature of seeing, the image, and the relationship of art to the brain, memory and creativity; Deborah Buzan for sustained encouragement and support over the many years of this project; Michael J. Gelb for his persistent and impassioned support of us, this book, and a Mind Mapping World; our friends who spent so much time both reading and helping us with the various drafts – Lynn and the late Paul Collins, who among many other things helped us realise that a quantum leap was a small one!; Judy Caldwell, who was able to criticise in the true sense of the word, firing us with enthusiasm as she did so; John Humble, whose support for the concept of Mind Mapping over the years has provided a constant emotional strength; Sean Adam, for his enormous personal support, his 10-year commitment to the project and his consistent friendly cajoling of Tony to 'get that book out'; George Hughes, the first to apply successfully the Mind Map Family Study Technique; Edward Hughes, who applied Radiant Thinking and Mind Mapping to 'ace' Cambridge University; Dr Andrew Strigner, for helping to keep the radiant mind radiating; Peter Russell, the *Brain Book* man, for his continuing support; Geraldine Schwartz, who has done so much to help nurture the concept; Phyllida Wilson for regularly finding her way through the most complex of mazes while wrestling with the typing of this book; Tony's office staff – Carol Coaker, Kate Morrell and Lesley Bias – for keeping all systems going throughout the creation of *The Mind Map Book*, and for their Mind Map contributions to the work; my entire BBC team: Nick Chapman, Chris Weller, Sheila Ableman, Deborah Taylor, Kelly Davis, Kate Gee, Sara Kidd, and Jennifer Fry; Martin and Alison Cursham, who provided the summer respite that helped initiate the work; Caro, Peter, Doris, Tanya and Julian Ayre for providing support, sustenance, and the beautiful home and grounds of Greenham Hall, where much of this was written; the Folley Family, for providing a home and work area of exquisite quality; Peter Barrett who was the first to develop a valid Mind Map computer software; and to all Mind Mappers, radiant thinkers and members of the Brain Club.

CONTENTS

ABOUT THE AUTHORS

Tony Buzan

Tony Buzan is the world's leading author, lecturer and adviser to governments, businesses, the professions, universities and schools on the brain, learning and thinking skills. He is the originator of Mind Maps®, the thinking tool popularly called 'the Swiss Army Knife of the Brain'! In addition, Tony is founder of the Brain Trust Charity and the Use Your Head/Brain Clubs, President of the Mind Sports Council and The Buzan Organisation, and the creator of Radiant Thinking and Mental Literacy.

Born in London in 1942, Tony Buzan graduated from the University of British Columbia in 1964, achieving double Honours in Psychology, English, Mathematics and the General Sciences. In the late 1960s and early 1970s he worked for the *Daily Telegraph*, and edited the *International Journal of MENSA*.

Among his 82 bestselling books, the classic *Use Your Head* and other members of **The Mind Set** have made him a top-selling international author. His books have been published in over 100 countries and translated into 30 languages. Waterstones bookshops, the *Express* newspaper group and their advisers recently selected *Use Your Head* as one of the 1,000 greatest books of the past millennium, and an essential title for the current millennium.

Tony Buzan has become an international media star featuring in, presenting and co-producing many satellite broadcasts, television, video and radio programmes, including *Use Your Head* (BBC TV), *Open Mind* (ITV), *The Enchanted Loom* (a one-hour feature documentary on the brain), and numerous talk shows. His two latest videos are the award-winning *MindPower* (BBC Video), which teaches the concepts of Mind Mapping for business use, and *Family Genius*, a video set incorporating the principles of **The Mind Set** aimed at improving the Brain Power of the whole family.

He is adviser to government departments and multinational organisations (including BP, IBM and Walt Disney), and is a regular lecturer to leading international businesses, universities and schools. At the time of going to press he was launching major educational initiatives with government organisations of England, Singapore, Mexico, Bahrain, Kuwait and Liechtenstein.

Tony Buzan is founder of The Memoriad, the World Memory Championships, founder of the World Speed Reading Championships, and co-founder of the Mind Sports Olympiad, the 'Mental Olympic Games', which by 2000 had attracted 25,000 entrants from 74 countries. He is also the holder of the world's highest 'creativity IQ', writing over 4,000 poems.

A prize-winning athlete, Tony Buzan is an adviser to international Olympic coaches and to the British Olympic Rowing Squad, as well as the British Olympic Chess Squads. He is an elected member of the International Council of Psychologists and a Fellow of the Institute of Training and Development. He is a member of the Institute of Directors and a Freeman of the City of London. Much of his work is devoted to helping those with learning disabilities. Adding to his list of honours, including the YPO Leadership Award, was his recognition by EDS with the Eagle Catcher Award – given to those who attempt the impossible and achieve it!

Barry Buzan

Barry Buzan is Professor of International Relations at the London School of Economics. Between 1995–2002 he was Professor of International Studies at the University of Westminster and a Research Director of the Centre for Peace and Conflict Research in the University of Copenhagen. He was also Chairman of the British International Studies Association 1988–90. He took his first degree at the University of British Columbia (1968), and his doctorate at the London School of Economics (1973). He has been extensively engaged in using and developing Mind Maps since 1970, and has been working with his brother on *The Mind Map Book* since 1981.

In his academic work, he specialises in the history and structure of the international system as a whole. He is therefore necessarily a generalist, with a broad knowledge of world history, politics, economics, science and sociology. He has written and lectured widely on the conceptual aspects of international security, on international relations theory, and on regional security in Europe, Southern Africa, South Asia, Southeast Asia, Northeast Asia, and the Middle East. He has been described by Lawrence Freedman as 'one of the most interesting theorists of contemporary international relations'.

Throughout his academic career Barry Buzan has used the Mind Map as a tool for grappling with massive and complex subjects, for preparing and giving academic and public presentations, and for planning and writing articles, papers and books. His previous publications include: *Seabed Politics* (1976); *People, States and Fear: The National Security Problem in International Relations* (1983, revised 2nd edition 1991); *South Asian Insecurity and the Great Powers* (1986, with Gowher Rizvi and others); *An Introduction to Strategic Studies: Military Technology and International Relations* (1987); *The Logic of Anarchy* (1993, with Charles Jones and Richard Little); *Security: A New Framework for Analysis* (1998, with Ole Waever and Jaap de Wilde); *Anticipating the Future* (1988, with Gerald Segal); *The Arms Dynamic in World Politics* (1998, with Eric Herring); *International Systems of World History: Remaking the Study of International Relations* (2000, with Richard Little) and *Regions and Powers: The Structure of International Security* (2003, with Ole Waever).

FOREWORD

Tony: In my second year at university, I strode purposefully into the library, and asked the librarian where I could find a book on my brain and how to use it. She immediately directed me to the medical section of the library!

When I explained that I did not wish to operate on my brain, but to *use* it, I was politely informed that there were no such books.

I left the library in astonishment.

Like others around me, I was going through the typical student's 'pilgrim's progress': the slow realisation that the volume of academic work is increasing and that the brain is starting to buckle under the strain of all the thinking, creativity, memory, problem-solving, analysis and writing required. Again, like others, I had begun to experience not only diminishing returns but accelerating *non-returns*. The more I took notes and studied, the less, paradoxically, I seemed to succeed!

The logical progression of either situation led me to catastrophe. If I cut down my studying, I would not absorb the necessary information and would consequently do progressively badly; if I were studying harder, making more notes, putting in more time, I was similarly spiralling into failure.

The answer, I assumed, must lie in the way I was using my intelligence and thinking skills – thus my visit to the library.

As I walked away from the library that day, I realised that the 'problem' of not being able to find the books I needed was actually a blessing in disguise. For if such books were not available, then I had happened upon virgin territory of the most staggering importance.

I began to study every area of knowledge I felt would help shed light on the basic questions:

- How do I learn how to learn?
- What is the nature of my thinking?
- What are the best techniques for memorising?
- What are the best techniques for creative thinking?
- What are the best current techniques for faster and efficient reading?
- What are the best current techniques for thinking in general?
- Is there a possibility of developing new thinking techniques or one master technique?

As a consequence of these questions, I began to study psychology, the neuro-physiology of the brain, semantics, neuro-linguistics, information theory, memory and mnemonic techniques, perception, creative thinking and the general sciences. Gradually I realised that the human brain functioned more effectively and efficiently if its various physical aspects and intellectual skills were allowed to work harmoniously with each other, rather than being divided.

The tiniest things produced the most significant and satisfying results. For example, simply combining the two cortical skills of words and colours transformed my note-taking. The simple addition of two colours to my notes improved my memory of those notes by more than 100 per cent, and perhaps even more importantly, made me begin to *enjoy* what I was doing.

Little by little, an overall architecture began to emerge, and as it did, I began to coach, as a hobby, pupils who had been described as 'learning disabled', 'hopeless', 'dyslexic', ESN, 'backward' and 'delinquent'. All these so-called 'failures' very rapidly changed into good students, a number of them rising to the top of their respective classes.

One young girl, Barbara, had been told that she had the lowest IQ her school had ever registered. Within a month of learning how to learn, she raised her IQ to 160, and eventually graduated as the top student from her college. Pat, a young American of extraordinary talent, who had been falsely categorised as learning disabled, subsequently said (after having shattered a number of creativity and memory tests), 'I wasn't learning *disabled*; I was learning DEPRIVED!'

By the early 1970s artificial intelligence had arrived and I could buy a megabyte computer and with that computer I could receive a 1,000-page operating manual. Yet, in our supposedly advanced stage of civilisation, we were all coming into the world with the most astoundingly complex biocomputer, *quadrillions* of times more powerful than any known computer, and where were *our* operating manuals?!

It was then that I decided to write a series of books based on my research: *An Encyclopedia of the Brain and Its Use.* I started in 1971, and as I did so the image on the horizon became ever clearer – it was the growing concept of Radiant Thinking and Mind Mapping.

In the early stages of its development, I envisaged Mind Mapping being used primarily for memory. However, after months of discussion, my brother Barry convinced me that creative thinking was an equally important application of this technique.

Barry had been working on the theory of Mind Mapping from a very different perspective, and his contribution enormously accelerated my development of the Mind Mapping process. His own story is an intriguing one, and is best told by himself.

Barry: I intersected with Tony's idea of Mind Maps in 1970, shortly after I had also settled in London. At that time, the idea was in its formative stages, only just beginning to take on an identity of its own, as distinct from mere keyword note-taking. It was just one part of Tony's broader agenda of learning methods and understanding of the human brain. As a sometime participant in Tony's work, I was on the fringes of this developmental process. My own serious engagement with the technique began when I started to apply it to the business of writing a doctoral thesis.

What attracted me about Mind Mapping was not the note-*taking* application that had captivated Tony, but the note-*making* one. I needed not only to organise a growing mass of research data, I needed also to clarify my thoughts on the convoluted political question of why peace movements almost always fail to achieve their stated objectives. My experience was that Mind Maps were a more powerful tool for thinking because they enabled me to sketch out the main ideas and to see quickly and clearly how they related to each other. They provided me with an exceptionally useful intermediate stage between the thinking process and actually committing words to paper.

I soon realised that the problem of bridging the gap between thinking and writing was a major deciding factor in success or failure for my fellow post-graduate students. Many failed to bridge this gap. They became more and more knowledgeable about their research subject but less and less able to pull all the details together in order to write about it.

Mind Mapping gave me a tremendous competitive advantage. It enabled me to assemble and refine my ideas without going through the time-consuming process of drafting and re-drafting. By separating thinking from writing, I was able to think more clearly and extensively. When it was time to start writing, I already had a clear structure and a firm sense of direction, and this made the writing easier, faster and more enjoyable. I completed my doctorate in under the prescribed three years, and also had time to write a chapter for another book, help to found, and then edit, a new quarterly journal of international relations, be associate editor of the student newspaper, take up motorcycling, and get married (doing a Mind Map with my wife-to-be to compose our wedding vows). Because of these experiences, my enthusiasm for the creative thinking side of the technique grew.

Mind Mapping remains a central element in my whole approach to academic work. It has made it possible for me to sustain an unusually high output of books, articles and conference papers. It has helped me to remain a generalist in a field where the weight of information forces most people to become specialists. I also credit it with enabling me to write clearly about theoretical matters whose complexity all too often inspires incomprehensible prose. Its impact on my career is perhaps best reflected in the surprise with which I am frequently greeted when first meeting people: 'You are much younger than I expected. How could you have written so much in such a short time?'

Having experienced the dramatic effect of Mind Mapping on my own life and work, I became a propagandist for the particular importance of creative thinking within the broader range of applications that Tony was developing.

At the end of the 1970s Tony decided that there should be a book about Mind Mapping, and we discussed how I might participate in this project. In the intervening decades we had developed very different styles. From his teaching and writing work, Tony had worked out a very wide range of applications, had begun to link the technique to brain theory, and had worked out many of the rules of form. As an academic writer, I had ploughed a much narrower furrow. My Mind Maps incorporated only a few elements of form, almost no colour or image, and evolved a rather different basic architecture. I used them almost exclusively for writing projects, though I increasingly, and with great benefit, took them up for lecturing and management tasks. I learned how to think deeply over long periods, using Mind Maps to structure and sustain large research projects.

There were several reasons why we wanted to collaborate on this book. One was the thought that by synthesising our two understandings, we would produce a better book. Another was that we shared a profound enthusiasm for Mind Maps, and wanted to make them more widely available to the world. A third reason was the frustration I had experienced when trying to teach some of my students the technology of Mind Mapping. Several unsuccessful attempts convinced me that Tony was right when he said that people needed to be taught not just a technique but also how to think. I wanted a book that I could give to people and say: 'This will teach you how to think and work as I do.'

The working process that ensued has been very long. It has taken the form of a sustained dialogue at regular but infrequent intervals in which each of us has tried to bring the other to a full understanding of his own ideas. About 80 per cent of the book is Tony's: all the brain theory, the linkage of creativity and memory, the rules, much of the technique, nearly all the stories, and all the linkage to other research. His also is the prose, for he did nearly all the drafting. My main contributions were in the structuring of the book, and the argument that the real power of Mind Maps is unleashed through the use of Basic Ordering Ideas. Beyond that, I played the role of critic, foil, nag, support and co-idea-generator.

It took a long time before we fully understood and appreciated each other's insights, but eventually we reached an almost complete consensus. Although slow, joint writing can sometimes produce a book that has much more range and depth than either author could have achieved alone. This is such a work.

Tony: As Barry has stated, we have practised what we preached, and preached what we practised, in that we have used the Mind Map itself to write *The Mind Map Book*. Over a period of 15 years, we have composed individual brainstorming Mind Maps, and then met and interlinked our two sets of ideas. After deep discussion, we have incubated and blended the next set of ideas, spent time observing natural phenomena, individually Mind Mapped our conceptions of the next stage, and once again met in order to compare and move on.

The Mind Map of the complete book generated the individual Mind Maps for the chapters, each Mind Map forming the basis for the text of that chapter. The process has given new meaning to the word 'brother', and especially to the word 'brotherhood'. Even as we were writing about it, we realised that we ourselves had created a group mind that contained all the elements of our individual minds as well as the explosively synergetic results of their meeting.

We hope that *The Mind Map Book* gives you the same thrill of discovery, excitement in exploration, and sheer delight in the creative generation of ideas and communication with the universe of another human being that we have ourselves experienced.

Foreword's Afterword

Mind Maps were formally introduced to the world in spring 1974, with the publication of *The Mind Map® Book*'s parent book – *Use Your Head*. A big birthday party at the Royal Albert Hall in London on 21 April 1995 commemorated the launch of *The Mind Map® Book*.

As each year has gone by, the number of people using Radiant Thinking and Mind Mapping has increased at a near logarithmic pace. It is now estimated that there are over 250 million Mind Mappers worldwide, and that they are practising the technique in every country on earth.

To build up support and communication among Radiant Thinkers and Mind Mappers, and to help charities that champion the concept of thinking as a necessary part of every school curriculum, a Mind Mappers' Society has been formed. Its goal is to introduce Radiant Thinking, Mind Mapping and Mental Literacy to 100 per cent of the earth's population by the year 2010.

Join us.

INTRODUCTION

The Mind Map® Book and How to Use It

Preview
- Purposes of *The Mind Map Book*
- Organisation of divisions
- Organisation of chapters
- Doing the exercises
- Levels of Mind Map knowledge
- Feedback
- *The Mind Map Book* and you

PURPOSES OF *THE MIND MAP BOOK*

This book is designed as an adventure to entice, delight, stimulate and challenge you. You will discover some astonishing facts about your brain and its function, and will take your first major steps on the path to freedom of mind.

The Mind Map Book has five main purposes:

1 To introduce you to a new concept in the development of thought – *Radiant Thinking*.

2 To introduce you to the revolutionary new tool that allows you to use Radiant Thinking to best advantage in all aspects of your life – The Mind Map.

3 To give you a profound intellectual freedom by demonstrating that you can control the nature and development of your thinking processes, and that your ability to think creatively is theoretically infinite.

4 To give you practical experience of Radiant Thinking, and in so doing to raise significantly the standard of many of your intellectual skills and intelligences.

5 To give you a sense of excitement and discovery as you explore this new universe.

ORGANISATION OF DIVISIONS
To accomplish these goals, the book has been arranged in six major divisions:

1 *Natural Architecture*

In this division you are introduced to the most up-to-date information about the human brain, its design, architecture and function. You are shown that many of the great thinkers of history (referred to in this book as the Great Brains) used skills that are available to everyone. You are then shown why, despite this, more than 95 per cent of people experience major problems in such areas as thinking, memory, concentration, motivation, organisation of ideas, decision-making and planning.

This division also introduces you to Radiant Thinking and Mind Mapping, demonstrating how each is a natural offshoot of the brain's fundamental structure, and how each can improve dramatically your mental performance.

2 *Foundations*

The Foundations division guides you through the practical applications of the skills of the left and right hemispheres of your brain, demonstrating how you can use each separately, and how you can then combine them in specific ways that multiply dramatically the advantages you get from using your brain. The result is the complete Mind Mapping technique (explained in chapter 9).

3 *Structure*

In this division you are given the complete set of laws and recommendations for using Radiant Thinking and Mind Mapping to best advantage. These laws and recommendations are designed to increase the precision and freedom of your thinking.

In conjunction with this advice on how best to do a Mind Map, you are given guidance and encouragement to develop your own personal style of Mind Mapping.

4 *Synthesis*

The Synthesis division gives you an overview of all the different intellectual tasks you can successfully tackle with Mind Maps. These include: making choices (decision-making), organising your own ideas (note-making), organising other people's ideas (note-taking), creative thinking and advanced brainstorming, improving memory and imagination, and creating a group mind.

5 *Uses*

The Uses division is your menu of Mind Map applications. This is itself subdivided into:
● Personal
● Family
● Educational
● Business and Professional
● The Future

These headings represent the areas in which Mind Maps are most frequently used. In each area you will learn a full range of specific and practical Mind Mapping skills. These are designed to give you a comprehensive tool kit for your intellectual life and work. Specific applications include self-analysis, problem-solving, memory, essay-writing, management and meetings. The division ends with the first-ever introduction of computer-Mind Maps and a glimpse of a mentally literate future.

6 *Addenda*

This division has been included as a back-up for all that has gone before, and also for your amusement and entertainment. Consequently you will find information, which is given on the Natural Architecture Plates and Notes by the Great Brains, presented as straight data or, alternatively, as quizzes.

6.1 Notes by the Great Brains Quiz

This is a collection of 17 notes from 14 of the world's great thinkers selected from the fields of art, science, politics and literature. To make this a quiz,

OPPOSITE: *Natural Architecture Plate 2*

examine each note and attempt to identify its creator. The highest score on this quiz at the time of going to press was seven out of 17 – see if you can beat it! (For the answers to this quiz, see page 315.)

6.2 Natural Architecture Plates

Throughout the book you will find images taken from the animal, vegetable, mineral and conceptual worlds which demonstrate nature's architecture. These have also been arranged as an optional quiz. The object is to see if you can recognise nature's maps, each of which mirrors in its own special way the structure and thinking patterns of your brain. At the time of going to press, the highest score in this quiz was 15 out of a possible 31. (See page 313 for the answers.)

6.3 Brain Foundation information

This section includes details of books, training courses, video tapes and audio tapes, as well as the Mind Map Kit, the Universal Personal Organiser, and other Buzan products. You can also find out how to join the Brain Club, an international organisation designed to promote Mental Literacy and help you increase your mental, physical and spiritual awareness.

6.4 Bibliography

The Bibliography includes novels, popular science and more traditional scientific volumes on the brain. It also mentions a number of research papers, should you wish to go further into this endlessly fascinating subject. References to the bibliography are indicated by the following symbol: †

ORGANISATION OF CHAPTERS

1 *Chapter design*

Each chapter in *The Mind Map Book* contains the following main elements:
- a natural architecture plate shows an image from the natural world reflecting Mind Map and Radiant Thinking forms
- a preview of the chapter content
- a foreword introducing the main thrust of the chapter
- the chapter itself
- an onword, linking each chapter with the next.

2 *Boxed text*

Throughout *The Mind Map Book* you will find boxed areas in the text. These are the passages our students have repeatedly asked us to emphasise, as they have proved especially helpful in their learning.

3 *Research*

Throughout the book a † at the start of a paragraph indicates the beginning of an area of text in which research stories are provided to show why it is so important to follow the recommendations made throughout *The Mind Map Book*.

DOING THE EXERCISES

You will gain a new dimension of understanding and expertise if you do the exercises offered in *The Mind Map Book*. These take the form of quizzes, challenges and explorations. It is best to use a Mind Map pad (a blank white A3 pad), a set of 12 or more good-for-writing felt-tip pens, four or more bright and different-coloured highlighters, and a standard writing pen.

Mind Map kits are available by post (see pages 317–19).

With these materials, you will be able to make full use of your Radiant Thinking and Mind Mapping abilities, and will learn these new techniques easily, enjoyably and rapidly. Another advantage of following the recommended exercises is that your Mind Map pad becomes a visual record of your progress.

LEVELS OF MIND MAP KNOWLEDGE

Regardless of your level of knowledge concerning Mind Maps, your initial approach should be to browse through the book fairly rapidly, scanning its structure, observing those areas that will be of particular interest to you, and formulating your initial goals.

After this, your approach will differ according to your level of knowledge and experience:

1 *Beginners*

If you are a beginner, meaning that you have had either no experience with Mind Maps or only the slightest acquaintance, continue by reading *The Mind Map Book* as a study text. For a succinct summary of how to approach this, see

Chapter 14, page 139. (For a fuller explanation of the study technique, see *Use Your Head*, 1989 edition, Chapter 9.)

2 *Intermediate students*

If you are an intermediate, meaning that you have some knowledge of Mind Maps and have started some form of basic application, once again use the study technique. Try to perfect your technique in the light of this book, as well as pursuing your specific goals from the Mind Map Menu in Division 5 (Uses).

3 *Advanced students*

If you are advanced, meaning that you have considerable experience with Mind Maps, you are advised to concentrate more on the first three divisions, focusing on those areas where either you need more in-depth knowledge, or where the information is new to you. Then scan Division 5 (Uses) in order to reinforce, refine and supplement your existing skills.

Whatever your level, we encourage you to construct – either during or after reading *The Mind Map Book* – a Master Mind Map of the entire book.

FEEDBACK

The Mind Map Book will always be a work-in-progress. As such, we would enormously appreciate your feedback in many ways:

1 *Stories*

Any stories you have, or indeed stories of friends or acquaintances who have been able to use Mind Mapping in some notable or extraordinary way.

2 *Research*

If you are aware of any research, experiments or studies that support any of the points we make in this book, please do let us know, care of the Buzan Centres (see pages 317–19), with references that are as detailed as possible.

3 *Additions*

If there are any general additions, new chapters, or even new divisions that you would like to see incorporated in future editions, please let us know.

4 *Great Brains' Notes*

We need as many examples as we can get!

5 *Exercises/Games*

If you yourself have developed, or know of other people who have developed, exercises or games that can enhance the development of Mind Mapping techniques, please send us an outline, with full details of who to credit.

6 *Mind Maps*

Similarly, if you have superb examples of Mind Maps that could go into future editions, please send originals or coloured photocopies for our consideration.

7 *Bibliography*

If there are other books or research papers you think are useful, please send us publication details.

THE MIND MAP BOOK AND YOU

You who now read these words are doing so with your own unique personality and uniquely developed set of learning skills. You will therefore progress at a pace and rhythm particularly suited to you. In the light of this, it is important that you measure yourself primarily against yourself. The examples contained within *The Mind Map Book* should be used not as standards that must be attained but as beacons to guide you towards your goal.

When you have completed *The Mind Map Book* we recommend that you read it again rapidly. This 'after completion reading' will be like meeting an old friend again, and will give you a knowledgeable reader's enhanced perspective on each of the developing segments.

DIVISION 1
NATURAL
ARCHITECTURE

Whoever, wherever, you are, you are using – to read these words – the most beautiful, intricate, complex, mysterious and powerful object in the known universe: your brain.

We are, as an evolutionary model, a mere 45,000 years old, and we now stand on the brink of a revolution that will change the course of human development. For the first time in the three and a half million year history of human intelligence, that very intelligence has realised that it can understand, analyse and nurture *itself*. By applying itself to itself it can develop new ways of thinking that are far more flexible and powerful than the traditional modes of thought currently in use throughout the world.

Only during the last few centuries have we begun gathering information about the structure and workings of our brains. As excitement about what we find gains momentum, so does the number of papers and articles published on the subject. Indeed it has been calculated that in the last 10 years we have accumulated as much as 95 per cent of all information ever gathered about the human brain. Although still a very long way from a complete understanding (we are increasingly aware that what we do know is only a tiny fraction of what there is to be known), we now know enough to change, for ever, our view of others and ourselves.

What then are these discoveries and what are the answers to the following questions?

1 What are the component parts of our brains?

2 How do we process information?

3 What are the brain's main functions?

4 How are the skill centres distributed through the brain?

5 How do we learn and what do we recall most easily?

6 Is the human brain fundamentally a pattern-making and pattern-seeking device?

7 What are the techniques used by those extraordinary yet normal people who have been able to remember so much more than their peers?

8 Why are so many people in despair over the capacity and function of their brains?

9 What is the natural and appropriate way to think?

10 What is the natural and appropriate expression of human thought?

Division 1 answers all these questions, introducing you to the amazing natural architecture of your brain on both the cellular and macro levels, and to the major principles of brain function. You are shown how the Great Brains used skills that are available to everyone, and why it is that 95 per cent of people are dissatisfied with their mental functioning. In the final chapters of this division you are introduced to the new, brain-based mode of advanced thought: Radiant Thinking, and its natural expression, the Mind Map.

CHAPTER 1

THE AMAZING BRAIN

Preview
- Foreword
- Modern brain research
- The psychology of learning – remembering
- Gestalt – wholeness
- The brain as a Radiant Thinking Association Machine
- The development of the history of human intelligence
- Onword

FOREWORD

This chapter takes you on a Concorde-flight overview of the latest bio-physiological and neurophysiological research into that amazing bio-computer – the human brain.

You will discover how many brain cells you have, and how they interact in astoundingly complex and sophisticated ways. You will also discover the true nature of your brain's information-processing systems, and will learn about state-of-the-art research into the left and right hemispheres.

As you read about the nature and workings of your memory, and about your brain's other major functions, you will realise the extraordinary extent of its capacity and potential.

MODERN BRAIN RESEARCH

The brain cell

It was after studying the brain cell that Sir Charles Sherrington, considered by many to be the grandfather of neurophysiology, was moved to make the following poetic statement:

'The human brain is an enchanted loom where millions of flashing shuttles weave a dissolving pattern, always a meaningful pattern, though never an abiding one, a shifting harmony of sub-patterns. It is as if the Milky Way entered upon some cosmic dance.'

In each human brain there are an estimated one million, million (1 000 000 000 000) brain cells.

Each brain cell (neuron) contains a vast electrochemical complex and a powerful micro-data-processing and transmitting system that, despite its complexity, would fit on the head of a pin. Each of these brain cells looks like a superoctopus, with a central body and tens, hundreds, or thousands, of tentacles.

As we increase the level of magnification, we see that each tentacle is like the branch of a tree, radiating from the cell centre or nucleus. The branches of the brain cell are called dendrites (defined as 'natural tree-like markings or structures'). One particularly large and long branch, called the axon, is the main exit for information transmitted by that cell.

Each dendrite and axon may range from a millimetre to 1.5 metres in length, and all along and around its length are little mushroom-like protuberances called dendritic spines and synaptic buttons (see overleaf).

Moving further into this super-microscopic world, we find that each dendritic spine/synaptic button contains bundles of chemicals which are the major message-carriers in our human thinking process.

A dendritic spine/synaptic button from one brain cell will link with a synaptic button from another brain cell, and when an electrical impulse travels through the brain cell, chemicals will be transferred across the minute, liquid-filled space between the two. This space is called the synaptic gap.

The chemicals 'slot into' the receiving surface, creating an impulse that travels through the receiving brain cell from whence it is directed to an adjoining brain cell (see illustration detail, page 31).

Although simply illustrated, the cascade of biochemical information that surges across the synapse is awe-inspiring in its volume and complexity. It is, in microcosmic terms, a Niagara Falls.

A brain cell may receive incoming pulses from hundreds of thousands of connecting points every second. Acting like a vast telephone exchange, the cell

OVERLEAF: *A single one of the brain's million million (1 000 000 000 000) brain cells, demonstrating a radiant natural architecture.*

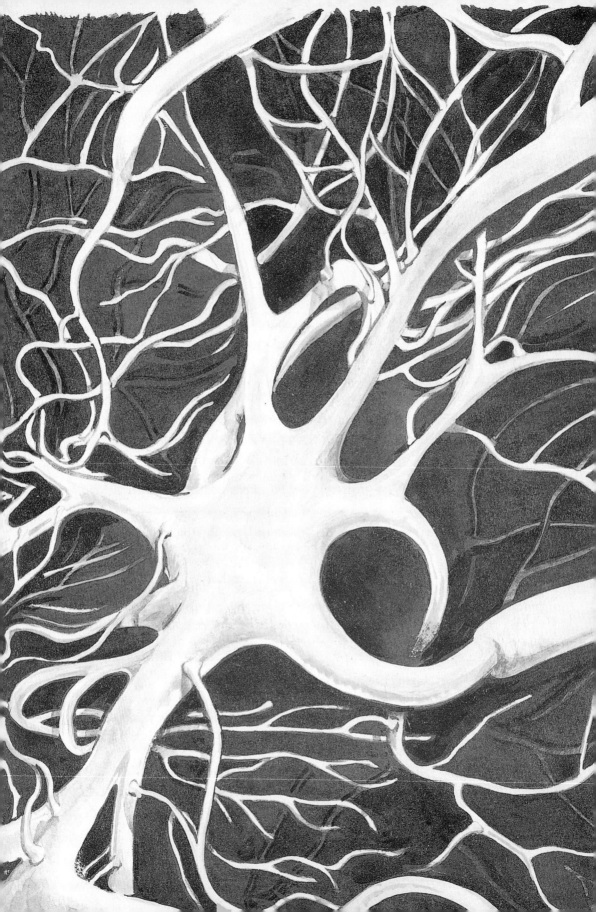

will instantaneously compute, microsecond by microsecond, the sum data of all incoming information and will redirect it along the appropriate path.

As a given message, or thought, or re-lived memory is passed from brain cell to brain cell, a biochemical electromagnetic pathway is established. Each of these neuronal pathways is known as a 'memory trace'. These memory traces or mental maps are one of the most exciting areas of modern brain research and have brought us to some startling conclusions.

Every time you have a thought, the biochemical/electromagnetic resistance along the pathway carrying that thought is reduced. It is like trying to clear a path through a forest. The first time is a struggle because you have to fight your way through the undergrowth. The second time you travel that way will be easier because of the clearing you did on your first journey. The more times you travel that path, the less resistance there will be, until, after many repetitions, you have a wide, smooth track which requires little or no clearing. A similar function occurs in your brain: the more you repeat patterns or maps of thought, the less resistance there is to them. Therefore, and of greater significance, *repetition in itself increases the probability of repetition*. In other words, the more times a 'mental event' happens, the more likely it is to happen again.

To return to the forest analogy, repeated use keeps the track clear, thus encouraging further 'traffic'. The more tracks and pathways you can create and use, the 'clearer', faster and more efficient your thinking will become. The boundaries of human intelligence can, in many ways, be related to the brain's ability to create and use such patterns.

In the winter of 1973, Professor Petr Kouzmich Anokhin of Moscow University made his last public statement on the results of his 60-year investigation into the nature of our brain cells. His conclusion, in his paper 'The Forming of Natural and Artificial Intelligence', was as follows:

'We can show that each of the ten billion neurons in the human brain has a possibility of connections of one with twenty-eight noughts after it! If a single neuron has this quality of potential, we can hardly imagine what the whole brain can do. What it means is that the total number of possible

OVERLEAF: *Natural Architecture Plate 3*

combinations/permutations in the brain, if written out, would be 1 followed by 10.5 million kilometres of noughts!'

'No human yet exists who can use all the potential of his brain. This is why we don't accept any pessimistic estimates of the limits of the human brain. It is unlimited!'

How is all this accomplished? By the biggest 'embrace' in the known universe – your brain cells embracing your brain cells. Each individual brain cell is capable of contacting and embracing as many as 10 000 *or more* proximate brain cells in the same instant.

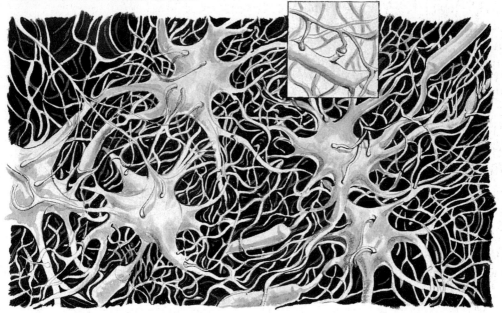

Five brain cells demonstrating part of the 'neuronal embraces' throughout the brain. This image is simplified a thousand times and represents a microscopic area of the brain.

It is in these shimmering and incessant embraces that the infinite patterns, the infinite Maps of your Mind, are created, nurtured and grown. Radiant Thinking reflects your internal structure and processes. The Mind Map is your external mirror of your own Radiant Thinking and allows you access into this vast thinking powerhouse.

R   L

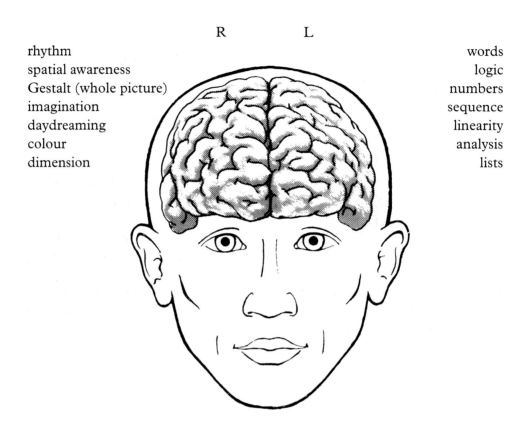

rhythm	words
spatial awareness	logic
Gestalt (whole picture)	numbers
imagination	sequence
daydreaming	linearity
colour	analysis
dimension	lists

The brain's cerebral cortex shown face-on. The cortical faculties shown make up the power-house of intellectual skills that can be used in noting and thinking.

Your brain's cerebral hemispheres

In the late 1960s, Professor Roger Sperry of California, who was subsequently awarded the Nobel Prize for his research, announced the results of his investigation into the brain's most highly evolved area, the cerebral cortex ('cortex' meaning 'outer shell' or bark).

Sperry's initial findings indicated that the two sides, or hemispheres, of the cortex tend to divide the major intellectual functions between them (illustration above). The right hemisphere appeared to be dominant in the following intellectual areas: rhythm, spatial awareness, gestalt (wholeness), imagination, daydreaming, colour and dimension. The left hemisphere appeared dominant in a different but equally powerful range of mental skills: words, logic, numbers, sequence, linearity, analysis and lists.

Subsequent investigations by Ornstein, Zaidel, Bloch et al, have confirmed these findings. In addition the following has been discovered:

> Although each hemisphere is *dominant* in certain activities, they are both basically skilled in *all* areas, and the mental skills identified by Roger Sperry are actually distributed *throughout* the cortex.

The current fashion for labelling people either left- or right-side dominant is therefore counter-productive. As Michael Bloch stated in his Tel/Syn paper: 'If we call ourselves "right brain" or "left brain" people, we are limiting our ability to develop new strategies.'

Saying 'I am bad at or do not possess mental skill X' is both an untruth and a misunderstanding. If one *is* weak in any skill area, the correct statement must be 'I have yet to develop mental skill X.' The only barrier to the expression and application of all our mental skills is our knowledge of how to access them.

The range of skills available to all of us include those previously attributed to either the left or right hemisphere:

1 Language
- Words
- Symbols

2 Number

3 Logic
- Sequence
- Listing
- Linearity
- Analysis
- Time
- Association

4 Rhythm

5 Colour

6 Imagery
- Daydreaming
- Visualisation

7 Spatial awareness
- Dimension
- Gestalt (whole picture)

Radiant Thinking and Mind Mapping take all these elements into account.

THE PSYCHOLOGY OF LEARNING – REMEMBERING

Research has shown that, during the learning process, the human brain primarily remembers the following:
- Items from the beginning of the learning period ('the primacy effect')
- Items from the end of the learning period ('the recency effect')
- Any items *associated* with things or patterns already stored, or linked to other aspects of what is being learned
- Any items which are *emphasised* as being in some way outstanding or unique
- Any items which appeal particularly strongly to any of the five senses
- Those items which are of particular interest to the person

This list of findings, taken together with the graph opposite, gives you information that is of critical importance in understanding the way your brain works.

Indeed it was this information (and not the 'left/right brain theory', as many have assumed) which gave rise to my development of Mind Mapping. In the 1960s, while lecturing at various universities on the psychology of learning and memory, I began to notice the enormous discrepancy between the theory I was teaching and what I was actually doing.

My lecture notes were traditional linear notes, providing the traditional amount of forgetting and the traditional amount of non-communication. I was using such notes as the basis of lectures on memory in which I was pointing out that two of the main factors in recall were *association* and *emphasis*. Yet these elements were singularly lacking in my own notes!

By constantly asking myself the question 'What, in my notes, will help me to associate and emphasise?' I arrived, in the late 1960s/early 1970s, at an embryonic concept of Mind Mapping. (For a fuller discussion of recall during learning, see *Use Your Head*, or for readers in the USA, *Use Both Sides of Your*

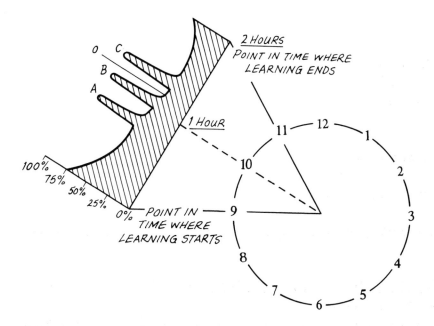

Graph predicting the high and low points of recall during a learning period. The reasons for the high points can be used to construct the basis for a new theory of learning (see page 34).

Brain.) My subsequent investigations into the nature of information processing, the structure and functioning of the brain cell, and research into the cerebral cortex, confirmed and buttressed the original theory, and Mind Maps were born.

GESTALT – WHOLENESS

Our brains tend to look for pattern and completion. For instance, most people, reading the words 'One, two, three...' will have to fight the impulse to add 'four'. Similarly, if someone says, 'I have the most *fascinating* story to tell you ... Oops! Sorry, I've just realised I'm not supposed to tell anyone', your mind will scream for completion! This in-built tendency of the brain to search for completion is satisfied by the structure of the Mind Map. The Mind Map allows an infinite sequence of associative 'probes' which comprehensively investigate any idea or question with which you are concerned.

THE BRAIN AS A RADIANT THINKING ASSOCIATION MACHINE

This amazing machine, your brain, has five major functions – receiving, holding, analysing, outputting and controlling – explained as follows:

1 *Receiving*

Anything taken in by *any* of your senses.

2 *Holding*

Your memory, including retention (the ability to store information) and recall (the ability to access that stored information).

3 *Analysing*

Pattern-recognition and information-processing.

4 *Outputting*

Any form of communication or creative act, including thinking.

5 *Controlling*

Referring to all mental and physical functions.

These five categories all reinforce each other. For example, it's easier to *receive* data if you are interested and motivated, and if the receiving process is compatible with brain functions. Having received the information efficiently, you will find it easier to *hold* and *analyse* it. Conversely, efficient *holding* and *analysis* will increase your ability to *receive* information.

Similarly, *analysis*, which involves a complex array of information-processing tasks, requires an ability to *hold* (retain and associate) that which has been *received*. The quality of the *analysis* will obviously be affected by your ability to *receive* and *hold* the information.

These three functions converge into the fourth – the *outputting* or expression by Mind Map, speech, gesture, etc. of that which has been *received*, *held* and *analysed*.

The fifth category, *controlling*, refers to the brain's general monitoring of all your mental and physical functions, including general health, attitude and environmental conditions. This category is particularly important because a healthy mind and a healthy body are essential if the other four functions of *receiving*, *holding*, *analysing* and *outputting* are to operate at their full potential.

THE DEVELOPMENT OF THE HISTORY OF HUMAN INTELLIGENCE

The history of human intelligence can be seen as the brain's search for ways of communicating effectively with itself.

When the first human made the first line, a revolution in human consciousness was precipitated, of which the Mind Map is the latest developmental stage. (For an in-depth discussion, see Lorraine Gill's paper, 'Line is man-made'.)

Once human beings realised that they could externalise their internal 'mental pictures', development was rapid. The first marks evolved into pictures, beginning with the early Australian Aboriginal cave paintings. As civilisations developed, pictures were condensed into symbols and thence into alphabets and scripts, such as Chinese characters or Egyptian hieroglyphics. With the development of Western thought and the spreading influence of the Roman Empire, the transition from picture to letter was complete. Subsequently, for 2000 years the not inconsiderable power of the letter held evolutionary sway over the momentarily derided image.

> The first humans to make marks were thus *literally* marking a gigantic leap in the evolution of intelligence, for they were externalising the first traces of the mental world. In so doing, they were fixing their thoughts in time and space, and also enabling their thoughts to span those same dimensions. Human intelligence could now communicate with itself across the infinite reaches of time and space.

Symbols, images and codes eventually developed into writing, and this major advance was the key to the emergence and development of large-scale civilisations such as those in Mesopotamia and China. These peoples enjoyed obvious advantages over those who had yet to develop writing, and therefore had no access to the wisdom and knowledge derived from great minds of the past.

Like a broad river being forced into a narrow sluice, the trend towards gathering information gradually accelerated over the centuries, giving rise to today's 'information explosion'. In recent times this 'explosion' has been partly caused by the assumption that writing is the only correct vehicle for the learning, analysis and dissemination of information.

If writing is indeed the best way of taking in, analysing and passing on information, why are so many people having problems in the fields of learning, thinking, creativity and memory? Why do they complain of basic inability, loss of self-confidence, diminishing interest, and reduced powers of concentration, memory and thinking?

Common responses to these problems include self-denigration, under-achievement, apathy and the acceptance of rigid and dogmatic rules, all of which further impede the natural functioning of the brain.

We have taken the word, the sentence, logic and number as the foundation stones of our civilisation, forcing our brains to use limiting modes of expression which we assume are the only correct ones.

Why have we done this? Because, in universal evolutionary terms, we are still only newborn babies. It is therefore understandable that we should have 'experimented ourselves' into the momentarily uncomfortable position which the next chapter describes, and which subsequent chapters resolve.

ONWORD

From the physiological and psychological evidence, we know that the brain contains vast power waiting to be unleashed. To find out more about the brain's true potential and how to utilise it, we need to look at those brains historically considered to be 'great'. In the next chapter we meet some great thinkers of the past and ask whether they did indeed use a fuller range of associative, outputting and Radiant Thinking capabilities.

THE GREAT BRAINS

Preview
- Foreword
- The Great Brains
- Using the full range of mental skills
- Onword

FOREWORD

Those considered to be 'Great Brains' in the fields of art, science, politics, literature, the military, business and education have all used notes to help them think. In the light of information revealed in Chapter 1 about the workings of the brain, Chapter 2 examines the degree to which some great figures in history have utilised their vast thinking power. This is your chance to analyse and copy!

THE GREAT BRAINS

For those of you who have been criticised for making 'messy notes' or 'doodling', what follows will provide consolation and vindication!

During my lectures over the past 25 years I have frequently displayed the notes of an unidentified thinker generally recognised as 'great'. I have then invited course participants to identify the originator of the notes. In every group, the participants have mentioned – usually guessing wrongly – the names of da Vinci, Einstein, Picasso, Darwin, and at least one other major musician, scientist or politician.

This experiment shows that we *assume* that people like da Vinci and Einstein must have achieved their greatness by using a wider range of mental skills than their peers. The examples that follow support this assumption, providing evidence that the Great Brains did indeed use more of their natural ability, and that – unlike their more linear-thinking contemporaries – they were intuitively beginning to use the principles of Radiant Thinking and Mind Mapping.

USING THE FULL RANGE OF MENTAL SKILLS

A quick way of judging the excellence of your own or any set of notes is to look at the list of mental skills on pages 33–4 and check how many of these skills are incorporated in the notes – the more the better.

The notes opposite, by Leonardo da Vinci, demonstrate the point. He used words, symbols, sequence, listing, linearity, analysis, association, visual rhythm, numbers, imagery, dimension and gestalt – an example of a complete mind expressing itself completely. The notes, also opposite, by Picasso are similarly comprehensive. You can try to guess which notes have been written by da Vinci and which by Picasso as a limbering up exercise before trying the Notes by the Great Brains Quiz (pages 303–312) in the Addenda. See also page 18.

In Notes by the Great Brains Quiz (page 303), you will find more examples of great thinkers expressing themselves in ways that reflect the full range of their mental skills.

For a full discussion of the nature, manifestation and unleashing of genius, with life histories of many of those mentioned in *The Mind Map*, see *Buzan's Book of Genius and Mental World Records*.

ONWORD

These notes, the external expressions of the thought processes of Great Brains of the past, reveal that they did indeed use a greater proportion of their inherent mental power than those around them. We know that we could all utilise the same inherent mental power. So why are so many people now experiencing such massive problems with thinking, creativity, problem-solving, planning, memory, and dealing with change? The reasons are explored in the next chapter, 'Brains in Quandary'.

Great Brain Note 1

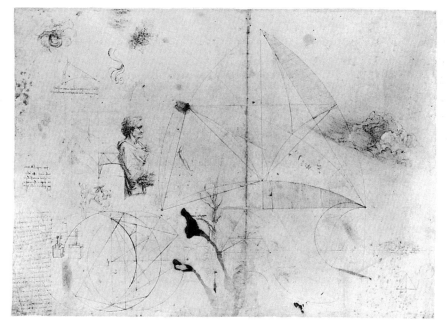

Great Brain Note 2

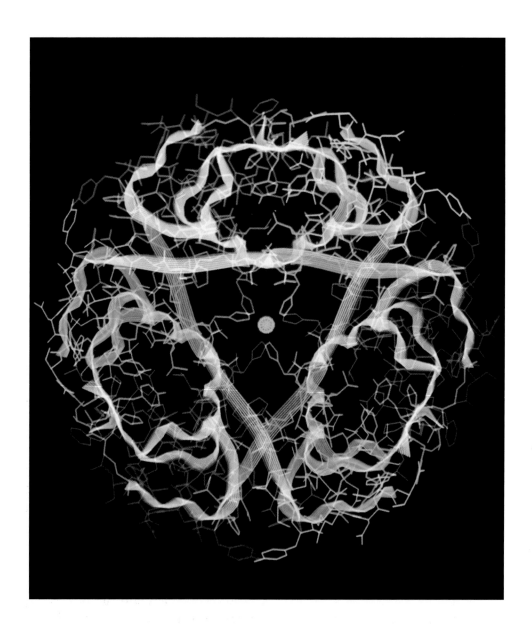

Natural Architecture Plate 4

CHAPTER 3

BRAINS IN QUANDARY

Preview
- Foreword
- Standard linear notes
- The major styles of standard note-making/taking
- The tools used for standard note-making/taking
- The disadvantages of standard notes
- The consequences for our brains
- The results of research on note-making/taking
- Onword

FOREWORD
This chapter reveals the inherent weaknesses of note-making/taking systems currently used all over the world. By analysing the effectiveness of various styles of note-making/taking, we can begin to evolve a system that works *with* our brains rather than *against* them.

STANDARD LINEAR NOTES
It is important, at the outset, to make a clear distinction between note-*making* and note-*taking*. Note-making means organising your own thoughts, often in a creative, innovative way. Note-taking means summarising someone else's thoughts, as expressed in a book, article or lecture.

For the past two decades, my colleagues and I have researched the note-making/taking styles of individuals at all levels in schools, universities and various professions. This research has been carried out in many different countries and has included observation, questioning and practical experiments.

One of the experiments consisted of asking each member of the group to prepare, within five minutes, an innovative, creative speech on the topic 'The

STYLE	PURPOSES	TOOLS
1	MEMORY COMMUNICATION & PRESENTATION	WORDS NUMBERS SEQUENCE
2	INNOVATION & CREATIVITY PLANNING ANALYSIS DECISION MAKING ETC	LINES LISTS LOGIC ANALYSIS ONE-COLOUR
3		

The three major note-taking styles used by 95 per cent of note-takers and note-makers in all schools and professions around the world, regardless of language or nationality. Can you see why they leave 'brains in quandary' (see pages 44–51)?

Brain, Innovation, Creativity and the Future'. They were allowed to use a wide variety of papers, coloured pens and other writing materials, and were asked to include the following purposes in their notes:

- Memory
- Communication and presentation
- Innovation and creativity
- Planning
- Analysis
- Decision-making
- Time management
- Problem-solving
- Humour
- Audience involvement

Despite being offered a wide range of materials, the majority chose standard lined paper and a single (usually black, blue or grey) pen. The results are intriguing.

THE MAJOR STYLES OF STANDARD NOTE-MAKING/TAKING

The three major styles used in the experiment are illustrated above.

1 The sentence/narrative style consists of simply writing out whatever is to be communicated in narrative form.

2 The list style involves noting down the ideas as they occur.

3 The outline numerical/alphabetical style consists of making notes in a hierarchical sequence consisting of major categories and sub-categories.

Many people combine various elements of these three major styles. However, there is also a fourth, and more rare style, which is often described as 'disorganised' or 'messy'. This fourth style, as we shall see, could be very much akin to Mind Mapping.

All over the world, the current standard systems of note-making/taking are identical. While Middle Eastern and Asian notes may *look* different from Western notes, they actually use exactly the same elements. Although languages like Chinese, Japanese and Arabic are written vertically or right-to-left, rather than left-to-right (see page 48), the presentation is still linear.

In every school, university and business we visited, the three major styles outlined above were used by *more than 95 per cent* of those tested.

THE TOOLS USED FOR STANDARD NOTE-MAKING/TAKING

In each of the three major styles described, the main tools used were:

1 **Linear patterning**
The notes were usually written in straight lines. Grammar, chronological sequence and hierarchical sequence were also used.

2 **Symbols**
These included letters, words and numbers.

3 **Analysis**
Analysis was used but its quality was adversely affected by the linear patterning,

reflecting too great an emphasis on the linear nature of presentation rather than content.

A quick look back at Chapter 1 ('Modern brain research', page 33) reminds us that symbols, linear patterning, words, numbers and analysis, the major elements of current standard note-making/taking, are only three of the many tools available to the cerebral cortex of the human brain. These standard notes show an almost complete absence of:

- Visual rhythm
- Visual pattern or just pattern
- Colour
- Image (Imagination)
- Visualisation
- Dimension
- Spatial awareness
- Gestalt (Wholeness)
- Association

As these missing elements are essential in overall brain function, and specifically in recall during learning, it is not surprising that most of those participating in our research found the whole business of taking notes frustrating. The words most commonly associated with note-making/taking were: 'boring', 'punishment', 'headaches', 'finger cramps', 'homework', 'exams', 'wasted time', 'failure', 'rigidity', 'depression', 'fear', 'study', 'learning'.

Furthermore, over 95 per cent of the notes were written in a single colour, a monotone (usually blue, black or grey). The word 'monotone' is the root of the word 'monotonous'. And what does a brain do when it is bored? It tunes out, turns off, and goes to sleep. So 95 per cent of the literate human population is making notes in a manner designed to bore themselves and others to distraction, and to send many of them into a state of unconsciousness.

And the method is *working*. We need only look at libraries in schools, universities, towns and cities around the world. What are half the people doing in those libraries? Sleeping! Our places of learning are becoming giant public bedrooms!

OPPOSITE: *Natural Architecture Plate 5*

سيداتي وسادتي، السلام عليكم وأصلاً بكم

إلى عالم الدفاع والأمن . ومنه هذا الأسبوع :

★ لماذا تررت كوريا الشمالية مساعدة منع انتشار الأسلحة

النووية ؟

★ وعملية بناء القوات الجوية في منطقة الخليج .

★ و النقاش الاستراتيجي الدائر في فرنسا حول مستقبل العلاقة

العسكرية مع حلف شمالي الأطلسي .

عالم الدفاع والأمن يأتيكم لمشاهد من القسم العربي

في هيئة الإذاعة البريطانية في لندن .

Arabic notes exemplifying the similarity of global note-taking styles, regardless of whether the direction is left-to-right, right-to-left, or even, as in Asian languages, vertical (see page 45).

This global 'sleeping sickness' in response to learning is due to the fact that for the last few centuries the vast majority of us have been making notes that use considerably *less* than half of the capacity of our cerebral cortex. This is due to the fact that the skills associated with our left and right hemispheres are not able to interact with each other in a way that produces an upward spiral of movement and growth. Instead we have saddled our brains with a note-making/taking system that encourages them to reject and forget! The combined disadvantages of these two factors take a heavy toll.

THE DISADVANTAGES OF STANDARD NOTES

There are four disadvantages of current standard note-making/taking systems:

1   They obscure the key words

Important ideas are conveyed by key words – those words, usually nouns or strong verbs, that bring back sprays of relevant associations whenever they are read or heard. In standard notes these key words often appear on different pages, obscured by the mass of less important words. These factors prevent the brain from making appropriate associations between the key concepts.

2   They make it difficult to remember

Monotonous (single colour) notes are visually boring. As such, they will be rejected and forgotten. In addition, standard notes often take the form of endless similar-looking lists. The sheer monotony of making such lists puts the brain in a semi-hypnotic trance, making it almost impossible to remember their content.

3   They waste time

Standard note-making/taking systems waste time at all stages:
- By encouraging unnecessary noting
- By requiring the reading of unnecessary notes
- By requiring the re-reading of unnecessary notes
- By requiring the searching for key words

4   **They fail to stimulate the brain creatively**

By its very nature, the linear presentation of standard notes prevents the brain from making associations, thus counteracting creativity and memory. In addition, especially when faced with list-style notes, the brain constantly has the sense that it has 'come to the end' or 'finished'. This false sense of completion acts almost like a mental narcotic, slowing and stifling our thought process.

THE CONSEQUENCES FOR OUR BRAINS

Repeated use of inefficient note-making/taking systems has a number of consequences for our brains:

- We lose our powers of concentration, as a result of the brain's understandable rebellion against mistreatment.
- We acquire the time-consuming habit of making notes on notes in an attempt to discover the ever more elusive essence of whatever we are studying.
- We experience loss of confidence in our mental abilities and in ourselves.
- We lose the love of learning so evident in young children and those who have been fortunate enough to learn how to learn.
- We suffer from boredom and frustration.
- The harder we work, the less we progress, because we are unwittingly working against ourselves.

> Our current note-making/taking systems produce ever diminishing returns. What we need is a system that produces *increasing* returns.

† Two stories are relevant at this point. The first concerns the case history of an autistic girl recorded in Springer and Deutch's 'Left Brain Right Brain' (1985). The authors report that superior artistic ability is often to be found in autistics who also have a severe language disability. They comment that 'At the age of three and a half, Nadia was producing lifelike drawings with considerable detail...' They suggest that these special abilities reflect the contribution of the right hemisphere, and later note that Nadia's drawing skills *diminished as therapy continued*.

Had Nadia been taught in a manner compatible with her brain's function, she would probably have continued to develop her already strong artistic skills *in addition to* developing verbal skills. Mind Maps would have been the appropriate tool.

The second story concerns a young girl in New York, who at the age of nine was an A student. By the time she was 10, she had become a B student; by the age of 11 a C student; and by the age of 12 a D student, verging on total failure. She, her teachers and her parents were all mystified, as she had been studying as hard, if not harder, every year, and was obviously intelligent.

Her parents arranged for me to meet her. After a long and sad conversation, she suddenly brightened up and said, 'There *is* one area in which I am doing better and better every year.'

'Which one?' I asked.

'My notes,' she replied.

Her answer hit me like a thunderbolt, for it solved the mystery. In order to do better at school, she had assumed that she must make more and better notes. 'Better', to her, meant 'more sentency', as close as possible to verbatim, and more traditionally 'neat'. As a result, she was innocently pouring more and more effort into the very activity that was making her misunderstand and forget what she was studying. This method was used deliberately by a Russian called Shereshevsky, who had a perfect memory, to help him to *forget*! As soon as she realised what she was doing, she was able to apply Mind Mapping and reverse the trend.

THE RESULTS OF RESEARCH ON NOTE-MAKING/TAKING

These findings are supported by many academic studies on note-making/taking, especially those by Dr Howe of Exeter University.

† Dr Howe's studies aimed to evaluate the effectiveness of different types of noting. Effectiveness was judged by how well students were able to talk from their notes, indicating a full and integrated understanding. They also had to be able to use the notes for review purposes, to provide accurate recall and considered responses in examination conditions where the notes were no longer available. These were the results, from worst to best:

1 Complete transcript notes given.

2 Complete transcript notes personally made.

3 Sentence summary notes given.

4 Sentence summary notes personally made.

5 Key word notes given. (These sometimes proved to be particularly poor because the person who received them was unable to make appropriate mental associations.)

6 Key word notes personally made.

> Howe's studies show that brevity, efficiency and active personal involvement are of crucial importance in successful noting.

ONWORD

As we have seen, current systems of note-making/taking utilise only a fraction of the brain's enormous learning potential. We also know that the Great Brains used a much greater proportion of the mental capacity that is available to all of us. Armed with this knowledge, we can move forward into the next chapter which introduces Radiant Thinking – a clearer, more natural and more efficient way of using our brains.

CHAPTER 4

RADIANT THINKING

FOREWORD

This chapter integrates the information from Chapters 1 to 3 and introduces you to Radiant Thinking, a major evolutionary step in the understanding, accessing and nurturing of the human brain.

INFORMATION – YOUR BRAIN'S PROCESSING SYSTEM

What happens in your brain when you taste a ripe pear, smell flowers, listen to music, watch a stream, touch a loved one, or simply reminisce?

The answer is both simple and amazingly complex.

Each bit of information entering your brain – every sensation, memory or thought (incorporating every word, number, code, food, fragrance, line, colour, image, beat, note and texture) can be represented as a central sphere from which radiate tens, hundreds, thousands, millions of hooks (see page 54).

Each hook represents an association, and each association has its own infinite array of links and connections. The number of associations you have already 'used' may be thought of as your memory, your database, or your library. As you read these words you may rest assured that contained within the mind that reads them is a data-processing system that dwarfs the combined analytical capacities and storage facilities of the world's most advanced computers (see page 56).

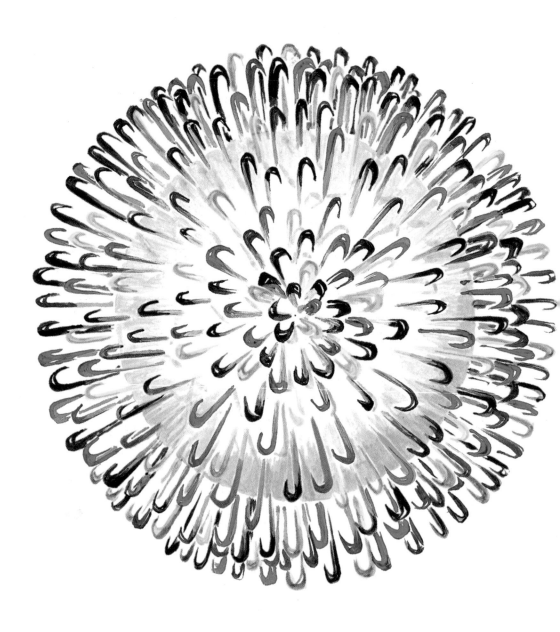

Graphic representation of a single 'unit' of information in the brain (see pages 53–4).

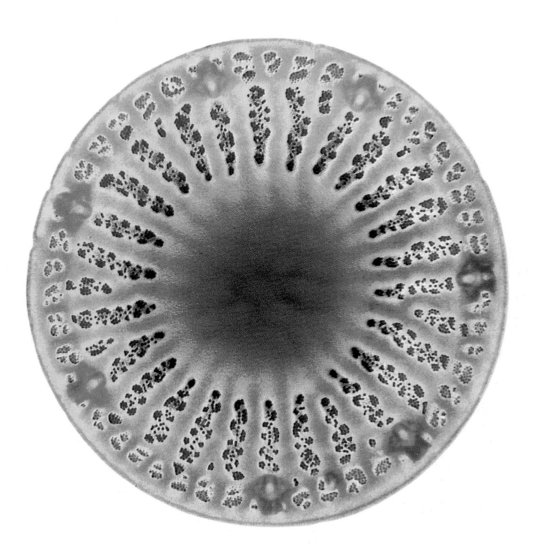

Natural Architecture Plate 6

As a result of using this many-hooked – multi-ordinate – information-processing and storage system, your brain already contains maps of information that would have the world's great cartographers gasping in disbelief, could they but see them.

> Your brain's thinking pattern may thus be seen as a gigantic, Branching Association Machine (BAM!) – a super bio-computer with lines of thought radiating from a virtually infinite number of data nodes. This structure reflects the neuronal networks that make up the physical architecture of your brain.

A quick calculation will reveal that your already existing database of items of information, and the associations radiating from them, consists of *multiple quadrillions* of data associations.

† Some people use this vast database as an excuse to stop learning, explaining that their brains are nearly 'full up', and that for this reason they are not going to learn anything new because they need to save the precious, remaining space for the 'really important stuff'. But there is no cause for concern because we now know, through the work of Dr Mark Rosenweig in Paris, that even if your brain were fed 10 items of data (each item being a simple word or image) every second for 100 years, it would still have used less than one-tenth of its storage capacity.

This astounding storage capacity is made possible by the almost unbelievable sophistication of the intricate pathways that constitute our metabolic processes. Even a single sub-section of one metabolic pathway is amazingly complex (see Chapter 1, 'Modern brain research', pages 29–31). And as Professor Anokhin has emphasised, even this phenomenal storage capacity is dwarfed by the brain's ability to make patterns using the data it already possesses (also see page 134).

However many items of data you have already stored, and however many associations you have already made, your potential to radiate new patterns and combinations of ideas exceeds it by *multiple* quadrillions!

> The more you learn/gather new data in an integrated, radiating, organised manner, the easier it is to learn more.

From this gigantic information processing ability and learning capacity derives the concept of Radiant Thinking of which the Mind Map is a manifestation.

Radiant Thinking (from 'to radiate', meaning 'to spread or move in directions, or from a given centre') refers to associative thought processes that proceed from or connect to a central point. The other meanings of 'radiant' are also relevant: 'shining brightly', 'the look of bright eyes beaming with joy and hope' and 'the focal point of a meteoric shower' – similar to the 'burst of thought'.

How do we gain access to this exciting new way of thinking? With the Mind Map, which is the external expression of Radiant Thinking. A Mind Map always radiates from a central image. Every word and image becomes in itself a subcentre of association, the whole proceeding in a potentially infinite chain of branching patterns away from or towards the common centre. Although the Mind Map is drawn on a two-dimensional page it represents a multi-dimensional reality, encompassing space, time and colour.

Before learning how to apply this powerful tool, it is essential to understand the operational principles of the brain that generates it. It is also essential to understand that Radiant Thinking is the *natural* and virtually automatic way in which all human brains have always functioned. In the evolutionary development of our thinking processes, we have used single beams of the radiation, rather than the full multi-dimensional powerhouse.

ONWORD

A Radiant Thinking brain should express itself in a radiant form which reflects the pattern of its own thought processes. As we shall see in the next chapter, 'The Way Ahead', the Mind Map is that form.

CHAPTER 5

THE WAY AHEAD

Preview
- Foreword
- The Mind Map – a definition
- What Mind Map users have said
- Onword

FOREWORD
This chapter defines the natural expression of Radiant Thinking: the Mind Map, the next evolution in human thought.

THE MIND MAP – A DEFINITION

The Mind Map is an expression of Radiant Thinking and is therefore a natural function of the human mind. It is a powerful graphic technique which provides a universal key to unlocking the potential of the brain. The Mind Map can be applied to every aspect of life where improved learning and clearer thinking will enhance human performance. The Mind Map has four essential characteristics:
a) The subject of attention is crystallised in a central image.
b) The main themes of the subject *radiate* from the central image as branches.
c) Branches comprise a key image or key word printed on an associated line. Topics of lesser importance are also represented as branches attached to higher level branches.
d) The branches form a connected nodal structure.

OPPOSITE: *Natural Architecture Plate 7*

Mind Maps may be enhanced and enriched with colour, pictures, codes and dimension to add interest, beauty and individuality. These in turn aid creativity, memory and specifically the recall of information.

Mind Maps help you to make a distinction between your mental storage *capacity*, which your Mind Map will help you demonstrate, and your mental storage *efficiency*, which your Mind Map will help you achieve. Storing data efficiently multiplies your capacity. It is like the difference between a well-packed or badly packed warehouse, or a library with or without an ordering system.

WHAT MIND MAP USERS HAVE SAID

Mind Maps have been described by those who have used them, from five-year-olds to those at all levels of business and education, in the following ways:

'a Neme Machine!' ('neme' meaning 'a thought as a gene')
'the device that helps you look after yourself'
'*the* mental training tool'
'a Mind-Mirror'
'a brain-caring device'
'my mental volcano'
'a device for accessing intelligence'
'a goal-centred thought network'
'a device for manifesting intelligence'
'the epitome of summarising devices – use a Mind Map, save a tree! Save a tree? Save a forest!'
'the embryonic manifestation of Super-Logical Thought'
'the most comprehensive creative thinking technique'
'a multi-dimensional mnemonic [memory-enhancing] technique'
'a consciously self-controlled electroencephalogram!'
'an externalisation of the brain's internal thought patterns/maps'
'the way, at last, in which I can enjoy using my brain!'
'the pathway(s!) to mental Freedom'
'a Mind Map is an externalisation of all aspects of cortical skills and intelligences, allowing the brain to gain access more fluidly, gracefully and rapidly to its vast store of abilities'
'to the Information and Space Age, what linear note-taking was to the Industrial Age'

Or, as one user put it when first using Mind Maps: 'It is as if I'd been driving all my life with a dirty windscreen and suddenly the Mind Map cleared it for me.'

> All these descriptions are appropriate and relevant. Taken together, they reveal the Mind Map as the next step in the progression from linear ('one-dimensional'), through lateral ('two-dimensional'), to Radiant or multi-dimensional thinking.

ONWORD

Armed with the knowledge you have gained about the workings and potential of your brain, you are now ready to travel through the intricate world of your cerebral cortex. This journey will lay the foundations for expressing and releasing your mental potential, and will lead you, through a series of brainstorming exercises, to the full art of Mind Mapping.

DIVISION 2
FOUNDATIONS

This division (Chapters 6 to 9) investigates the twin worlds of words and images, showing how you can unleash extraordinary mental energy through the use of powerful brainstorming and association techniques. These chapters take you from basic Radiant Thinking brainstorming, through mini-Mind Map brainstorming, to the Mind Map itself.

CHAPTER 6

BRAINSTORMING WORDS

Preview
- Foreword
- Mini-Mind Map word exercise
- Implications
- Applications
- Onword

OPPOSITE: *Natural Architecture Plate 8*

The 'Happiness' exercise (see pages 64–6).

FOREWORD

This chapter, 'Brainstorming Words', explores in depth your brain's Radiant Thinking information-processing system. Through the brainstorming exercises, you will discover the vast potential of your associative machinery as well as gaining an insight into your own and other people's uniqueness as individuals.

You will be introduced to a new brainstorming technique and some interesting research findings. In particular, you will gain a deeper understanding of communication and how we can avoid misunderstanding each other.

MINI-MIND MAP WORD EXERCISE

The Mini-Mind Map is the embryonic form of a Mind Map. 'Mini' though this Mind Map is, its implications are gigantic.

To do the following exercises, you will need pens and a Mind Map notepad (see page 317), the image above or several large sheets of blank paper.

Doing the exercises

Fill in quickly, with printed single key words on the lines, and without pausing to choose, the first ten associations that radiate from the centre when you think of the concept 'happiness'. It is important to put down the *first* words that come into your mind, no matter how ridiculous they may seem. This exercise is not a test and should take you no more than 1 minute.

If possible, ask two or three other people to do the exercise at the same time. Do not discuss your associations while doing the exercise.

Analysing the results

Your aim is to find those words which are common to all members of the group. (In this instance 'common' means *exactly* the same word – 'sun', for example, is not the same as 'sunshine'.)

Before counting up the results, you should each predict, individually and privately, how many words will be common to *all* members of the group; how many words common to all but one member; and how many words will have been chosen by only one person.

When you have finished the exercise and made your estimates, compare the words you have noted with those of your friends or associates. Then check and discuss the number of common words. (If you are doing the exercise on your own, simply compare your set of associations with the author's, below.)

Each person in turn can read out his/her list of words while the others write them down, underlining any words that are identical and identifying by colour or code who chose which words (see page 67).

Most people predict that there will be many words common to the whole group, with only a few words unique to any individual. Yet, after thousands of trials, we have found that for there to be even *one* word common to all members of a group of four is a rarity.

When this 'common' word is itself made the centre of the next mini-Mind Map, and the same four people are asked to repeat the exercise on the 'common' word, the same result is observed, showing that even the commonality is rooted in fundamental difference!

The more people there are in the group, the less chance there is of any one word being common to all members of the group (see graph, overleaf).

Sample from 'Happiness' exercise.

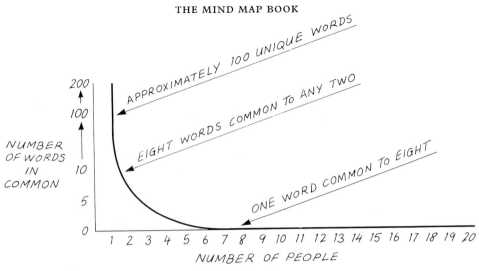

AS THE NUMBER OF PEOPLE INCREASES
THE NUMBER OF WORDS IN COMMON DECREASES

Graph illustrating the incredible uniqueness of each human being's thinking networks.

Results of similar exercises

The exercise you have just completed with the word 'happiness' produces similar results with any word.

For instance, a group of senior bank managers, all 40 to 55 years old and all from similar backgrounds, did the same exercise with the word 'run'. As we predicted, there were on average no words common to all four members of the group; occasionally one word common to three people; a few pairs of words common to two people; and most words unique to one individual.

The group complained that this was not fair because the word was not one of major interest to them. Had it been so, they predicted that their results would have been far more 'common'.

Accordingly they were given a second exercise, using 'money' instead of 'run'. To their amazement, their results were even *more* uncommon.

This finding contradicts a popular misconception: that the more you educate people, the more clone-like they will become. Radiant Thinking demonstrates that the opposite is true: *the more you educate people, the more unique their vast, and growing, networks of associations become.*

Opposite you will find the results from three groups of four people who recorded their associations with the word 'run'. Colour coding is used to indicate words common to more than one individual.

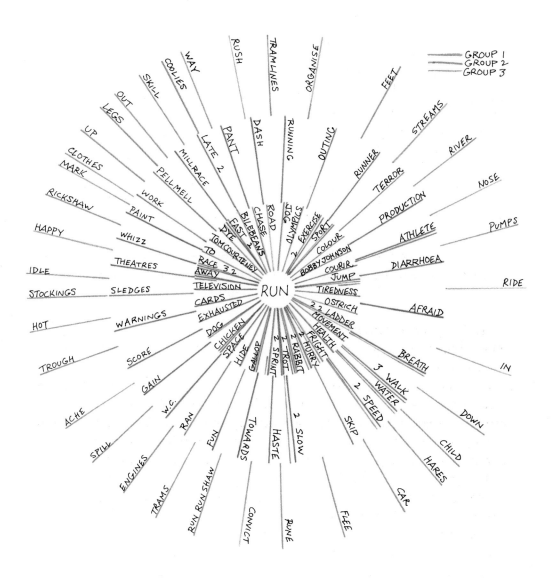

*The 'Multi-ordinate' run exercise by three groups of four people searching for commonality
(see page 66).*

IMPLICATIONS

The vast potential of your associative machinery

Consider the fact that every sight, sound, smell, taste or sensation you have ever received – either consciously or paraconsciously – is like a tiny radiant centre with millions of associations emanating from it.

Now think about trying to note down all these associations.

It would be impossible, because every time you noted something you would have a thought about what you had noted. That would be another association which you would be obliged to note down, and so on, *ad infinitum*. The human brain can make an infinite number of associations; and our creative thinking potential is similarly infinite.

In the average human brain there are multiple quadrillions of 'used' associations. This vast network may be considered not only as your memory or personal reference library, but also as your entire conscious and paraconscious self (see Tony Buzan, *Harnessing the ParaBrain*).

The uniqueness of each individual

The fact that individuals share so few common associations for a given word, image or idea means that we are all magically and eerily different from each other. In other words, every human being is far more individual and unique than has hitherto been surmised. You who are now reading this sentence contain, in your brain, trillions of associations shared by no one else, past, present or future.

If we find a unique mineral we call it: 'a gem', 'priceless', 'a jewel', 'invaluable', 'precious', 'a treasure', 'rare', 'beautiful', 'irreplaceable'.

In view of what research has revealed about us, we should start applying these terms to ourselves and our fellow human beings.

APPLICATIONS

Our extraordinary uniqueness has many benefits. For example, in any brainstorming or problem-solving situation, the greater the diversity of ideas the better. Each individual thus becomes an extremely valuable part of the process.

In the wider social context, so-called 'delinquent', 'abnormal' or 'eccentric' behaviour may often now be perceived in a new light as 'appropriate divergence from the norm, leading to increased creativity'. In this way many apparent social problems may actually turn out to be *solutions*.

The results of these exercises also highlight the dangers involved in viewing people as groups rather than individuals. Appreciating our uniqueness can help in resolving misunderstandings and conflicts, both personal and social.

Association exercises reveal the unlimited power of every human brain, both those of 'gifted' people and those previously considered to be 'average'. These exercises can therefore liberate billions of people from their self-imposed mental limitations. By simply performing the 'happiness' exercise described in this chapter, anyone can experience an instant explosion in mental power.

Take the example of an eight-year-old boy in a deprived area of London who was considered to be virtually a moron, both by his teacher and by himself. After he had completed the 'happiness' exercise I asked him whether he could find further associations for any of the ten words he had written down. He paused for a moment, wrote down two, then looked up with the beginnings of a gleam in his eyes and asked, 'Can I keep going?'

When I said, 'Yes,' he started tentatively, like someone going into the sea for the first time. Then, with an increasing beat, almost like a drum roll, words and associations started to pour from him. His entire physical posture was transformed into one of eagerness, energy and happiness, as he filled the page, literally shouting, 'I'm smart! I'm smart!' *He* was right. His *education* was lacking.

> Understanding the radiant nature of reality gives us an insight, not only into the nature of understanding but also the nature of mis-understanding, and consequently helps us to avoid many of the emotional and logical traps that bedevil our attempts to communicate.

In the context of this book, brainstorming is the first step towards the Mind Map. These exercises can strengthen and tone your associative abilities in readiness for the full development of Radiant Thinking.

ONWORD

If the Radiant Thinking ability of the brain can be applied to the 'left cortical skill' of words, can the same power be applied to the 'right cortical skill' of imagination and images? The next chapter explores this question.

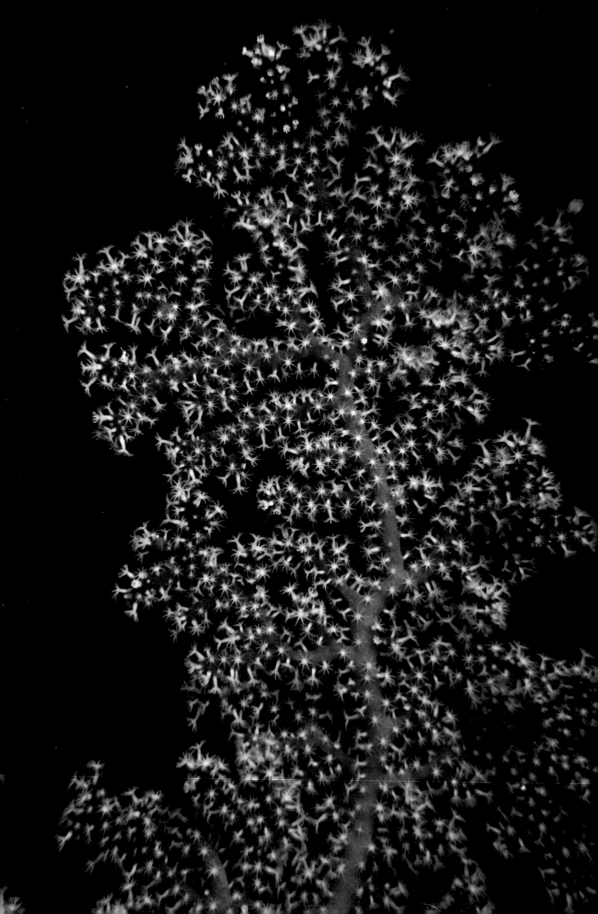

CHAPTER 7

BRAINSTORMING IMAGES

Preview
- Foreword
- The power of images
- Mini-Mind Map image exercise
- Onword

FOREWORD

This chapter discusses recent brain research which has astounded experts around the world. Together with the practical exercises described here, this knowledge will enable you to access the vast store of imaginative skills that lie dormant in 95 per cent of the population.

THE POWER OF IMAGES

† In 1970 *Scientific American* magazine published the results of a fascinating experiment carried out by Ralph Haber. Haber had shown his subjects a series of 2560 photographic slides, presenting one image every 10 seconds. It took approximately 7 hours for the subjects to view all the slides, but this viewing time was divided into separate sessions over a period of several days. An hour after the last slide had been shown, the subjects were tested for recognition.

Each person was shown 2560 pairs of slides, in which one slide came from the series they had seen, while the other came from a similar set which they had not seen. On average, the accuracy of their recognition was between 85 and 95 per cent.

Having confirmed the unrivalled accuracy of the brain as a receiving, holding

OPPOSITE: *Natural Architecture Plate 9*

and recalling mechanism, Haber carried out a second experiment to check the brain's ability to recognise at speed. In this experiment one slide was shown every second.

The results were identical, indicating that not only does the brain have an extraordinary capacity to imprint and recall, but that it can do so, with no loss of accuracy, at incredibly high speeds.

To test the brain even further, Haber conducted a third experiment in which slides were still presented at the rate of one per second but were all shown as mirror images. Again, the results were identical, indicating that even at high speeds the brain can juggle images in three-dimensional space with no loss of efficiency.

Haber commented: 'These experiments with visual stimuli suggest that RECOGNITION OF PICTURES IS ESSENTIALLY PERFECT. The results would probably have been the same if we had used 25 000 pictures instead of 2500.'

Another researcher, R. S. Nickerson, reported in the *Canadian Journal of Psychology* the results of experiments in which each subject was presented with 600 pictures at the rate of one per second. When tested for recognition immediately after the presentation, average accuracy was 98 per cent!

Like Haber, Nickerson expanded on his research, increasing the number of pictures from 600 to 10 000. Significantly, Nickerson emphasised that each of his 10 000 pictures were 'vivid' (i.e. striking, memorable images like the ones used in Mind Maps).

With the vivid pictures, subjects achieved a recognition accuracy rate of 99.9 per cent. Allowing for some degree of boredom and exhaustion, Nickerson and his colleagues estimated that had their subjects been shown a *million* pictures, rather than 10 000, they would have recognised 986 300 – an accuracy rate of 98.6 per cent.

In his article 'Learning 10 000 Pictures' in the *Quarterly Journal of Experimental Psychology*, Lionel Standing commented that 'the capacity of recognition memory for pictures is almost limitless!'

The reason why, to quote the old adage, pictures are 'worth a thousand words' is that they make use of a massive range of cortical skills: colour, form, line, dimension, texture, visual rhythm, and especially *imag*ination – a word taken from the Latin *imaginari*, literally meaning 'to picture mentally'.

Images are therefore often more evocative than words, more precise and potent in triggering a wide range of associations, thereby enhancing creative thinking and memory. This shows how ludicrous it is that over 95 per cent of note-taking/making is done without the benefit of images.

The reason for this rejection of the image is partly our modern over-emphasis on the word as the primary vehicle of information. However it may also be due to many people's (mistaken) belief that they are incapable of creating images.

Over the last 30 years we and others, including the artists Dr Betty Edwards and Lorraine Gill, have surveyed opinion in this area. In these experiments as many as 25 per cent of subjects said they had *no* visualisation capability, and more than 90 per cent believed they had a genetic inability to draw or paint in *any* way. Further research has shown that anyone with a 'normal' brain (i.e. not genetically or physically damaged) can learn to draw to good art school level (see below).

LEFT: *Best artistic effort of dominantly right-handed author using right hand.*
RIGHT: *Best artistic effort of author two hours later, after training, using left hand.*

The reason why so many people assume that they are incapable of creating images is that, instead of understanding that the brain always succeeds through continued experimentation, they mistake initial failure for fundamental incapacity and as its true measure of their talent. They therefore leave to wither and die a mental skill which could have flourished naturally.

† In his book *Ghosts in the Mind's Machine*, S. M. Kosslyn states that 'in most of our imagery experiments people definitely improve with practice'.

Mind Mapping reawakens this exceptional visualising capacity. Where the brain develops its ability to image, so it develops its thinking capacity, its perceptual abilities, its memory, its creativity, and its confidence.

Two widespread and damaging beliefs have led to the modern rejection of our visualising skills:

1
That images and colours are somehow primitive, childish, immature and irrelevant.

2
That the power to create and reproduce images is a god-given talent dispensed to a tiny minority. (It is in fact a god-given talent bestowed on everyone!)

With a more complete understanding of the human brain, we are beginning to realise that a new balance must be established between the skills of the image and those of the word. In the computer industry this is reflected in the increasing development of machines that allow us to link and manipulate words and images together. On the personal level it has given rise to the Mind Map.

MINI-MIND MAP IMAGE EXERCISE

The exercise recommended for people wishing to build up their visual 'mental musculature' is identical to the 'happiness' exercise described in the previous chapter, except that an image is placed in the centre, and on each of the ten branches surrounding the image, the first ten 'image associations' are drawn.

In an exercise like this, it is essential for people to overcome their inhibitions about drawing 'bad' images. No matter how 'bad' the initial images may seem, because of the trial and success (not error) nature of the human brain they will simply form the first experimental stage from which there will be continued and inevitable improvement.

Example by Vanda North of Mini-Mind Map image exercise (see pages 74–77).

A good, and recommended, central image to begin with is 'home' because it provides plenty of opportunities for easy associative image development.

Aims of the exercise

The aims of this visual association exercise are:

1 To unleash the enormous power of the visual cortex.

2 To enhance the memory's storing and recalling capabilities through the use of images for emphasis and association.

3 To increase aesthetic pleasure – simple enjoyment of the images themselves.

4 To break down resistance to the use of images in learning.

5 To aid mental relaxation.

6 To begin to develop the extraordinary powers of visualisation and perception utilised by great artists/thinkers such as Leonardo da Vinci.

Image association in practice

Here is an entertaining and exhilarating example of how image association works in practice.

A number of adults were joined in a seminar by the five-year-old son of one of the participants. The little boy, Alexander, who was only able to write a few disjointed letters of the alphabet, valiantly and persistently insisted that he join in the exercise. Over the adult protestations, he was finally allowed to join in.

Alexander chose the human brain as his central image because he had heard it mentioned so many times during the preceding days. He then began to 'image aloud' in the following manner.

'Now, let's see, what does my brain do?... Ah yes, it asks questions!' So saying, he drew a rough image of a question mark and immediately continued: 'Now, what else does my brain do?... Ah yes, it has friends!' And so saying, he quickly drew a little image of two hands holding each other, and proceeded: 'What else does my brain do? . . .'

'Ah yes, it says "thank you"!' And so saying, he drew a tiny envelope and proceeded, with increasing joy and bouncing up and down in his seat with every realisation: 'What *else* does my brain do? . . .'

'Ah yes, it loves Mummy and Daddy!' And so saying, he drew a little heart, making his ten visual associations without a moment's hesitation, and with a whoop of excitement on completion. This was a brain working totally naturally – radiantly flowing, open and elegantly associative.

Doing the exercise
Armed with all this information about your inbuilt capacity for image association, proceed exactly as you did with the word association exercise, creating your own central image for the concept of 'home' (or using one similar to that on page 75) and adding the images that spring to mind.

ONWORD
Having completed these two brainstorming exercises using different cortical skills, you now need to integrate the two worlds of words and images. The next chapter continues the journey from basic brainstorming to Mind Mapping.

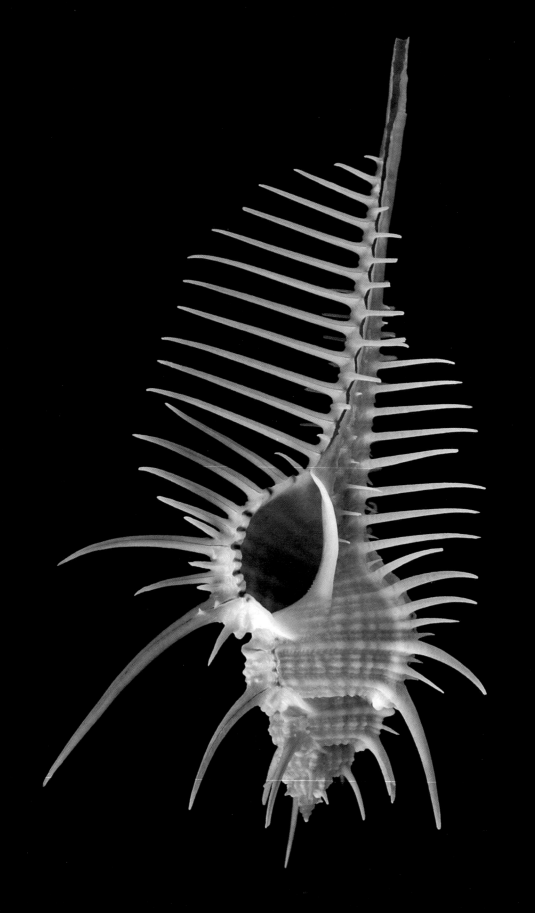

CHAPTER 8

FROM BRAINSTORMING TO MIND MAPPING

Preview
- Foreword
- Expanding your powers of association
- Exercise
- Onword

FOREWORD

This chapter continues the process begun in Chapter 6 with the 'happiness' exercise. Moving on from the Mini-Mind Map stage, this chapter takes you to the threshold of full Mind Mapping by showing you how to expand any Mini-Mind Map to any size you want.

EXPANDING YOUR POWERS OF ASSOCIATION

The next step is to extend the original 'happiness' exercise, following the guidelines already laid down.

In exactly the same way that your ten original words or images radiated from the central concept of 'happiness', each of these ten words can also radiate its *own* associations.

By 'free-associating' on each of the ten words or images, connecting the concepts that spring from them with lines and clearly printing single key words on lines which are the same length as the words, you can begin to build a verbal Mind Map 'tree' of associations like the one on page 80.

OPPOSITE: *Natural Architecture Plate 10*

When you look at the illustration you will notice that the original ten words have been written in larger letters, and that the lines on which they rest are thicker than the secondary ones. This serves to emphasise their significance as the ten key concepts which originally sprang to mind.

As you make connections between words in your Mini-Mind Map you will be increasing the sophistication and power of your memory.

† In 1985 Anderson and Parlmutter carried out an interesting experiment on memory. They presented the subjects with key central words and asked them to generate associations beginning with a given letter.

For example, one group was given the key word and letter sequence 'dog – c, bone – m'. A second group was given the sequence 'gambler – c, bone – m'. The subjects were then tested on the speed with which they generated the word 'meat'. The people in the first group were faster because the preceding word 'dog' activated the memory link of 'dog – bone – meat'. As a result of their observations, Anderson and Parlmutter suggest that:

> 'Memory works by an activation process, which *spreads from word to associated word via these links.*'

EXERCISE

Take a quick look at the illustration opposite. Then expand each of *your* ten original key words with further associations. Spend 1 minute on each key word (10 minutes in all).

When you have completed this exercise, you will be at the second, third and fourth branch levels on your Mini-Mind Map. At this point you will realise that you can go on for ever!

This exercise demonstrates that, using appropriate techniques, your brain is capable of exploring and manifesting its infinite creative ability.

ONWORD

Having exercised, integrated and expanded your powers of image and word association, you are now ready to express your full range of cortical and mental skills in the Mind Map itself.

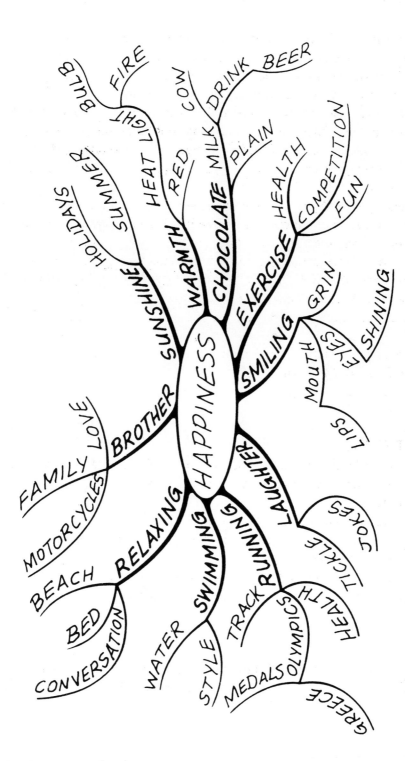

The extended original 'Happiness' exercise, leading to basic verbal Mind Mapping.

CHAPTER 9

MIND MAPPING

FOREWORD

This chapter introduces you to techniques for ordering and structuring your thinking; and the 'Journey through the mind of a Mind Mapper' enables you to see the process of Mind Mapping 'from the inside'. In addition, you will be presented with further evidence of your brain's infinite linking and creative capacity.

HARNESSING THE FULL RANGE OF YOUR CORTICAL SKILLS

The full power of the Mind Map is realised by having a central image instead of a central word, and by using images wherever appropriate rather than words. Combining the two cortical skills of words and images multiplies your intellectual power, especially when you create your own images.

† In 1989 W. M. Matlin described an experiment showing this. It was carried out by Bull and Whittrock 16 years earlier to discover effects of images on learning.

Bull and Whittrock asked 9 and 10-year-old children to learn words such as 'brain', 'magazine', 'trouble' and 'truth'. The children were divided into three groups. Group 1 read the word and its definition, wrote them down and then created their own images of both the word and its definition. The children in Group 2 did the same as those in Group 1, except that instead of creating their own images they traced a picture. The children in Group 3 simply wrote down the word and its definition over and over again.

A week later the children were tested for their recall of the words and their definitions. The children in Group 1, who had created their own images, did by far the best, while the children in Group 3, who had done no drawing, did worst.

This finding supports the argument that the Mind Map is a uniquely appropriate learning tool. It not only uses images, it *is* an image.

The Mind Map harnesses the full range of cortical skills – word, image, number, logic, rhythm, colour and spatial awareness – in a single, uniquely powerful technique. In so doing, it gives you the freedom to roam the infinite expanse of your brain.

INTRODUCTION TO HIERARCHIES AND CATEGORIES

In order to control and apply this vast mental power, you need to structure your thoughts and your Mind Map using hierarchy and categorisation. The first step is to identify your Basic Ordering Ideas (BOIs).

Basic Ordering Ideas are key concepts within which a host of other concepts can be organised. The term 'machines', for example, contains a vast array of categories, one of which is 'motor vehicles'. This in turn generates a large range, one of which is 'cars'. 'Cars' in turn contains a host of types, including Fords, which can themselves be subdivided into various models.

Seen from this perspective, 'machines' is a more powerful word than Fords because it encompasses and potentially structures a huge range of information. 'Machines' both suggests a set of categories and puts them in a hierarchical order subordinate to itself.

Likewise this hierarchy can be extended upwards to even higher levels of generalisation: 'artefacts', for example, has 'machines' as one of its subjects. These power words or Basic Ordering Ideas are the key to shaping and steering the creative process of association. To put it another way, they are the chapter headings you would use if you were writing a book on the subject.

† A classic study carried out by Bower, Clark, Lesgold and Wimzenz in 1969 demonstrated the importance of hierarchies as an aid to memory. In this experiment the subjects were divided into two groups. Each group was shown four cards, with 28 words written on each card.

The people in Group 1 were shown words organised hierarchically. For example, the word 'instrument' was placed at the top, and there were branches down to 'strings' and 'percussion'. On the next level there were branches from the word 'strings' down to 'violin', 'viola' and 'cello', while 'percussion' branched down to 'timpani', 'kettledrum', 'bongo' and so on.

The people in Group 2 were shown exactly the same words but arranged randomly. Both groups were then tested on their ability to recall the words. As you would now expect, those in Group 1, who had been shown words in hierarchies, did far better than those in Group 2, who had been shown random lists of the same words.

JOURNEY THROUGH THE MIND OF A MIND MAPPER, PART 1

This is your chance to 'get inside' the mind of an individual and explore his or her ideas on the nature of happiness. In the process, you will have an opportunity to apply all the Mind Mapping techniques you have learnt so far, as well as a few new ones.

The Mind Mapper starts with a central image that expresses the concept of happiness. This image needs to incorporate dimension and at least three colours.

The first Basic Ordering Idea that comes to the mind of our mapper is 'ACTIVITIES'. This is printed in large capital letters on a thick, curving line connecting to the centre, the line being the same length as the word.

A quick spray of associations – a sailing boat, a heart, a person running and the word 'sharing' – radiates from the idea of 'activities'.

Our Mind Mapper's brain now flashes to another BOI – 'PEOPLE'. This is placed on the left side of the Mind Map, again enlarged, again attached to the central image by a thick line. The multiple colours used to write the word reflect the multiple colours of the various races, including Martian!

Another spray of ideas – 'family', 'friends', 'performers', 'supporters', 'animals' radiates from this key word.

Some of these thoughts themselves generate ideas. To 'family' is added 'brother', 'mum', 'dad'. To 'performers' is added 'magicians', 'actors', 'clowns'. And 'supporters' generates 'doctors', 'nurses', 'teachers' and 'coaches'.

The next three thoughts are all BOIs – 'FOODS', 'ENVIRONMENTS' and 'SENSATIONS' – and as such are given appropriate status on the Mind Map.

The next two thoughts are triggered by the word 'environments'. Our host immediately adds a picture of mountains and the word 'rural'. At this point, let's pause to consider the implications of what has been done so far.

IMPLICATIONS

On considering the Mind Map our host has created, it is clear that any of the key words or images could be placed at the centre of a new Mind Map which would again radiate outwards.

Bearing this in mind, any Mind Map is potentially infinite. In view of its radiant nature, every key word or image added to a Mind Map itself adds the possibility of a new and greater range of associations, which themselves add the possibilities of new and greater ranges, and so on *ad infinitum*. This demonstrates yet again the infinite associative and creative nature of every normal human brain.

It also completely contradicts the widely held belief that the *generation* of ideas is much more difficult than the *editing and organising* of those ideas. If our Mind Mapping ability is infinite, the only difficulty is deciding when to stop; though the Mind Map can help with this decision as well.

By contrast, linear notes in the form of lists directly oppose the workings of the mind, in that they generate an idea and then deliberately cut it off from the ideas preceding and following it. By continually disassociating each idea from its context, they stunt and cauterise the natural thinking process.

Lists rein in the free-ranging movement of the brain, eventually reducing it to stasis and establishing narrow neural pathways of thought that increasingly reduce the probability of creativity and recall.

† The reason why lists do this is that they act in direct opposition to the associative nature of the brain. As an idea is set down it is 'finished with', divorced from the ideas which precede or follow it. This constant guillotining of new thoughts is one of the major factors behind the appalling international

statistics on the generation of creative ideas. In the Torrance tests, for example, where subjects are asked to think of as many uses (associations) for a given idea as possible, the average number – given as much time as the student wishes – is a paltry 26. This, in the face of evidence that had the student known about Radiant Thinking, he or she would have scored in the multiple millions before giving up through sheer exhaustion.

JOURNEY THROUGH THE MIND OF A MIND MAPPER, PART 2

Returning to our Mind Mapper, we find our host – momentarily affected by previous education – experiencing a mental block.

Due to lack of knowledge about our own minds, such mental blocks strike some people dumb for seconds, minutes, hours, years, sometimes even for life. However, once you have understood the infinite associative nature of your brain, you are in a position to help it help itself.

Harnessing the brain's tendency to function in gestalts or wholes, our host simply adds blank lines to the key words on the Mind Map, enticing the brain to 'fill in' the beckoning areas.

Once the human brain realises that it can associate anything with anything else, it will almost instantaneously find associations, *especially when given the trigger of an additional stimulus.*

From this point on, we watch with delight as our host completes the associative network: adding more images; second, third and fourth level ideas; linking areas; appropriate codes; and embracing outlines when a major branch is considered to be complete.

At this stage another major aspect of Radiant Thinking/Mind Mapping becomes apparent: that the Mind Map is based on the *logic of association*, and not the logic of time. The Mind Map reaches out in any direction and catches any thought from any angle.

Having generated enough ideas to satisfy the requirements for his or her speech, presentation, essay or exploration, our host decides to order the ideas further by giving them each a number, thus putting the Mind Map into a chronological sequence should that be necessary. (For more on chronological sequencing, see Chapters 22 (page 211), 23 (page 221), 25 (page 245), 27 (page 261) and 28 (page 274).)

MORE ABOUT HIERARCHIES AND CATEGORIES

The Basic Ordering Ideas in any Mind Map are those words or images which are the simplest and most obvious ordering devices. They are the key concepts, gathering the greatest number of associations to themselves.

It is the use of hierarchy and categorisation which distinguishes the full Mind Map from the Mini-Mind Maps described earlier. In these, the first ten words or images gained their importance simply by occurring first. In the full Mind Map, they are placed according to their inherent importance.

A simple way of discovering primary Basic Ordering Ideas is to ask such questions as:

- What knowledge is required?
- If this were a book, what would its chapter headings be?
- What are my specific objectives?
- What are the most important seven categories in the area under consideration?
- What are my basic questions? 'Why?', 'What?', 'Where?', 'Who?', 'How?', 'Which?', 'When?' often serve remarkably well as major branches in a Mind Map.
- What is a larger or more encompassing category into which these fit?

Very often, just asking yourself these questions will unearth the desired Basic Ordering Ideas. If not, start with the central image or subject and draw between four and seven lines branching out from it. Then ask the above questions.

Alternatively, you can go back to the Mini-Mind Map technique, write down the first ten words or images that spring to mind, then ask yourself which of them can be combined under more general headings.

ADVANTAGES OF HIERARCHY, CATEGORISATION AND BOIs

1 The primary ideas are in place so that secondary and tertiary ideas can follow quickly and easily to facilitate a harmonious thought structure.

2 BOIs help to shape, sculpt and construct Mind Maps enabling the mind to think in a naturally structured way.

Exercise

Using all the Mind Mapping techniques you have learnt so far, make your own complete Mind Map on the concept of happiness, and compare it with the one on page 81.

ADVANTAGES OF MIND MAPPING OVER LINEAR NOTE-MAKING/TAKING

By reversing the disadvantages of modern note-taking (described on pages 49–50), it is possible to summarise the advantages of Mind Mapping:

1   Time saved by noting only relevant words: between 50 and 95 per cent.

2   Time saved by reading only relevant words: more than 90 per cent of total.

3   Time saved reviewing Mind Map notes: more than 90 per cent of total.

4   Time saved by not having to search for key words amongst unnecessary verbiage: more than 90 per cent of total.

5   Concentration on real issues enhanced.

6   Essential key words made more easily discernible.

7   Essential key words juxtaposed in time and space, thus improving creativity and recall.

8   Clear and appropriate associations made between key words.

9   The brain finds it easier to accept and remember visually stimulating, multi-coloured, multi-dimensional Mind Maps, rather than monotonous, boring linear notes.

10 While Mind Mapping, one is constantly on the verge of new discoveries and new realisations. This encourages a continuous and potentially endless flow of thought.

11 The Mind Map works in harmony with the brain's natural desire for completion or wholeness, replenishing our natural desire for learning.

12 By constantly utilising all its cortical skills, the brain becomes increasingly alert and receptive, and confident in its abilities (see Chapter 3, 'The consequences for our brains', page 50).

ONWORD

Having completed Divisions 1 and 2, you have familiarised yourself with the architecture and foundations of Radiant Thinking. You have also progressed from basic brainstorming to Mini-Mind Mapping, and from there to full Mind Mapping.

You now need a structure within which to express your Radiant Thinking. Division 3 provides the fundamental guidelines that will release rather than inhibit your natural creativity.

DIVISION 3
STRUCTURE

Division 3 introduces all the Mind Map laws and recommendations. These guidelines will lead you towards being able to increase massively your mental precision, creativity, power and freedom. Once you have understood and absorbed the basic Mind Map laws, you will be able to develop more rapidly your personal Mind Mapping style.

CHAPTER 10

THE GUIDING PRINCIPLES

Preview
- Foreword
- A Martian view of human intelligence
- The three 'A's of Mind Mapping
- The Mind Map laws and recommendations
- Summary of the Mind Map laws
- Rationale of the Mind Map laws
- Summary of the Mind Map recommendations
- Rationale of the Mind Map recommendations
- Four danger areas
- Onword

FOREWORD

Chapter 10 begins by looking at the development of human intelligence from the viewpoint of an imaginary Martian. This extra-terrestrial perspective enables you to explore the guiding principles of Radiant Thinking with greater objectivity than would otherwise be possible.

The Mind Map laws and recommendations are set out – supplemented by practical exercises – to help you break mental blocks, remember what you have Mind Mapped, and to prepare appropriate working conditions. Finally you are shown how to avoid the most common pitfalls awaiting fledgling Mind Mappers.

A MARTIAN VIEW OF HUMAN INTELLIGENCE

Imagine you are a Martian from a billion-year-old civilisation who has been asked to study, help and eventually befriend the racially young but very talented inhabitants of Earth.

You study the Earth-dwellers intensively and find that they have a staggeringly complex cortex, with a wide range of advanced mental skills, an infinite associative capacity, a virtually limitless storage capacity, and a similarly limitless ability to generate new ideas and associations. In addition, they have a magnificently complex and flexible physical body to support and transport this intelligence, the psychological ability to enhance their own skills, and an inbuilt curiosity that drives them to explore all aspects of the universe.

You next observe that, in attempting to gain access to their vast mental capabilities, the members of this race are squeezing their intelligences out only through the incredibly narrow and restrictive channel of language. As a result, many of them experience actual nausea at the mere prospect of learning, and in the millions of learning institutions dotted around the planet most of the students are either sleeping or trying to get out!

Moved by this tragicomic situation, you decide to give the humans a set of Mind Mapping laws to help them release their incredible capabilities. These laws must be valid from any academic perspective to which the humans may choose to apply them – semantics, neurophysiology, information processing theory, cortical hemisphere theory, physics, psychology, philosophy, memory research or learning theory. What follows are the laws, theories and recommendations you propose.

THE THREE 'A'S OF MIND MAPPING

In many ancient Eastern cultures, master teachers traditionally gave new students only three basic instructions: 'obey', 'cooperate' and 'diverge'. Each of these instructions characterised a specific learning stage.

'Obey' indicated that the student was to imitate the master, only asking for clarification when necessary. Any other questions were to be noted and raised in the next stage.

'Cooperate' referred to the second stage in which the student, having learnt the basic techniques, began to consolidate and integrate the information by asking appropriate questions. At this stage the student would assist the master in analysis and creation.

'Diverge' meant that, having thoroughly learnt all that the master could teach, the student would honour the master by continuing the process of mental evolution. In this way the student could use the master's knowledge as a platform from which to create new insights and paradigms, thus becoming a master of the next generation.

The Mind Mapping equivalents of these three instructions are the three 'A's: 'ACCEPT', 'APPLY' and 'ADAPT'.

● 'ACCEPT' means that, in the first stage, you should set aside any pre-conceptions you may have about your mental limitations, and follow the Mind Mapping laws *exactly*, imitating the models given as precisely as you can.

● 'APPLY' is the second stage, when you have completed the basic training given in this book. At this point, we suggest that you create a minimum of 100 Mind Maps, applying the laws and recommendations contained in this chapter, developing your personal Mind Mapping style, and experimenting with the different types of Mind Maps outlined in the following chapters. Mind Maps should be used for all aspects of your note-taking and note-making until you feel them to be an entirely natural way of organising your thoughts.

● 'ADAPT' refers to the ongoing development of your Mind Mapping skills. Having practised several hundred 'pure' Mind Maps, this is the time to exper-iment with ways of adapting the Mind Map form. Let us know the results . . .

THE MIND MAP LAWS AND RECOMMENDATIONS

The laws

The Mind Map laws are intended to increase, rather than restrict, your mental freedom. In this context, it is important not to confuse order with rigidity or freedom with chaos. All too often, order is perceived in negative terms as rigid and restrictive. Similarly, freedom is mistaken for chaos and lack of structure. In fact true mental freedom is the ability to create order from chaos. The Mind Map laws will help you do exactly this. They are divided into the laws of technique and the laws of layout:

Techniques

1   Use emphasis

2   Use association

3   Be clear

4   Develop a personal style

Layout

1   Use hierarchy

2   Use numerical order

The recommendations
The recommendations supplement the laws and are sub-divided as follows:

1   Break mental blocks

2   Reinforce

3   Prepare

OPPOSITE: *Natural Architecture Plate 12*

SUMMARY OF THE MIND MAP LAWS

Techniques

1 Use emphasis

- Always use a central image.
- Use images throughout your Mind Map.
- Use three or more colours per central image.
- Use dimension in images and around words.
- Use synaesthesia (the blending of the physical senses).
- Use variations of size of printing, line and image.
- Use organised spacing.
- Use appropriate spacing.

2 Use association

- Use arrows when you want to make connections within and across the branch pattern.
- Use colours.
- Use codes.

3 Be clear

- Use only one key word per line.
- Print all words.
- Print key words on lines.
- Make line length equal to word length.
- Make major branches connect to central image.
- Connect lines to other lines.
- Make the central lines thicker.
- Make your boundaries 'embrace' your branch outline.
- Make your images as clear as possible.
- Keep your paper placed horizontally in front of you.
- Keep your printing as upright as possible.

4 Develop a personal style

Layout

1 Use hierarchy

2 Use numerical order

RATIONALE OF THE MIND MAP LAWS

Techniques

1 **Use emphasis**

Emphasis, as we have already seen, is one of the major factors in improving memory and creativity. All the techniques used for emphasis can also be used for association, and vice versa. The following laws enable you to achieve maximum and appropriate emphasis in your Mind Maps.

Always use a central image

An image automatically focuses the eye and the brain. It triggers numerous associations and is astoundingly effective as a memory aid. In addition an image is *attractive* – on many levels. It attracts you, it pleases you and it draws your attention to itself.

If a particular word (rather than an image) is absolutely central to your Mind Map, the word can be made into an image by using dimension, multiple colours, and attractive form.

Use images throughout your Mind Map

Using images wherever possible gives all the benefits described above, as well as creating a stimulating balance between your visual and linguistic cortical skills, and improving your visual perception.

If you set aside your fear of being a poor artist, and attempt to draw a butterfly, for example, you may find your first image unsatisfactory. In some instances, you might fail magnificently! But the advantage is that you have tried, and the next time you see a butterfly you will want to look at it more closely in order to remember and duplicate it.

Thus, by using images in your Mind Maps, you will focus more clearly on real life and will strive to improve your depiction of real objects. You will literally 'open your eyes' to the world around you.

Use three or more colours per central image
Colours stimulate memory and creativity, enabling you to escape the danger of monochrome monotony. They add life to your images and make them more attractive.

Use dimension in images and around words
Dimension makes things 'stand out', and whatever stands out is more easily remembered and communicated. Thus, the most important elements in your Mind Map can be emphasised by being drawn or written in three dimensions.

Use synaesthesia (the blending of the physical senses)
Wherever possible, you should include in your Mind Maps words or images that refer to the senses of sight, hearing, smell, taste, touch and kinaesthesia (physical sensation). This technique has been used by many of the famous memorisers, as well as by great writers and poets.

For example in his epic poem *The Odyssey*, an astounding work of memory, Homer uses the full range of human sensation to convey the excitement and danger of Ulysses' voyage home after the siege of Troy. In the following scene Ulysses has made the mistake of angering Neptune, god of the sea, who gets his revenge by raising a terrible storm:

'As he spoke a sea broke over him with such terrific fury that the raft reeled again, and he was carried overboard a long way off. He let go the helm, and the force of the hurricane was so great that it broke the mast halfway up, and both sail and yard went over into the sea. For a long time Ulysses was under water, and it was all he could do to rise to the surface again, for the clothes Calypso had given him weighed him down; but at last he got his head above water and spat out the bitter brine that was running down his face in streams. In spite of all this, however, he did not lose sight of his raft, but swam as fast as he could towards it, got hold of it and climbed on board again so as to escape drowning. The sea took the raft and tossed it about as Autumn winds whirl thistledown round and round upon a road. It was as though the South, North, East and West winds were all playing battledore and shuttlecock with it at once.'

Notice the rhythm, the repetition, the sequencing, the imagery, the appeal to all the senses, the movement, the exaggeration, the colour and feeling, all contained in one masterful and memorable paragraph.

It is interesting to observe how young children experience nature with all their senses. They touch, taste, move and explore; then chant, sing, rhyme and tell each other stories, creating captivating Mind Map fantasies and daydreams.

Like these children, the great memoriser Shereshevsky, known as 'S', used synaesthesia to help him remember virtually every instant of his life. In his book about 'S', *The Mind of a Mnemonist*, Alexander Luria reports:

> *'For "S", too, it was the meaning of words that was predominantly important. Each word had the effect of summoning up in his mind a graphic image, and what distinguished him from the general run of people was that his images were incomparably more vivid and stable than theirs. Further, his images were invariably linked with synaesthetic components . . .'*

Movement, too, is a major mnemonic technique, and can also be used to advantage in your Mind Maps. Your words, your pictures, your whole Mind Map can *move* – like the wonderfully memorable animations created by Walt Disney. To make your images move, simply add appropriate visual indicators of movement, as in the following examples:

Use variations of size of printing, line and image
Variation in size is the best way of indicating the relative importance of items in a hierarchy. Expanded size adds emphasis, thereby increasing the probability of recall.

Use organised spacing
Organised spacing increases the clarity of the image, helps in the use of hierarchy and categorisation, leaves the Mind Map 'open' to additions, and is aesthetically pleasing.

Use appropriate spacing

Leaving the right amount of space around each item gives your Mind Map order and structure. Taken to its logical conclusion, the space between items can be as important as the items themselves. For example, in Japanese flower-arranging, the entire arrangement is based on the space between the flowers. Likewise, in music the sound is often arranged around the silence. For instance, Beethoven's famous Fifth Symphony actually starts with a rest or silent note.

2   Use association

Association is the other major factor in improving memory and creativity. It is the integrating device our brains use to make sense of our physical experience, the key to human memory and understanding.

Having established your central image and your Basic Ordering Ideas, the power of association can take your brain into the depths of any subject.

As already mentioned, any technique used for association can also be used for emphasis, and vice versa.

Use arrows when you want to make connections within and across the branch pattern

Arrows automatically guide your eye to connect one part of a Mind Map with another. They can be uni-directional, multi-headed, and varied in size, form and dimension. They give spatial direction to your thoughts.

Use colours

Colour is one of the most powerful tools for enhancing memory and creativity. Choosing specific colours for coding purposes or for specific areas of your Mind Map will give you faster access to the information, will improve your memory of the information, and will increase the number and range of your creative ideas. Such colour codes and symbols can be developed both by individuals and by groups.

Use codes

Codes enable you to make instant connections between different parts of your Mind Map, however far apart they may be on the page. These codes can take the form of ticks and crosses, circles, triangles and underlinings, or they can be more elaborate, as in the Mind Map on page 106.

Codes can also save a lot of time. For instance, you could use a range of simple codes in all your notes to represent people, projects, elements or processes that frequently recur.

Codes reinforce and enhance categorisation and hierarchy through the simple application of colours, symbols, shapes and images. They can also be used to link source material (such as biographical references) to your Mind Map.

3 Be clear

Obscurity veils perception. If you scribble your notes they will hinder rather than help your memory; it will also hinder the associative nature and clarity of your thinking.

Use only one key word per line
Each individual word has thousands of possible associations. Placing one per line gives you associational freedom, like giving a limb extra joints. Important phrases are *not* lost and *all* your options are kept open. (For an extended discussion of this rule, see 'The idea that phrases are more meaningful', on pages 111 and 114.)

Print all words
Printed letters have a more defined shape and are therefore easier for your mind to 'photograph'. The extra time spent printing is more than made up for by the advantages of rapid creative association and recall. Printing also encourages brevity, and both upper and lower case letters can be used to show the relative importance of words on your Mind Map.

Print key words on lines
The line forms a 'skeleton' for the 'flesh' of the word. It therefore provides organisation and neatness which improve clarity and aid recall. Lines also encourage further connections and additions (see the Figures on page 114).

Make line length equal to word length
This law makes it easier to place words near each other, thus facilitating association. In addition, the space saved enables you to include more information in your Mind Map. (For more on this, see page 224.)

Connect lines to other lines and major branches to central image
Connecting the lines on your Mind Map enables you to connect the thoughts in your mind. Lines can be transformed into arrows, curves, loops, circles, ovals, triangles, polyhedrons or any of the other shapes from your brain's limitless store.

Make the central lines thicker and organic
Through emphasis, thicker lines immediately signal to your brain the importance of your central ideas. If your Mind Map is at the exploratory stage, you may discover during the Mind Mapping process that some of the peripheral ideas are actually more important than the central ones. In such cases you can simply thicken the outer lines where appropriate. The organic, curved lines add more visual interest.

Make your boundaries 'embrace' your branch outline
When a boundary line 'hugs' the outline of a completed Mind Map branch, it defines the unique shape of that branch. This unique shape can then trigger the memory of the information contained in that branch. For more advanced mnemonic thinkers, such shapes can become 'living pictures', dramatically enhancing the probability of recall.

Many of us do this almost unconsciously as children. For instance, do you ever remember lying outside on a sunny day, looking up at a blue sky dappled with clouds? If you did, the chances are that you looked up at the drifting clouds and thought: 'Oh, there's a sheep!' 'There's a dinosaur!' 'There's a boat!' 'There's a bird' . . .

Your brain was creating images from random shapes, thus making the shapes more memorable. In the same way, creating shapes in your Mind Map will enable you to organise many bits of data in a more memorable form. This gathering of data, known as 'chunking', is a well-known mnemonic technique.

According to psychologists, our short-term memory is on average only capable of storing seven items of information. Chunking can help us use this storage space more effectively.

For example, an untrained brain-user may use all their short-term memory capacity to store a seven-digit phone number. The skilled brain-user, on the other hand, will chunk the seven digits in some meaningful way, thus leaving space for other information.

In 1982 Chase and Erickson carried out an experiment on this aspect of memory, described by Glass and Holyoak in 1986. One subject proved to be particularly interesting. Initially he could only remember the average seven digits. However, after more than two years of practice in chunking techniques, he could remember 82 digits. His particular strategy was to chunk digits that matched information he had already stored in his long-term memory. For example, the sequence '351' was associated with a previous world record for running the mile (3 minutes 51 seconds).

So drawing boundaries on a Mind Map has obvious mnemonic advantages. If you wish to add further branches after you have drawn a boundary then the new set of branches can be enclosed by a new boundary, rather like the rings on a sawn-off tree trunk.

Make your images as clear as possible
External clarity encourages internal clarity of thought. A clear Mind Map will also be more elegant, graceful and attractive.

Keep your paper placed horizontally in front of you
The horizontal ('landscape') format gives you more freedom and space to draw your Mind Map than the vertical ('portrait') position. A horizontal Mind Map is also easier to read.

Inexperienced Mind Mappers often keep the body and pen in the same position while rotating the paper. This may not cause any problems while Mind Mapping, but re-reading the Mind Map will require physiological contortions that would test the abilities of a yoga master!

Keep your printing as upright as possible
Upright printing gives your brain easier access to the thoughts expressed, and this law applies as much to the angle of the lines as to the printing itself. If you keep your lines as close to horizontal as possible, your Mind Map will be much easier to read. Try to keep to a maximum angle of 45°.

4 Develop a personal style while maintaining the Mind Map Laws

As already discussed, we are all astoundingly unique. Our Mind Maps should reflect the unique networks and patterns of thought in our individual brains; the more they do so, the more our brains will be able to identify with them.

In order to develop a truly personal Mind Mapping style, you should follow the '1 +' rule. This means that every Mind Map you do should be slightly more colourful, slightly more three-dimensional, slightly more imaginative, slightly more associatively logical, and/or slightly more beautiful than the last.

In this way you will constantly develop and refine all your mental skills. You will also produce Mind Maps which you *want* to review and use for creation and communication. In addition, the more you personalise your Mind Maps, the more easily you will remember the information they contain. (For more on this, see Chapter 11, page 115.)

Layout

1 Use hierarchy

As discussed in Chapter 9 (page 83), the use of hierarchy and categorisation in the form of Basic Ordering Ideas enormously enhances the power of your brain.

2 Use numerical order

If your Mind Map is the basis for a specific task, such as a speech, an essay or an examination answer, you will want to communicate your thoughts in a specific order, whether chronological or in order of importance.

To do this, you can simply number the branches in the desired order, even allotting the appropriate time or emphasis to each branch if necessary. Letters of the alphabet can be used rather than numbers if you prefer. Either way, this use of order will automatically result in more logical thought.

SUMMARY OF THE MIND MAP RECOMMENDATIONS

Break mental blocks

1 Add blank lines.

2 Ask questions.

3 Add images.

4 Maintain awareness of your infinite associational capacity.

Reinforce

1 Review your Mind Maps.

2 Do quick Mind Map checks.

Prepare

1 Prepare your mental attitude
- Develop a positive mental attitude.
- Copy images around you.
- Commit yourself to your Mind Map.
- Commit to the absurd!
- Make your Mind Map as beautiful as possible.

2 Prepare your materials

3 Prepare your workspace / environment
- Ensure that you have a moderate temperature in the room.
- Use natural light where possible.
- Ensure that you have plenty of fresh air.
- Furnish the room appropriately.
- Create pleasing surroundings.
- Play appropriate music, or work in silence if you prefer.

RATIONALE OF THE MIND MAP RECOMMENDATIONS

The Mind Map recommendations are designed to help you implement the laws, to release the flow of your thoughts, and to provide the best possible environment for your brain and body.

Break mental blocks

1 Add blank lines

Should you come up against a temporary block, simply add a line or lines to your on-going Mind Map. This will challenge your brain to complete what has been left unfinished and will 'tap in' to your infinite associative power.

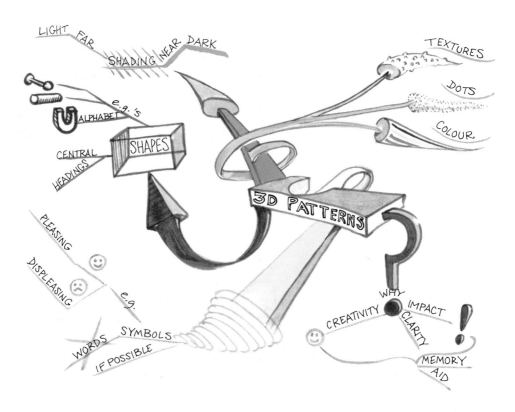

Mind Map by Mark Brown demonstrating spectacularly the use of images, shape and dimension (see pages 97–100).

2 Ask questions

Questions are the main device by which the brain accumulates networks of knowledge. When you challenge your brain with appropriate questions you stimulate a block-breaking response.

3 Add images

Adding images to your Mind Map increases the possible triggers for further associations and recall.

4 Maintain awareness of your infinite associational capacity

Maintaining this awareness will free your brain from its accustomed restrictions. Remember the happiness exercise – any word can be the centre of a radiating spray of associations.

Exercises

You may find it useful to do two exercises at this stage.

Firstly, choose any piece of data from your memory and link it, logically or fantastically, with any randomly chosen object.

Secondly, take any part of a Mind Map on which you have got 'stuck' and make it the centre of a new Mini-Mind Map. Do a quick word association burst to get your mental flow going again.

Reinforce

1 Review your Mind Maps

Research has shown that memory after review alters according to a specific time curve (see *Use Your Perfect Memory* by Tony Buzan, page 82). If you need an active (as opposed to passive) memory of your Mind Map, perhaps for an exam or a specific project, you should plan to review it at a certain time. This will enable you to refine or correct certain areas, fill in any areas which may have been missed, and reinforce particularly important associations.

After a 1 hour learning period you should ideally review your Mind Map:
- After 10–30 minutes
- After a day
- After a week
- After a month
- After three months
- After six months

The Mind Map will become part of your on-going long-term memory.

2 Do quick Mind Map checks

Occasionally, while reviewing your Mind Map, you should quickly do a speed Mind Map (taking only a few minutes) which summarises all you can recall from your original.

When you do one of these fresh Mind Maps you are actually recreating and refreshing your memories, demonstrating yet again that creativity and memory are two sides of the same coin.

If you only check your original Mind Map, your brain remains dependent on the external stimulus of the Mind Map to recognise what it has already done. Producing a fresh Mind Map, on the other hand, enables you to check what you can recall *without* external stimulus. You can then compare the result with your original Mind Map and adjust any errors, inconsistencies or omissions.

Prepare

To maximise your performance, you need to create the ideal context – mental and physical – within which to create your Mind Maps. The following recommendations should help you ensure that you have the best possible attitude, materials and working environment.

1 Prepare your mental attitude

Develop a positive mental attitude
A positive mental attitude unblocks the mind, increases the probability of making spontaneous connections, relaxes the body, improves perception, and creates a general expectation of positive results. All these benefits will be reflected in your Mind Map. It is therefore vital to approach each Mind Mapping task positively, even if it takes place in a traditionally 'negative' situation such as an exam.

Copy images around you
Wherever possible, you should copy other Mind Maps, images and works of art. This is because your brain is designed to learn by copying and then creating new images or concepts from those it has copied. Your reticular activating system (a sophisticated 'sorting station' at the base of your brain) will automatically look out for information that will help you improve your Mind Mapping skills.

Commit yourself to your Mind Map
Many people get worried or frustrated if their Mind Maps do not live up to their expectations. In such cases, you should analyse your Mind Map *non-judgementally* and renew your resolution to continue and improve.

Commit to the absurd!
Especially in the initial, creative stages of any Mind Map, all 'absurd' or 'silly' ideas should be recorded, allowing any additional ideas to flow from them. This is because ideas that seem absurd or silly are usually those that are far from the norm. These same ideas often turn out to be the ones that contain the great breakthroughs and new paradigms which are also, by definition, far from the norm.

Make your Mind Map as beautiful as possible
Your brain is naturally attuned to beauty. So the more beautiful your Mind Map is, the more you will create and remember from it. (For more on the power of images, see Chapter 7, page 71.)

2 Prepare your materials
On a paraconscious level we tend to 'tune in to' or 'tune out of' any sensory input, depending on how attractive it is. Your paper, pens, highlighters and filing systems should all therefore be the best you can obtain, so that you are attracted to them and *want* to use them.

3 Prepare your workspace / environment
Like your materials, your working environment can evoke in you a negative, neutral or positive response. Your surroundings should therefore be as pleasant and comfortable as possible in order to put you in the best frame of mind.

Ensure that you have a moderate temperature in the room
Extremes of temperature will distract you from your work. In a moderate temperature you can easily adjust your clothing for optimum comfort.

Use natural light where possible
Natural light is the most relaxing light for your eyes, and also gives your brain more accurate information on form, colour, line and dimension.

Ensure that you have plenty of fresh air
One of your brain's main foods is oxygen. Fresh air provides your brain with this fuel, thus increasing your perception and mental stamina.

Furnish the room appropriately
Make sure that your chair and desk or table are of the best quality available and that their design allows you to maintain a relaxed, comfortable, upright posture. Good posture increases the supply of blood to your brain, improves perception and enhances mental and physical stamina. In addition, well-designed, attractive furniture will make you *want* to use your workspace.

Create pleasing surroundings
Like good-quality materials and furniture, attractive surroundings will encourage you to use your workspace. Because learning is often associated with punishment, many people paraconsciously make their study or workspace into a prison cell. Make yours a place where you actively *want* to go, even if you have no particular learning task in mind. A few favourite pictures on the wall, an attractive rug – these little touches can all make your workspace a more welcoming, appealing environment.

Play appropriate music, or work in silence if you prefer
We all react differently to music. Some people like to have music while they Mind Map; others prefer silence. It is important to experiment both with and without music, and to choose music – whether classical, jazz, pop, rock or some other type – which is appropriate to you and the way you are feeling at a particular time.

FOUR DANGER AREAS
There are four major pitfalls for any Mind Mapper:

1 Mind Maps that aren't really Mind Maps

2 The idea that phrases are more meaningful

3 The idea that a 'messy' Mind Map is no good

4 A negative emotional reaction to any Mind Map

All these danger areas can easily be avoided as long as you bear in mind the principles explained below.

1 Mind Maps that aren't really Mind Maps

The Figures overleaf are often created by people at an early stage in Mind Mapping who have not yet fully absorbed all the Mind Map laws.

At first glance, they look like Mind Maps and seem to obey the fundamental Mind Mapping principles. There are, however, a number of differences. As both figures develop, their structure becomes increasingly random and monotonous. Furthermore, all the ideas are reduced to the same level and each one becomes *dis*associated from the others.

Because the laws of clarity, emphasis and association have been neglected, what appeared to be developing into order and structure has in fact resulted in confusion, monotony and chaos.

2 The idea that phrases are more meaningful

This danger area can best be explained with a practical example.

Let's say that someone has had a very unhappy afternoon and wishes to make the Mind Map diary entries shown in Figures 1 and 2 on page 114.

Initially this may appear to be a perfectly adequate record of an afternoon that was indeed 'very unhappy'. However, on closer examination, a number of disadvantages become clear. Firstly, this note makes it extremely difficult to revise the interpretation of the afternoon. The phrase expresses a fixed concept which is not open to any other possibility.

By contrast, Figure 2 breaks the phrase into its individual word meanings, allowing each word the freedom to radiate its own unique associations. The importance of this can be seen even more dramatically in Figure 3 (page 114), where the single-word rule is taken to its logical conclusion, and where the additional guidelines of image and colour have been added. Here you can see that the *main concept* in the afternoon is the concept of *happiness* with the major emphasis on the *un* in unhappy. You may have been ill, failed dramatically, or received some exceptionally bad news, all of which is true. It is *also* true that the afternoon contained some positives (the sun may have shone, even if very briefly!) which the single-word/image rule allows you to record truthfully. The single unit Mind Map rule allows you to see both your internal and external environments more clearly and realistically, and therefore to be more 'true' to yourself.

At their worst, negative phrases can wipe out days, years, and even decades of people's lives. 'Last year was the worst year of my life', 'My school years were pure hell!', to quote two commonly heard examples.

If such thoughts are constantly repeated they eventually take on the appearance of truth. But they are not true. Certainly, we all experience disappointment and frustration at times. But there are always underlying positive factors – if nothing else, the fact that we are still alive and conscious of being depressed! And of course there is the fact that we still possess the potential for positive change and development.

Mind Maps that aren't really Mind Maps. These structures, often named clustering or spider diagrams, lead to confusion, monotony and chaotic thought. Check for yourself just how many cortical skills they include, and, more importantly, how many they exclude.

Using single words in your Mind Maps enables you to see your internal and external environment more clearly and realistically. It also provides balance, allowing you to see the 'other side' of any issue. It is especially helpful for problem-solving and creative thinking because it opens your mind to all the options.

3 The idea that a 'messy' Mind Map is no good

In certain situations, perhaps when you are short of time or you are listening to a rather confusing lecture, you may produce a 'messy'-looking Mind Map. This does not mean it is 'bad'. It is simply a reflection of your state of mind at the time, or of the input your mind was receiving.

Your 'messy'-looking Mind Map may lack clarity and beauty but it will still be an accurate record of your mental processes while making it.

Neatly written linear notes may look aesthetically pleasing, but what kind of information retrieval do they give? As we have seen, such notes appear to be very precise and organised but – lacking emphasis or association – they are usually almost impossible for the eye to decode.

Realising this can eliminate a lot of guilt and self-denigration. Looking at your Mind Map may help you realise that it was not you but the lecturer you were listening to, or the author of the book you were reading, who was disorganised, messy and confused!

4 A negative emotional reaction to your Mind Map

You may occasionally produce a 'final' Mind Map straight away but you will often produce a 'first attempt'. If you are disappointed or depressed by the standard of your Mind Map you should simply remind yourself that it is only a first draft which will require revision before it reaches maturity.

Exercise

Throughout this book the Mind Maps have been selected or prepared to illustrate as many of the laws and applications as possible. At this point you may find it useful to look quickly at all the Mind Maps in this book, checking them against the laws and criticising where appropriate. Having done this, you should copy elements from the best ones in order to produce your own, even more radiant, beautiful and memorable Mind Maps!

FIGURE 1: *Standard phrase noting, which at first glance appears adequate, but which contains dangerous inaccuracies.*

FIGURE 2: *More concise noting, which illustrates the freedom for each word to radiate its own associations.*

FIGURE 3: *Note following the full Mind Map guidelines, which allows the noter to reflect a more comprehensive, true and balanced picture of reality.*

Progression of noting a 'very unhappy afternoon' in which application of the Mind Map laws brings the noter much closer to the truth (see pages 101 and 111–12).

ONWORD

This chapter has given you all the knowledge you need to launch yourself into the infinite universe of Radiant Thinking! Having absorbed all the laws and recommendations, you need to make your Mind Maps truly your own. The next chapter, 'Developing a Personal Style', explains how you can enhance your Mind Maps by using them to express your particular personal combination of skills and characteristics.

CHAPTER 11

DEVELOPING
A PERSONAL STYLE

Preview
- Foreword
- The art of Mind Mapping
- Examples of Mind Map art
- Benefits of creating artistic Mind Maps
- The story of a great Mind Map artist
- Onword

FOREWORD

In this chapter you will learn how to use the Mind Map laws and recommendations to express your individual personality. We begin with some very
varied examples of the Mind Mapping art, and then explore the potential
benefits of creating artistic Mind Maps. There is also the tantalising story of a
Mind Mapper who, almost by accident, made a dream come true.

THE ART OF MIND MAPPING

Mind Maps provide the ideal opportunity to improve your hand/eye coor-
dination and to develop and refine your visual skills. With a little more practice,
the image-making skills you have already developed can be used to take your
Mind Maps into the realms of art. Such Mind Maps enable your brain to express
its own artistic and creative personality. In developing your own personal style
it is especially useful to apply the guiding principles of image, colour, dimension,
and spacing.

EXAMPLES OF MIND MAP ART

The extraordinary tree-like Mind Map on page 119 is by Claudius Borer, who is becoming famous throughout Europe for his art Mind Maps on the structuring of organisations. This generic Mind Map covers the fundamental routes, the main branches and the possible 'fruits' for a growing business.

The Mind Map on page 120 (top) was drawn by Kathy De Stefano, a marketing consultant, to express her idea of the ideal job. The result is a brilliantly creative work of art as well as a vibrant and creative Mind Map.

The other Mind Map on page 120 (bottom) was created by Dr John Geesink, an international computer industry consultant. He wanted to express the concept of 'love' artistically, humorously and without using words. People who saw his Mind Map begged him for colour copies!

BENEFITS OF CREATING ARTISTIC MIND MAPS

1 Development of artistic skills and visual perception, which in turn enhance memory, creative thinking and self-confidence.

2 Stress-reduction, relaxation and self-exploration.

3 Pleasure.

4 Providing good 'role models' for other Mind Mappers.

5 Achieving a greater understanding of the work of great artists.

6 Commercial. (For example, a five-year-old English boy became entranced with Mind Maps, started to do at least two a day, and sold each one for five times his weekly pocket money!)

THE STORY OF A GREAT MIND MAP ARTIST

In 1984 Ulf Ekberg, a Swedish ship's captain who was also an expert on computer systems, took a Mind Mapping course. Great things were expected of him, for he regularly contributed cartoons to his company's journals, and he had also started studying portrait and landscape painting.

At the end of the course, when all the students had to complete their final Mind Maps, Ulf's mind went blank!

Disappointed and frustrated, he went home for the weekend, vowing to devote several hours to completing the course in the grand manner he had dreamed of.

Partly to rid himself of the day's frustrations, he went to work on the large boat he kept in his back garden. It was a freezing winter's day in Stockholm, and as Ulf finished his task he slipped and fell 10 feet on to the ice-hard ground. To his delight, he landed on his feet perfectly. But, as he confidently took a step, he fell to the ground in pain and literally had to crawl back inside. The doctor confirmed that Ulf had two hairline fractures in the heel of each foot, and that he would not be able to walk properly for at least two months.

After his anger at his enforced immobility had subsided, Ulf decided to fulfil one of his lifetime ambitions – to do a painting in the style of Salvador Dali. He planned to use as his subject a single-image Master Mind Map which incorporated everything he had learnt on his course as well as his own interpretations and extrapolations.

Among the concepts he wished to include were:

- Introspection – the brain seeing itself seeing itself seeing itself . . .
- The Roman ideal of *mens sana in corpore sano* ('a healthy mind in a healthy body/a healthy body in a healthy mind')
- Love as an essential element for healthy brain function.
- The brain as synergetic – its parts adding up to more than its whole.
- Time as a variable.
- The mind's ability to create whatever it wishes.
- Juggling as a metaphor for balance and self-control.
- The strong sense of justice found in a highly trained brain.
- The biggest brain on the planet.
- The brain as musical.
- The basic question of existence.
- Einstein's theory of relativity seen in the context of the brain as an infinite association machine.
- Understanding bringing an end to war.
- The brain as magical.
- Mistakes as acceptable and enjoyable parts of the learning process.
- The breaking of all known boundaries.

Ulf Ekberg's single-image Master Mind Map (see pages 116–7).

Natural Architecture Plate 13

Mind Map by Claudius Borer showing how application of basic principles (the roots) will lead to appropriate fruits! (See page 116.)

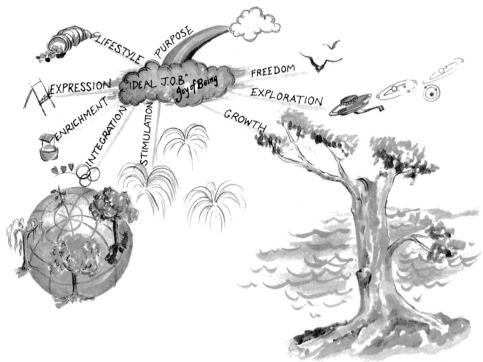

Kathy de Stefano's Mind Map expressing her idea of the ideal job (see page 116).

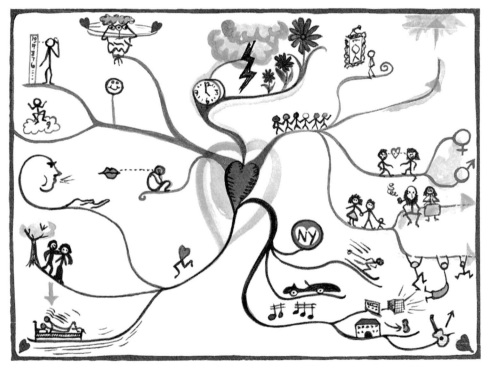

Mind Map by Dr John Geesink of Digital Corporation, exploring the concept of love without the use of word (see page 116).

This first true example of Mind Map art has already been published in limited editions and is rapidly becoming a collectors' item.

Exploring Ekberg's Art-Mind Map will introduce you to many ideas not yet mentioned in this chapter and will inspire you to develop your personal Mind Mapping style even further.

ONWORD

At this stage you may be feeling a bit like a child who has just been given a whole set of incredibly complex and beautiful toys but doesn't quite know what to do with them. The next division explores the huge range of possible applications for the Mind Mapping skills and techniques you have learnt.

DIVISION 4
SYNTHESIS

This division explores the many distinct tasks which can be successfully accomplished using Mind Maps. These tasks include the following main areas of intellectual activity: making choices; organising your own and other people's ideas; creative thinking and brainstorming; and creating a group mind or Meta-mind.

CHAPTER 12

MAKING CHOICES

Preview
- Foreword
- General decision-making
- Simple decision-making
- Journey through the mind of a Mind Mapper, Part 3
- Making the choice
- Dealing with indecision
- Decision-making exercises
- Benefits of dyadic Mind Maps
- Onword

OPPOSITE: *Natural Architecture Plate 14*

FOREWORD

The Mind Map is a particularly useful tool for clarifying personal choices. By using the Mind Map to set out your needs and desires, priorities and constraints, you will be able to make decisions based on a clearer view of the questions involved. Having gained a comprehensive knowledge of the Mind Mapping laws, use this chapter to help you utilise your new-found skills to make decisions.

GENERAL DECISION-MAKING

In general decision-making the Mind Map helps you to balance competing factors.

Let's take the example of deciding whether or not to buy a new car. You require a certain degree of comfort and quality but you don't have a great deal of money. You may therefore have to go for a second-hand car and so you will have to weigh up the financial saving against the reduction in reliability and durability.

The Mind Map does not make the choice for you. However it dramatically increases *your* ability to make the choice by highlighting the key trade-offs.

SIMPLE DECISION-MAKING

A simple choice of this kind is known as a dyadic decision (derived from the Latin *dyas*, meaning 'two'). Dyadic decisions are the first stage in creating order. They can be broadly categorised as evaluation decisions, and they involve simple choices such as: yes/no, better/worse, stronger/weaker, more effective/less effective, more efficient/less efficient, more expensive/less expensive. The third journey through the mind of a Mind Mapper will provide a good example.

JOURNEY THROUGH THE MIND OF A MIND MAPPER, PART 3

Visiting our host once again, we find that he or she is involved in deciding whether or not to buy a house.

Following the Mind Mapping laws, a multi-dimensional, multi-coloured image is placed at the centre of the Mind Map. Because this is an evaluation decision, the Basic Ordering Ideas are the dyadic YES and NO.

Having established the central image and the major branches, our host follows the Mini-Mind Map method which allows the Mind Map to 'catch' whatever thoughts spring to mind in relation to buying the house. As soon as some of the main branches are in place our host follows the Mini-Mind Map method of allowing the sequence of thoughts in his/her head to flow naturally. Each is placed wherever it best fits on the Mind Map. Since association is rarely linear, the normal progression will involve quite a bit of leaping about from one branch to another as the sequence of thoughts dictates. Working on stress, for example, might trigger thoughts on dreams, or environment on the other side of the Mind Map. These thoughts, in turn might lead to considerations of alternatives. (A methodical branch-by-branch completion of the Mind Map is not desirable because it restricts the brain's workings and traps it into a semi-chronological method of thinking.) It is far better to let the mind range free, allowing the full range of thoughts and emotions to be incorporated within the growing web of associations.

The use, by our host, of images and colours is especially important in decision-making because these visual elements help to capture concepts and emotions. Contrary to widespread opinion, emotions are an integral part of any decision-making process and should therefore be given appropriate importance in the Mind Map.

MAKING THE CHOICE

Once all the relevant information, thoughts and emotions have been collated on to the Mind Map, there are five major methods for making a dyadic choice:

1 Process-generated

In many cases the process of Mind Mapping itself generates the solution. As the brain gets an overview of all the data it has gathered there is a sudden 'aha!' realisation which effectively concludes the decision-making process.

2 Number-weighting

If, after completion of the Mind Map, the decision is still not clear, the number-weighting method can be used. In this method, each specific key word on either side of the Mind Map is given a number from 1 to 100 according to its importance (see overleaf).

When each item has been given a number, the 'scores' are added up, first for the 'YES' side and then for the 'NO' side. The highest total 'wins'.

The Mind Map overleaf by Vanda North, past President of the International Society for Accelerated Learning and Teaching, and Co-founder of The Brain Trust, gives a clear example of the number-weighting Mind Map. Vanda had

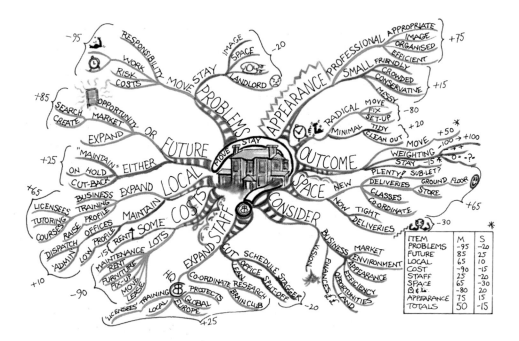

Mind Map by Vanda North helping her make a decision as to whether or not to move her business (see pages 125–6).

to weight a number of personal and professional factors in deciding whether to move her business headquarters or remain where she was. You can see which won!

3 Intuition/Superlogic

If neither the first nor the second method has generated a decision, a choice can be made on the basis of intuition or 'gut feel'.

Intuition is a much-maligned mental skill which I and neuropsychologist Michael Gelb prefer to define as a 'superlogic'. The brain uses superlogic in order to consider its vast data bank (consisting of many billions of items gained from previous experience) in relation to any decision it has to make.

In a flash the brain completes the most astounding mathematical calculations, considering trillions of possibilities and permutations, in order to arrive at a mathematically precise estimate of probable success which might be sub-consciously expressed as follows:

'Having considered the virtually infinite database of your previous life, and integrated that with the trillion items of data you have presented me with in the current decision-making situation, my current estimate of your probability of success is 83.7862 per cent.'

The result of this massive calculation registers in the brain, is translated into a biological reaction, and is interpreted by the individual as a simple 'gut feel'.

Studies at Harvard Business School have found that managers and presidents of national and multi-national organisations attributed *80 per cent of their success* to acting on intuition or 'gut feel'.

The Mind Map is especially useful for this form of super-thinking, in that it gives the brain a wider range of information on which to base its calculations.

4 Incubation

Another method is to simply allow your brain to incubate an idea. In other words, having completed your decision-making Mind Map, you allow your brain to relax. It is at times of rest and solitude that our brains harmonise and integrate all the data they have received. And it is at such times that we often make our most important and accurate decisions, because relaxation releases the gigantic powers of the parabrain – the 99 per cent of our unused mental ability, including that which is often called 'the paraconscious'. (For more on this, see Tony Buzan, *Harnessing the ParaBrain.*)

This method is supported by practical experience. For instance, many people report suddenly remembering where something is, suddenly having creative ideas, or suddenly realising that they need to make a particular choice, while lying in the bath, shaving, driving, long-distance running, lying in bed, day-dreaming, gardening, sitting on the beach, walking in the countryside, or being in any other calm, restful, solitary situation. It is advisable that you use this technique because it is in this kind of situation that your brain harmonises and integrates, and as a result, tends to make its most meaningful and accurate decisions.

5 If the weightings are equal

If you have completed your Mind Map, and none of the previous methods has generated a decision, there must be an equal weighting between 'YES' and 'NO'. In a case like this, either choice will be satisfactory, and you may find it useful simply to toss a coin (the ultimate dyadic device) – heads for one option, tails for the other.

During the coin-tossing you should monitor your emotions very carefully, in case you find that you really do have a preference. You may think you have decided that the choice is equal but your parabrain may already have made its superlogical decision.

If the coin shows heads, and your first reaction is one of disappointment or relief then your true feelings will finally be revealed and you will be able to make an appropriate choice.

DEALING WITH INDECISION

In a very few instances all the above decision-making methods will fail and you will be left swinging to and fro like a pendulum.

At this point the brain is undergoing a subtle shift from the dyadic (two-option) choice to a triadic (three-option) choice. The decision is no longer simply 'yes' or 'no'. It is now:

1 Yes.

2 No.

3 Continue thinking about the choice.

The third option is not only counter-productive but becomes more so the longer it is maintained. Eventually it *becomes* the choice because that is where your mental energy is being directed.

The simplest solution to this problem is to decide not to make the third decision! In other words, the minute you recognise this spiralling whirlwind on your mental horizon, you should immediately choose 'Yes' or 'No' (the first or second option). The basic principle here is that it is more fruitful to have made *some* decision and to be implementing it, than to be in a state of paralysis.

DECISION-MAKING EXERCISES

Like all forms of thinking, dyadic decision-making requires training. Practise your decision-making skills by asking yourself the following questions:
- Should I buy item X?
- Should I learn subject X?

- Should I change personal characteristic X?
- Should I join organisation X?
- Should I go to country/city X?

In the following 'object X' exercise, the basic idea is to find BOIs without having any data – in other words, to construct a set of questions that you can address to any object and which, as a set of enquiries, can serve as the basis for a full Mind Map once the object is identified. This exercise can also be done to help you analyse a question before you attempt to answer it. In the 'object X' exercise Mind Map overleaf, the main branches are explained as follows:

1 History – What are its origins? How did it develop?

2 Structure – What form does it take? How is it constructed? These enquiries can range from the molecular to the architectural.

3 Function – How does it work? What are its dynamics?

4 Role – What does it do: a) in the natural world? and b) in the human world?

5 Classification – How does it relate to other things? Again, this can range from very general animal, vegetable, mineral type questions to specific classifications such as species or the table of elements. You might like to try this exercise with one of the following 'object X' suggestions: horse, car, carbon, Spain, sun, God, stone, book, TV. Of course you can use anything else of your choosing. When you have finished this exercise, see if you can improve upon the basic set of basic Mind Map ideas (if so, let us have them!).

You can also create dyadic Mind Maps on areas of public debate, such as religion, politics, morality, the professions, or the educational system.

BENEFITS OF DYADIC MIND MAPS

1 Dyadic Mind Maps allow your brain to assimilate immediately a whole range of complex and inter-related items of information, bringing all the issues into clear focus. They also give the brain a pre-structured framework for association, ensuring that all the relevant elements are taken into consideration.

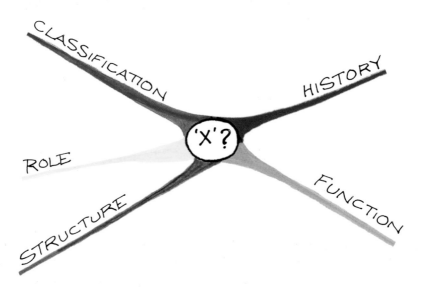

The 'X' Exercise! (See pages 128–9.)

2   They utilise the full range of cortical skills, resulting in a more comprehensively considered decision.

3   They use images, colours and dimensions to add the necessary creativity to the decision-making process.

4   They also use colours and images to bring vital emotional responses into the decision and help to highlight the major points of comparison.

5   The Mind Mapping process itself often results in or triggers a decision.

6   They generate a greater number of specific items than any list method, thus ensuring a more accurate final decision, especially if the number-weighting method is used.

7 They use a greater than usual range of cortical skills, thus releasing the brain's intuitive, superlogical abilities.

8 They provide a balanced and comprehensive environment in which appropriate choices can be incubated.

9 By clearly reflecting the internal decision-making process, they enable the individual to remain focused on all the elements relevant to that decision.

ONWORD

Having familiarised yourself with dyadic decision-making, you are ready to make the transition to polycategoric Mind Mapping. The next chapter introduces you to this exciting technique which will help you make more complex decisions and organise your own ideas.

CHAPTER 13

ORGANISING YOUR OWN IDEAS

Preview
- Foreword
- Note-making
- Complex Mind Mapping
- Journey through the mind of a Mind Mapper, Part 4
- Thought-building exercises
- Benefits of polycategoric Mind Maps
- Onword

FOREWORD

In this chapter you will learn how to organise your own ideas (make notes), using multiple-branched or polycategoric Mind Maps. These involve more complex hierarchies and a greater number of Basic Ordering Ideas than the simple dyadic model. Polycategoric Mind Maps can be used for most descriptive, analytic and evaluative tasks but we have used basic decision-making examples in order to ease your transition from dyadic to polycategoric Mind Mapping. You will also continue your journey through the mind of a Mind Mapper, and learn some enjoyable thought-building games and exercises.

NOTE-MAKING

Note-making is the process by which you extract information from either your memory or from your creative reservoirs and organise that information in an external form. It is the process by which you organise your *own* ideas in either a dyadic or polycategoric (more complex) way. It also helps tremendously with decision-making.

COMPLEX MIND MAPPING

Whereas simple dyadic Mind Maps have two major branches radiating from the centre, complex or polycategoric Mind Maps can have any number of major branches. In practice, the average number of branches or Basic Ordering Ideas (BOIs) is between three and seven.

This is because, as we saw in Chapter 10 ('Rationale of the Mind Map Laws', page 103), the average brain cannot hold more than seven major items of information in its short-term memory. You should therefore aim to select the minimum number of BOIs that will truly embrace your subject, using them as a way of breaking the information up into manageable chunks, rather like chapter titles in a book.

The following groups of BOIs have been found to be particularly useful in developing polycategoric Mind Maps:

- Basic questions – how/when/where/why/what/who/which?
- Divisions – chapters/lessons/themes
- Properties – characteristics of things
- History – chronological sequence of events
- Structure – forms of things
- Function – what things do
- Process – how things work
- Evaluation – how good/worthwhile/beneficial things are
- Classification – how things are related to each other
- Definitions – what things mean
- Personalities – what roles/characters people have

Learning to develop and manipulate polycategoric Mind Maps will enormously enhance your brain's ability to describe, analyse, evaluate and synthesise information. Interestingly, over the last century, the highly sophisticated hierarchical classification systems used in biology and astronomy (see overleaf) have increasingly come to resemble complex polycategoric Mind Maps – a case of Mind Maps reflecting nature and vice versa!

JOURNEY THROUGH THE MIND OF A MIND MAPPER, PART 4

Since we left our host in the last chapter, he or she has made the decision, based on the completed dyadic Mind Map, to buy a house. The question now is a rather more complex one: What *kind* of house shall I buy?

At first the process is identical. Our host places an appropriate three-dimensional, multi-coloured image at the centre. Then he or she selects BOIs which cover the full range of choices available: price, environment, purposes,

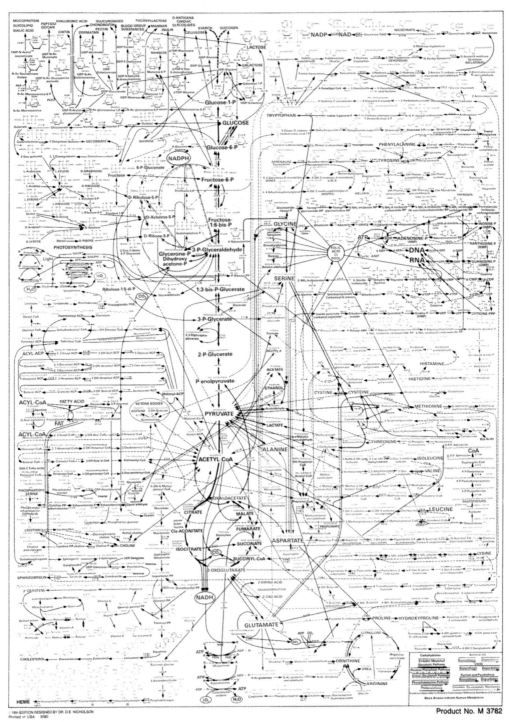

Diagram of a single metabolic pathway which resembles a complex polycategoric Mind Map (see page 133).

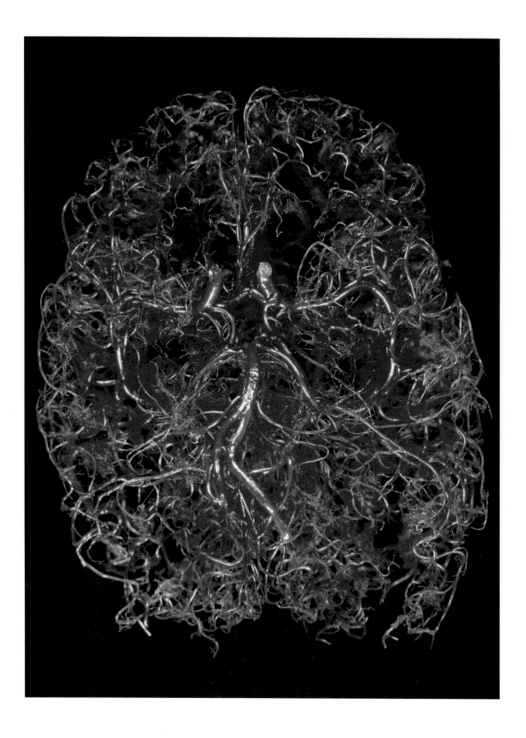

Natural Architecture Plate 15

additions, size, style.

Once these parameters have been established, our host can fill in his or her specific desires and priorities under each heading. This process immediately clarifies the range of choices to be made, highlighting the key trade-offs which will govern the purchase. The Mind Map does not make the decision itself – it presents the Mind Mapper with a 'smorgasbord' of choices from which the most appropriate decision can be taken.

Having completed the polycategoric Mind Map our host is ready to consult the estate agents' literature with a much clearer idea of what he or she wants and needs from a house.

THOUGHT-BUILDING EXERCISES

Like all forms of thinking, polycategoric Mind Mapping is a skill that can be learnt and developed. Here are two useful and enjoyable thought-building exercises.

Why would it be fun to?

Each of these exercises can be done as speed Mind Maps as they are an excellent way of improving your ability to select relevant BOIs quickly. Imagine, and then Mind Map, why it would be fun to:

1 Go out with a . . . .

2 Buy a . . . .

3 Learn a . . . .

4 Change a . . . .

5 Believe a . . . .

6 Withdraw from a . . . .

7 Begin a . . . .

8 Create a . . . .

9 Finish a . . . .

Make sure that you specify an object for each item on the list, and try choosing some 'absurd' objects in order to boost your imagination, memory and creative thinking abilities all at the same time. The next step is to do a very quick Mind Map for each one, choosing no more than seven major reasons why each item would be fun. (A secondary benefit of these exercises is that they often result in real action being taken when you realise how much fun you could be having!)

Object X

This is a more abstract, and therefore more demanding, way of testing your BOI selection skills. Your task is to prepare a Mind Map describing object X. The problem is that you do not know what object X is, so you must try to find a set of general-purpose BOIs which, if developed, could generate a full and ordered description of *any* object.

Making a decision

When your polycategoric Mind Map has been completed, the decision-making process will resemble that of the simple two-way choice, and the steps to be followed in this instance are the same as those outlined in the preceding chapter.

BENEFITS OF POLYCATEGORIC MIND MAPS

Having completed a polycategoric Mind Map, you may wish to apply one or more of the methods described in Chapter 12 ('Making the choice', pages 125–8) in order to reach your decision.

The major benefits of polycategoric Mind Maps are as follows:

1 They help you develop your mental powers of classification, categorisation, incisiveness and clarity.

THE MIND MAP BOOK

2 They enable you to collect complex data in an integrated form on a single page, thus increasing the chances of making an informed and intelligent decision.

3 They highlight the key trade-offs which must be considered in the decision.

4 Like dyadic Mind Maps, they utilise the full range of cortical skills, resulting in a more comprehensively considered decision.

5 By stimulating all these cortical areas, polycategoric Mind Maps encourage the brain to enter into a dialogue with itself. In other words they allow the brain to observe its own activity in an externalised whole picture and thus to learn more about itself. This new knowledge expands the brain's perspective, encouraging it to have even more advanced thoughts about the topic.

6 They can be filed away for future use as reminders of the reasons for previous decisions or as guides for other situations in which similar decisions have to be made.

ONWORD

Now that you have learnt how to organise your own ideas, to *make* notes using polycategoric Mind Maps, you will find it easy to organise other people's ideas, to *take* notes. The vital and enjoyable art of note-taking, traditionally the bane of many people's lives, is the subject of the next chapter.

CHAPTER 14

ORGANISING OTHER PEOPLE'S IDEAS

Preview
- Foreword
- Note-taking
- The four main functions of notes
- Establishing a productive 'mental set' for note-taking
- A practical example of polycategoric Mind Mapping
- Benefits of polycategoric Mind Maps for note-taking
- Onword

FOREWORD
This chapter looks at how you can use polycategoric Mind Maps to organise other people's ideas (take notes). After exploring the main functions of notes, you will learn how to prepare for note-taking so that you get the maximum benefit from each study session. There is also a practical example of poly-categoric note-taking and a summary of its benefits.

NOTE-TAKING
Note-taking is receiving other people's ideas from speeches, books and other media, and organising them into a structure that reflects their original thought or enables you to re-organise it to suit your own needs. Note-taking should be supplemented with the note-taker's own thoughts.

THE FOUR MAIN FUNCTIONS OF NOTES
Mnemonic – Analytic – Creative – Conversational.

Mnemonic

Sadly, most students in school and universities around the world seem to think that notes are nothing more than a memory aid. Their only concern is that their notes should enable them to remember what they have read just long enough to pass their exams, after which the information can be happily forgotten. As we have seen, memory is indeed a major factor but by no means the only one. Other functions, such as analysis and creativity, are equally important.

The Mind Map is a particularly effective mnemonic device for all the reasons outlined in the next chapter, 15 (page 147). As a note-taking technique, it has none of the disadvantages of standard linear note-taking, as described in Chapter 3 ('The disadvantages of standard notes', pages 49–50). Instead, it offers all the advantages of a method that works in harmony with your brain, utilising and releasing the full range of its capabilities.

Analytic

When taking notes from lectures or from written material, it is essential first of all to identify the underlying structure of the information being presented. Mind Mapping can help you extract the Basic Ordering Ideas and hierarchies from linear information.

Creative

The best notes will not only help you remember and analyse information, they will also act as a springboard for creative thought.

Mind Maps combine notes *taken* from the external environment (lectures, books, journals and the media) with notes *made* from the internal environment (decision-making, analysis and creative thought).

Conversational

When you take Mind Map notes from a lecture or book, your notes should record all the relevant information from that source. *Ideally, they should also include the spontaneous thoughts that arise in your mind while listening to the lecture or reading the book.* In other words your Mind Map should reflect the conversation between your intellect and that of the speaker or author. Special colour or symbol codes can be used to distinguish your own contribution to the exchange of ideas.

If the lecture or book happens to be badly organised or badly expressed, your Mind Map will reflect that lack of clarity. This may result in a messy-looking Mind Map but it will also reveal the source of the confusion. You will therefore have a much better grip on the situation than linear note-takers who disguise their confusion in pages of neatly written but functionally useless lines and lists.

The Mind Map thus becomes a powerful tool, for gathering information from others and for assessing the quality of their thinking and relating it to your personal needs and goals.

ESTABLISHING A PRODUCTIVE 'MENTAL SET' FOR NOTE-TAKING

In order to take best advantage of your note-taking opportunities, it is important for you to organise your approach in a way that allows you to build up a clearly structured Mind Map as your note-taking progresses.

To establish the best mental set for note-taking from a book, use the Mind Map Organic Study Technique (MMOST) as described in detail by Tony Buzan in *Use Your Head* (Chapter 9). There are eight basic steps:

1 Very quickly **browse** or look through the entire book or article, getting a general feel for the way it is organised.

2 Work out the length of **time** to be spent studying and determine the **amount** of material to be covered in that time.

3 Mind Map what you already **know** in that subject area in order to establish associative mental 'grappling hooks'.

4 Define your **aims** and **objectives** for this study session and complete a different Mind Map of all the questions that need to be answered.

Natural Architecture Plate 16

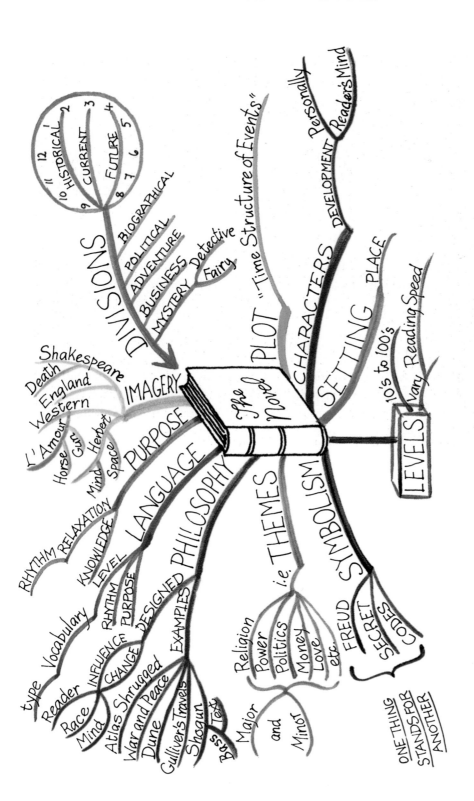

Mind Map by a father, Sean Adam, helping his daughter to pass her literature exams (which she did!) (See page 145)

5 Take an **overview** of the text, looking at the table of contents, major headings, results, conclusions, summaries, major illustrations or graphs, and any other important elements which catch your eye. This process will give you the central image and main branches (or Basic Ordering Ideas) of your new polycategoric Mind Map of the text. Many students report that they have often completed 90 per cent of their learning task by the time they finish the overview stage. By focusing on the overall structure and major elements of the text, the author's essential ordering impetus rapidly becomes clear and can easily be Mind Mapped.

6 Now move on to the **preview**, looking at all the material not covered in the overview, particularly the beginnings and ends of paragraphs, sections and chapters, where the essential information tends to be concentrated. Add to your Mind Map.

7 The next stage is the **inview**, in which you fill in the bulk of the learning puzzle, still skipping over any major problem areas. Having familiarised yourself with the rest of the text, you should now find it much easier to understand these passages and bulk out your Mind Map.

8 Finally there is the **review** stage, in which you go back over the difficult areas you skipped in the earlier stages and look back over the text to answer any remaining questions or fulfil any remaining objectives. At this point you should complete your Mind Map notes. See Chapter 24 (Mind Map, page 239).

The process can be likened to building up a jigsaw puzzle, beginning by looking at the complete picture on the box, then putting in the corners and outside edges, and gradually filling in the middle until you have a complete replica.

In a lecture situation, a similar approach is recommended. In order to make your note-taking task easier, you could ask the lecturer beforehand if he or she will give you a summary of the major topics, themes or categories that are to be dealt with in the session.

If this is not possible, simply construct a Mind Map while listening, searching for BOIs as the lecture progresses. After the lecture you can edit, re-order and refine your Mind Map, a process which will force you to make sense of the information, preparation and presentation, thus enhancing your understanding of it. For more on Mind Mapping a lecture, see Chapter 26 (page 252).

A PRACTICAL EXAMPLE OF POLYCATEGORIC MIND MAPPING

The polycategoric Mind Map on page 143 was produced by a father to help his daughter pass her university entrance examinations in English literature.

When confronted with a structure as complex as the novel, it is an enormous advantage for the brain to be able to refer to this type of mental 'grid' which sets out the major literary elements in the novel.

This type of Mind Map enables the reader to extract the essence of any text more accurately and comprehensively. It also makes it much easier to transform that essential information into spoken or written form (such as an essay or examination answer).

The Mind Map overleaf was prepared over a four month period by Pan Collins, producer of Eire's leading television programme, *The Late Late Show*. Pan had to organise the entire crew's thoughts on topics, presenters, and programme order, etc. For her own records, she noted, in the large arrows, how the programme ranked for the week.

BENEFITS OF POLYCATEGORIC MIND MAPS FOR NOTE-TAKING

1 All 12 benefits of Mind Mapping mentioned in Chapter 9 (pages 89–90).

2 Your enormous 'search-and-find' mental association powers are unleashed.

3 Learning objectives can be attained far more quickly.

4 Mind Map notes can be quickly and easily transformed into essays, presentations and other creative or communicative forms.

5 Ever-increasing clarity of analytical thought.

6 A growing delight in accumulating knowledge.

7   A permanent and easily accessible record of all your significant learning experiences.

ONWORD

Having used Mind Maps to organise your own and other people's ideas, you are ready to explore Mind Maps and memory – the subject of the next chapter.

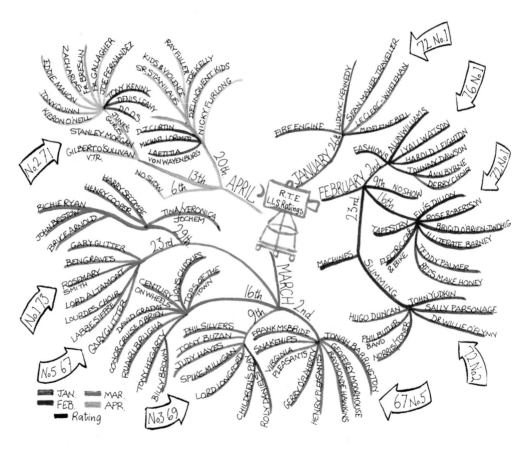

Mind Map by Pan Collins, Senior Producer of Radio Telefis Eirean's 'Late Late Show', planning and recording for major programmes (see page 145).

CHAPTER 15

MEMORY

FOREWORD

This chapter begins with a colourful Greek myth which has much to tell us about the relationship between memory, energy and creativity. We then explore Mind Maps as mnemonic and creative thinking devices, before summarising the benefits of mnemonic Mind Maps.

A GREEK MYTH

Zeus, the king of the gods, was well-known as a philanderer. He spent most of his time seducing – either directly or by means of deception – all the most beautiful women in the heavens and on earth.

Contrary to popular belief, his affections were not spread equally – there was one goddess with whom he spent far more time than any other. Her name was Mnemosyne, the goddess of memory. On one occasion he spent nine days and nights making passionate love to her, a coupling which resulted in the birth of the nine muses.

The muses represent creativity. Each is the goddess of a particular art:
- Erato – love poetry
- Calliope – epic poetry

- Euterpe – lyric poetry
- Polyhymnia – hymns
- Thalia – comedy
- Melpomene – tragedy

- Urania – astronomy
- Clio – history
- Terpsichore – dance

Zeus symbolises energy and power. So, according to the myth, applying energy or power to memory produces a fertilisation which results in creativity. This relationship has major implications for Mind Mapping theory. It is interesting to note that Tony originated the Mind Map entirely on the basis of his researches into recall during learning and mnemonics. The Mind Map was therefore originally a memory technique. It evolved naturally into a creative and multi-purpose thinking technique with the theoretical support of Sperry's brain research and the investigations of Torrance *et al* into creativity.

THE MIND MAP AS A MULTI-DIMENSIONAL MEMORY DEVICE

Mnemonic techniques involve the use of imagination and association in order to produce a new and memorable image. As well as imagination and association, the Mind Map combines *all* the cortical skills to create a highly advanced multi-dimensional memory device.

Multi-dimensional, in this context, means that rather than the one-dimensional (line) or two-dimensional (flat page) perspectives, the Mind Map allows you to create an internal, radiant, three-dimensional image that uses cross-association, colour and time.

A creative thought similarly combines two elements to produce a third for the purpose of projecting the present into the future. The creative device helps you project the present into the future for the purposes of changing or creating that future. *The mnemonic device helps you recreate the past in the present.*

The mnemonic Mind Map is therefore identical in mechanics and design to the multi-dimensional, *creative* Mind Map. In the same way that the mnemonic Mind Map multiplies dramatically your powers of memory, similarly the creative Mind Map multiplies the simple creative thinking model infinitely in all directions.

THE MNEMONIC MIND MAP AS A MIRROR OF CREATIVITY

Like memory, creative thinking is based on imagination and association. The aim is to link item A with item B, thus producing the new, innovative, far-from-the-norm idea we label 'creative'. The mnemonic and creative thinking processes are therefore identical in structure – the only difference is in intent.

A mnemonic device associates two items in order to enable the brain to recall (re-create) a third image in the future.

A creative device likewise combines two elements to project a third into the future, but the creative aim is to change or affect the future in some way, whereas the mnemonic aim is simply to remember.

Thus by making mnemonic Mind Maps, you are simultaneously training your creative thinking faculties. These in turn enhance memory capacity, and a mutually reinforcing upward spiral is created.

The illustration overleaf exemplifies the Mind Map as both mnemonic and creative thinking device. It was drawn by a leading American video producer called Denny Harris, and was originally made to remind him of what he wished to cover in a video on the subject of memory. His Mind Map summarises the content of the programme, including a preview, an in-depth explanation of the number/shape mnemonic system, the applications of a simple mnemonic system, and general discussion of the practice and theory presented in the programme. In this case, developing a mnemonic Mind Map became a genu-inely creative process, itself producing new ideas for the structure and content of the programme – memory feeding on creativity feeding on memory.

APPLICATIONS OF MNEMONIC MIND MAPS

Most of the specific applications are covered in Division 5, under the 'Personal', 'Family', 'Educational' and 'Business' section headings. However there are many other general memorising applications for Mind Maps, such as recalling radio and television programmes of particular interest, dreams, enjoyable family events, or general lists of 'things to do'.

One particularly useful application is searching for a 'lost' memory – perhaps a person's name or the whereabouts of an object.

In such cases, focusing on the missing item is usually counter-productive because 'it' has gone, and in focusing on 'it' you are focusing on an absence or nothingness.

Bearing in mind the associative power of your mind, leave the centre of your

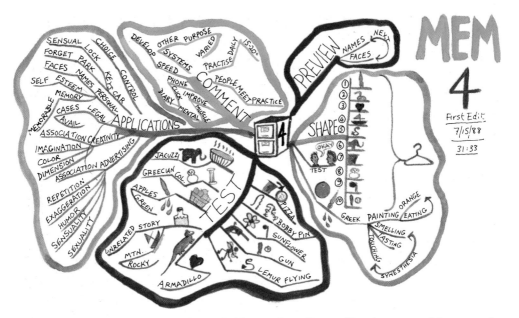

Mind Map by the well known film and video producer Denny Harris, summarising an entire programme on Memory (see page 149)

Mind Map blank, and surround it with words and images associated with the absent centre.

For example, if the 'missing' centre is the name of a person, the major surrounding branches would include sex, age, appearance, family, voice, hobbies, profession, and where first and last met. In this way you dramatically increase the probability of your brain recognising the centre from its memory banks. (For more on this, see Tony Buzan, *Use Your Memory*, Chapters 23–24.)

If you find it inconvenient to create a physical Mind Map to retrieve a 'missing' memory, you can simply visualise an internal screen on which you create the same sort of Mind Map.

BENEFITS OF MNEMONIC MIND MAPS

1 They utilise all the cortical skills, thereby enormously enhancing the probability of recall.

2 They activate the brain on all levels, making it more alert and skilful at remembering.

Natural Architecture Plate 17

3   Their attractiveness makes the brain want to return to them, and again encourages the probability of spontaneous recall.

4   They are intrinsically designed to aid memory.

5   The use of the memory *Mind Maps* activates the brain to become mnemonically alert and thus with each usage increases the base memory skill level.

6   They reflect the creative thinking process, thereby simultaneously enhancing creative thinking skills.

7   They maintain a high level of recall throughout a learning or listening period (contrary to the standard forgetting curves described in Tony Buzan, *Use Your Memory*, Chapter 5).

8   They utilise all the individual's associative capabilities, enhancing the brain's physical imprinting and network-making capabilities, and therefore increasing the probability of recall.

9   They provide a 'sure fire' method of remembering, thus increasing the individual's confidence, motivation and general mental functioning.

ONWORD

As we have seen, memory and creativity are two sides of the same coin. Having explored the mnemonic benefits of Mind Maps, the next chapter illuminates

CHAPTER 16

CREATIVE THINKING

Preview
- Foreword
- Aims of creative Mind Mapping
- The Mind Map as a creative thinking mechanism
- The stages of the creative thinking process
- Mind Mapping to gain new paradigms
- Benefits of creative thinking Mind Maps
- Onword

FOREWORD
In this chapter the focus is on creative thinking using Mind Maps. You will discover why Mind Maps are so startlingly effective in this area, and how you can use them to stretch and expand your own creative thinking and brainstorming abilities, thus gaining major new insights.

AIMS OF CREATIVE MIND MAPPING
Creative thinking or brainstorming Mind Maps have a great many objectives. The major ones are:

1 To explore all the creative possibilities of a given subject.

2 To clear the mind of previous assumptions about the subject, thus providing space for new creative thought.

3 To generate ideas that result in specific action being taken, or physical reality being created or changed.

4 To encourage more consistent creative thinking.

5 To create new conceptual frameworks within which previous ideas can be reorganised.

6 To capture and develop 'flashes' of insight when they occur.

7 To plan creatively.

THE MIND MAP AS A CREATIVE THINKING MECHANISM

The Mind Map is ideally suited to creative thinking because it utilises all the skills commonly associated with creativity, especially imagination, association of ideas and flexibility.

In psychological literature, especially in the testing manuals on creative thinking by E. Paul Torrance, flexibility has been identified as a vital element in creative thinking. Other important factors include the ability to:

- Associate new and unique ideas with pre-existing ones.
- Use different colours.
- Use different shapes.
- Combine unusual elements.
- Magnify and use dimension.
- Adjust conceptual position.
- Rearrange and link pre-existing concepts.
- Reverse pre-existing concepts.
- Respond to an aesthetically appealing object.
- Respond to an emotionally appealing object.
- Respond to an object which appeals to the senses of sight, touch, hearing, smell and taste.
- Use interchangeable shapes and codes.

Natural Architecture Plate 18

It can be seen from looking at the Mind Map laws and general theory that the Mind Map is in fact a sophisticated and elegant external manifestation of *all* of these defined categories: it is an external manifestation of the complete creative thinking process.

(My own researches have unearthed a striking similarity between the major factors in creative thinking, and the major factors in the history of the development of mnemonic techniques. For discussion see Chapter 15 ('The mnemonic Mind Map as a mirror of creativity', pages 148–9).

> The nearly identical nature of the creative thinking and mnemonic principles confirms the Mind Map as the essential and natural manifestation and tool for these forms of thought. It also lays the foundation for the claim that, in opposition to the bulk of literature on creativity and memory, the two processes, rather than being separate, distinct, and to many theoreticians opposites, *are* in fact mirror images of the same process.

The popular myth that the creative genius is absent-minded and forgetful fails to take note of the fact that the particular geniuses in question are only forgetful of those things which *psychologists* consider it important for them to remember. If attention were focused on their powers of memory in relation to the subject of their creative thoughts, we would find memories as vast as those of any of the great mnemonists.

THE STAGES OF THE CREATIVE THINKING PROCESS

Applying the creative thinking Mind Mapping technique correctly can enable individual Mind Mappers to produce *at least* twice as many creative ideas as a traditional large brainstorming group in the same period of time.

These are the five stages in the creative thinking Mind Mapping process.

1   The quick-fire Mind Map burst

Begin by drawing a stimulating central image. (For example, if you were trying to think of new possibilities in flight technology, you might draw a Concorde-like pair of wings.) Your image should be placed in the centre of a large blank page, and from it should radiate *every* idea that comes into your mind when you think of that subject.

For no more than 20 minutes you should let the ideas flow as fast as possible. Having to work at speed unchains your brain from its habitual thinking patterns, and encourages new and often apparently absurd ideas. These apparently absurd ideas should *always* be left in, because they contain the keys to new perspectives and the breaking of old and restrictive habits. To quote the philosopher Rudolf Flesch:

'Creative thinking may mean simply the realisation that there is no particular virtue in doing things the way they have always been done.'

It may also be useful for you to bear in mind Ezra Pound's famous dictum:

'Genius ... is the capacity to see ten things where the ordinary man sees one, and where the man of talent sees two or three, plus the ability to register that multiple perception in the material of his art.'

The reason for the page being as large as possible is to be found in Buzan's Precept: 'a Mind Map will expand to fill the space available'. In creative thinking, you need as much space as possible in order to entice your brain to pour out more and more ideas.

2   First reconstruction and revision

Have a short break, allowing your brain to rest and begin to integrate the ideas generated so far. You then need to make a new Mind Map, in which you identify the major branches or Basic Ordering Ideas, combining, categorising, building up hierarchies, finding new associations, and reconsidering in the context of the whole Mind Map any ideas that initially appeared 'stupid' or 'absurd'. As we have seen, the less conventional an idea, the better it often turns out to be.

During this first reconstruction stage, you may notice similar or even identical concepts appearing on the outer boundaries of your Mind Map. These should not be dismissed as unnecessary repetitions. They are fundamentally 'different' in that they are attaching themselves to different branches radiating from the central image. These peripheral repetitions reflect the underlying importance of ideas which are buried deep within your store of knowledge but which actually influence every aspect of your thinking.

To give such concepts their appropriate mental and visual weight, you should underline them on their second appearance; outline them with a geometric shape on their third appearance; and, if they recur a fourth time, box them in three-dimensional shapes.

Linking these related three-dimensional areas on your Mind Map, and dimensionalising the link, can literally create a new mental framework, leading to the flash of insight that occurs when old facts are seen from a new perspective.

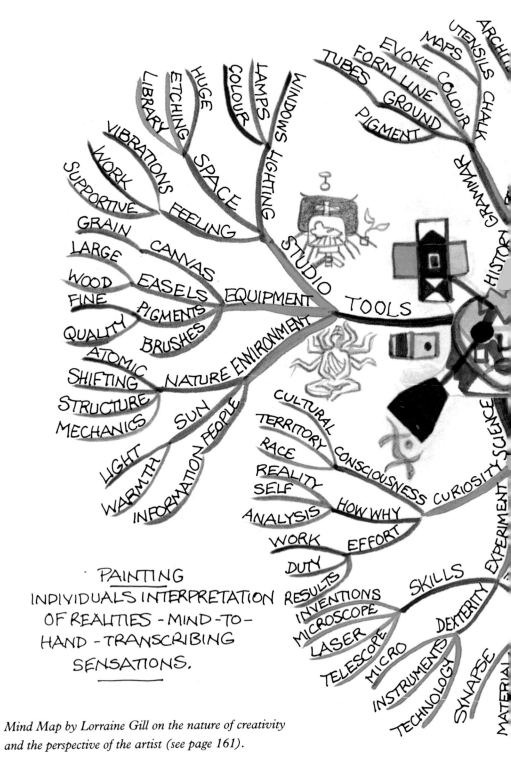

PAINTING
INDIVIDUALS INTERPRETATION
OF REALITIES - MIND -TO -
HAND - TRANSCRIBING
SENSATIONS.

*Mind Map by Lorraine Gill on the nature of creativity
and the perspective of the artist (see page 161).*

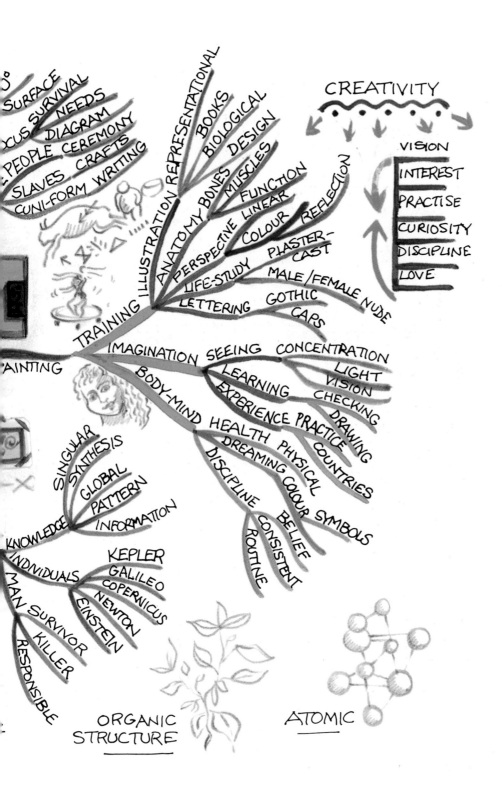

CREATIVITY

VISION
INTEREST
PRACTISE
CURIOSITY
DISCIPLINE
LOVE

SURFACE
SURVIVAL
NEEDS
DIAGRAM
PEOPLE CEREMONY
SLAVES CRAFTS
CUNI-FORM WRITING

REPRESENTATIONAL
BOOKS
BIOLOGICAL
DESIGN
ILLUSTRATION
ANATOMY BONES MUSCLES FUNCTION
PERSPECTIVE LINEAR
COLOUR REFLECTION
LIFE-STUDY PLASTER-CAST
TRAINING LETTERING GOTHIC MALE/FEMALE NUDE
CAPS

PAINTING

IMAGINATION SEEING CONCENTRATION
LIGHT
LEARNING VISION
EXPERIENCE PRACTICE CHECKING
DRAWING
BODY-MIND HEALTH PHYSICAL COUNTRIES
DREAMING COLOUR SYMBOLS
DISCIPLINE
SINGULAR
SYNTHESIS
GLOBAL
PATTERN
KNOWLEDGE INFORMATION
CONSISTENT BELIEF
ROUTINE

KEPLER
GALILEO
COPERNICUS
INDIVIDUALS NEWTON
MAN SURVIVOR EINSTEIN
KILLER
RESPONSIBLE

ORGANIC
STRUCTURE

ATOMIC

Such a shift represents a massive and instantaneous reorganisation of entire structures of thought.

In a sense, this type of Mind Map may appear to be 'breaking the rules', in that the central image and major branches no longer have central importance.

However, far from breaking the rules, such a Mind Map is using them to the full, particularly those of emphasis and imagery. A new idea discovered and repeated on the boundaries of thought may become the new centre. Following your brain's search-and-find workings, the Mind Map explores the furthest reaches of your current thought in search of a new centre to replace the old. And in due course this new centre will itself be replaced by a new and even more advanced concept.

> The Mind Map therefore aids and reflects intellectual exploration and growth.

3 Incubation

As we saw in Chapter 12 ('Making the choice', page 127), sudden creative realisations often come when the brain is in a relaxed, peaceful and solitary condition – perhaps when walking, running, sleeping or daydreaming. This is because such states of mind allow the Radiant Thinking process to spread to the farthest reaches of the parabrain, increasing the probability of mental breakthroughs.

The great creative thinkers have used this method throughout history. Einstein instructed his students to include incubation as a necessary part of all their cogitations; and Kekule, the discoverer of the benzene ring, scheduled incubation/daydreaming periods into his daily work programme.

4 Second reconstruction and revision

After incubation your brain will have a fresh perspective on your first and second Mind Maps, and you will find it useful to do another quick-fire Mind Map burst to consolidate the results of this integration.

During this reconstruction stage you need to consider all the information gathered and integrated in stages 1, 2 and 3 in order to make a comprehensive Mind Map.

The Mind Map on page 162 by Norma Sweeney was the result of intense incubation and a number of thought-revisions. It represents the culmination of ideas on the introduction of Brain Clubs to the world.

5 The final stage

At this stage you need to search for the solution, decision or realisation which was your original creative thinking goal. This often involves linking disparate elements in your final Mind Map, leading to major new insights and break-throughs.

MIND MAPPING TO GAIN NEW PARADIGMS

During deep and prolonged creative thinking, if new insights have been gained at the first reconstruction and revision stage, incubation may produce a new perspective on the collective insights, known as a paradigm shift.

The Mind Map on pages 158–159 is by Lorraine Gill. It summarises a series of lectures on the creative process as seen from the perspective of the practising artist. The Mind Map incorporates the History of Art, the growth of a 'grammar of seeing' and the tools for the accomplishment of creative tasks. Coinciding with modern brain research, the Mind Map emphasises Art as a Science (and Science as an Art) and also emphasises the training of both the imagination and the body in the creative process.

The *Mind Map* on page 163 by Benjamin Zander, Conductor of the Boston Philharmonic, is the result of such a process. The *Mind Map* reflects Zander's startlingly new approach to Beethoven's Symphony No. 9, an approach that was the result of years of study, internal Mind Mapping, and intense incubation.

A paradigm shift is a global change in thinking about assumptions that have become well-established worldwide. Examples include Darwin's theory of evolution and Einstein's theory of relativity, paradigms of thought that replaced previous paradigms. The Mind Map is the primary tool for recording the *process* of paradigm shifting.

For the creative thinking Mind Mapper, the new realisation is itself placed in a new framework by sudden realisations that have occurred within the parabrain during incubation. In this way the Mind Mapper adds further dimensions to his or her thinking, records the stages of the paradigm shift gaining mnemonic and macroscopic visions of the subject matter leading not only to new creative ideas but eventually to wisdom.

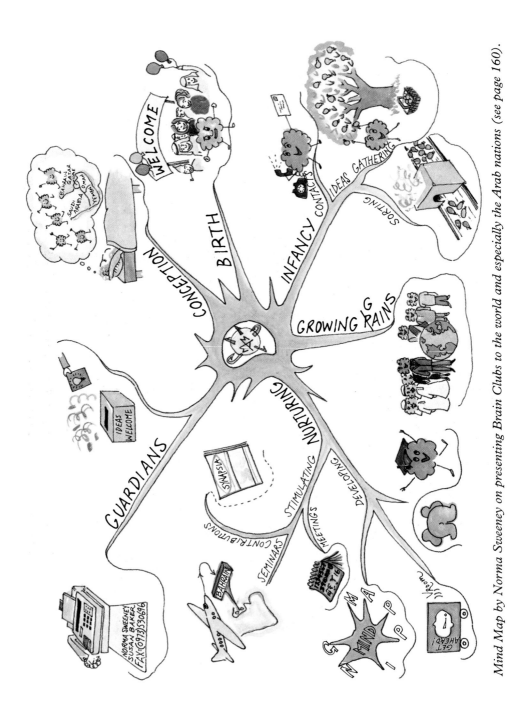

Mind Map by Norma Sweeney on presenting Brain Clubs to the world and especially the Arab nations (see page 160).

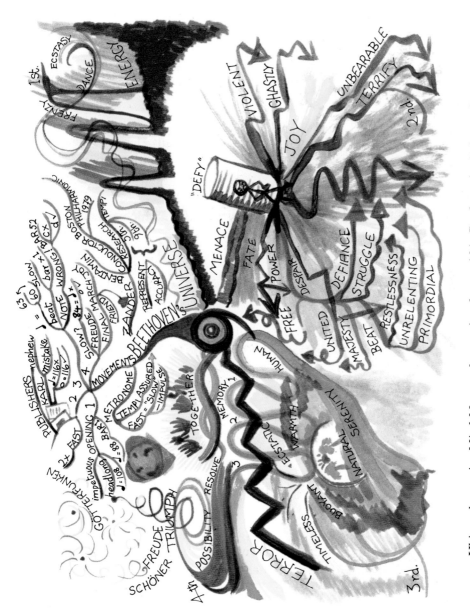

Ultimately creative Mind Map on the creation theme within Beethoven's ninth symphony,
by Benjamin Zander, Conductor of the Boston Philharmonic Orchestra (see page 161).

BENEFITS OF CREATIVE THINKING MIND MAPS

1   They automatically utilise all the creative thinking skills.

2   They generate ever-increasing mental energy as the Mind Mapper moves towards his or her goal.

3   They allow the Mind Mapper to view a great many elements all at once, thus increasing the probability of creative association and integration.

4   They enable people's brains to hunt out ideas which normally lie in obscurity on the periphery of their thinking.

5   They increase the probability of gaining new insights.

6   They reinforce and buttress the incubation process, increasing the probability of the generation of new ideas.

7   They encourage playfulness and humour, thus increasing the probability of the Mind Mapper straying far from the norm and producing a truly creative idea.

ONWORD
Once you have released your personal creativity through Mind Maps, you can gain enormous additional impetus by working with others to create a group mind. This is the subject of the next chapter.

CHAPTER 17

THE GROUP MIND MAP

FOREWORD

In this chapter we explore the exciting possibilities offered by group Mind Maps, in which groups of individuals can combine and multiply their personal creative abilities.

FUNCTIONS OF GROUP MIND MAPPING

The advantages of bringing individuals together in Mind Mapping groups were neatly summarised by Michael Bloch of the Sperry Laboratory in his Tel/Syn paper:

> *'In our daily lives, we learn a myriad of information that is unique to each of us. Because of this uniqueness, each of us has knowledge and a perspective that is strictly ours. Therefore it is beneficial to work with others during problem-solving tasks. By combining our Mind Map knowledge with others, we further the associations that we as well as others make.'*

During group brainstorming, the Mind Map becomes the external reflection, the 'hard copy', of the emerging group consensus and subsequently becomes a group record or memory. Throughout this process, the individual brains combine their energy to create a separate 'group brain'. At the same time the Mind Map reflects the evolution of this multiple self and records the conversation within it.

> At its best, it is impossible to distinguish the group Mind Map from one produced by a single great thinker.

CREATING A GROUP MIND

† Numerous studies have been done concerning the positive impact of checking knowledge and asking appropriate questions, an impact which is magnified by the use of the Mind Map. One of the most interesting was conducted by Frase and Schwartz (1975), who divided the subjects of their experiment into three groups of pairs. In Group 1, one person read a passage and then asked his or her partner questions regarding the passage. In Group 2, one person read a passage and was then *questioned* by their partner concerning the passage. In the third condition, they simply read the passage silently, and had no interactions with their partners. Groups 1 and 2 both performed well in subsequent tests of their recall, while the third group performed poorly.

The findings of this experiment lend further support to the suggestion that noting your own knowledge and questions in a Mind Map form will lead to far better comprehension of the material you read. Frase and Schwartz's findings also give added strength to the suggestion that it is extremely beneficial to work, either in pairs or in a group, rather than studying alone, and to engage in active conversation about the material you are studying, rather than studying in silence – very active verbalising leads to greater efficiency in the processing of the information, and to a greater recall. In addition, working with others will result in the unique perspectives and associations of each individual contributing to a greater overall Mind Map and a much more comprehensive and integrated learning.

The stages involved in group Mind Mapping are similar to those already described for individual creative thinking Mind Mapping. The main difference is that many of the functions that take place in the individual's parabrain during incubation are replaced by physical activity on the part of members of the Mind Mapping group. See pages 168–170 for the seven stages.

Natural Architecture Plate 19

These are the seven major stages in the group Mind Mapping process:

1 Defining the subject

The topic is clearly and concisely defined, the objectives are set, and the members of the group are given all the information that might be relevant to their deliberations.

2 Individual brainstorming

Each member of the group should spend at least 1 hour doing a quick-fire Mind Map burst and a reconstruction and revision Mind Map, showing major branches or Basic Ordering Ideas. (These are equivalent to stages 1 and 2 of the individual creative thinking Mind Mapping process in Chapter 16, pages 156–7.)

This method contrasts very markedly with traditional brainstorming in which one individual leads the group, noting the keyword ideas given by other members on a flip chart or central screen. This is counter-productive because each word or concept publicly mentioned will create mental eddies and currents that will draw all members of the group in the same direction. In this way, traditional brainstorming groups negate the non-linear associative power of the individual brain, thus losing the massive gains that could be made by initially allowing each brain to explore its own uninterrupted thoughts on the topic.

3 Small group discussion

The group now divides into groups of three to five. In each small group the members exchange their ideas and add to their own Mind Maps the ideas generated by other members. Allow 1 hour for this stage.

It is essential that a *totally* positive and accepting attitude be maintained. Whatever idea is mentioned by a group member should be supported and accepted by all the other members. In this way the brain which has generated the idea will be encouraged to continue exploring that chain of association. The next link in the chain may well turn out to be a profound insight, emanating from an idea that might have originally seemed weak, stupid or irrelevant.

4 Creation of first multiple Mind Map

Having completed the small group discussion, the group is ready to create its first multiple-mind Mind Map.

A gigantic screen or wall-sized sheet of paper is used to record the basic structure. This can be done by the whole group, one good Mind Mapper from each small group, or by one individual who acts as scribe for the whole group.

Colour and form codes should be agreed on in order to ensure clarity of thought and focus.

Basic Ordering Ideas are selected as the main branches, and *all* ideas are incorporated in the Mind Map, the group still maintaining its totally accepting attitude. For the group mind, this Mind Map represents the same stage as that reached by the individual Mind Mapper in Stage 2 of Individual Brainstorming.

5 Incubation

As in individual creative Mind Mapping, it is essential to let the group Mind Map 'sink in'.

Once again the Mind Mapping brainstorm process differs markedly from traditional methods, in which the pursuit of ideas tends to be non-stop verbal and analytical activity until a result is achieved. Such approaches use only a fraction of the brain's capabilities, and in so doing produce a result which is less than this fraction, for by eliminating so many of the brain's natural thinking skills, not only are they not used, but the synergetic relationship they have with the few skills that are used is also lost.

6 Second reconstruction and revision

After incubation the group needs to repeat stages 2, 3 and 4 in order to capture the results of the newly considered and integrated thoughts. This means doing individual quick-fire Mind Map bursts, then producing reconstructed Mind Maps showing main branches, exchanging ideas, modifying the Mind Maps in small groups, and finally creating a second group Mind Map.

The two giant group Mind Maps can then be compared, in preparation for the final stage.

The Mind Map on page 171 (top) is a group Mind Map created by a team of eight Digital executives: Matthew Puk, Microsystems Unit Manager, Thomas Spinola, Second Shift Unit Manager, Thomas Sullivan, Major Accounts Unit Manager, Chris Slabach, Field Service Manager, Lorita Williams, Unit Manager, Richard Kohler, Specialist Unit Manager, Tony Bigonia, Field Service Unit Manager, and John Ragsdale, Field Service Manager. They had been working for five days on the development of teamwork. Their conclusions were unremittingly positive!

7   Analysis and decision-making

At this stage, the group makes critical decisions, sets objectives, devises plans, and edits using the methods outlined in Chapter 12 (page 123).

GROUP MIND MAPPING APPLICATIONS

The major applications of group Mind Maps are as follows:

- Joint creativity.
- Combined recall.
- Group problem-solving and analysis.
- Group decision-making.
- Group project management.
- Group training and education.

EXAMPLES OF GROUP MIND MAPS IN ACTION

In recent years the group Mind Mapping method has been used very successfully by families, schools, universities and multinational companies.

A Boeing Aircraft engineering manual was condensed into a 25-foot long Mind Map, to enable a team of 100 senior aeronautical engineers to learn in a few weeks what had previously taken a few years. The result was an estimated saving of $11 million. See page 171 (bottom).

Electronic Data Systems (EDS), Digital Equipment Corporation and Nabisco have implemented group commando study programmes. Using group Mind Mapping and the Mind Mapping Organic Study Technique (MMOST), up to 120 senior members of staff were able to enter a seminar room in the morning and leave that same evening with between four and six books' worth of information understood, Mind Mapped, integrated, comprehensively remembered, and related to their professional situation.

At Oxford and Cambridge Universities, students like Edward Hughes (see Tony Buzan, *Use Your Head*, 1994 edition) have used group Mind Maps to obtain, with a minimal amount of time spent studying, exceptionally high firsts in their examination results.

Around the world, 'family genius groups' are being formed, in which the family becomes a group mind and the individual parents and children consistently rank first in whatever mental (and often physical!) activities they choose to pursue. For Mind Maps of a full 'family genius' study day, see Chapter 21 (page 207) and Chapter 24 (page 239).

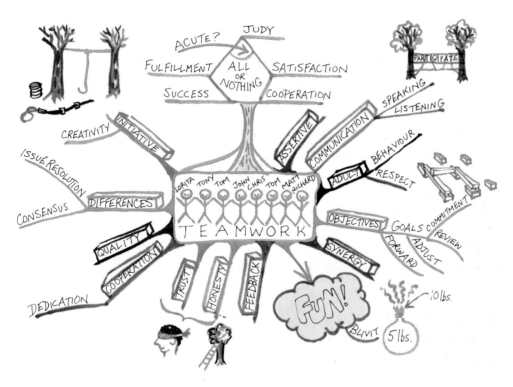

Mind Map on the development of team-work by Digital executives.

Dr Stanley with the 25-foot long Boeing Aircraft Mind Map (see pages 170 and 261).

THE DYADIC GROUP MIND

The most basic form of group mind is the dyadic mind, in which two individuals work as a partnership on a particular creative project. A similar procedure is followed as that described in Chapter 21 (page 199) for the larger group mind:

1 The subject is defined.

2 The individuals separate to prepare their individual quick-fire Mind Map bursts and basic Mind Maps.

3 They meet for discussion and exchange ideas.

4 The first joint Mind Map is created.

5 They incubate the newly integrated ideas.

6 A reconstructed, revised joint Mind Map is created.

7 They analyse and make decisions.

In long-term projects (like the writing of this book by my brother and me) joint Mind Mapping has several advantages. The Mind Maps can be used as a way of ordering, recording and stimulating conversation in the many meetings that such a project requires. They also enable you to conduct the process over a long time, and in numerous sessions, with continuity and momentum.

BENEFITS OF GROUP MIND MAPPING

1 This method of thinking and learning is natural to the human brain, and is *far* more enjoyable.

2   Throughout the group Mind Mapping process, there is equal and consistent emphasis on both the individual and the group. The more frequently individuals are allowed to explore their own mental universes, the more such explorers bring back and contribute to the group, without in any way losing their contribution.

3   The group mind benefits from individual contributions and instantaneously feeds back its own strength to the individual members, thus further increasing their ability to contribute to the group mind.

4   Even in its early stages, group Mind Mapping can generate many more useful and creative ideas than traditional brainstorming methods.

5   Group Mind Mapping automatically creates an emerging consensus, thus building team spirit and focusing all minds on the group's goals and objectives.

6   Every idea expressed by every member is accepted as valid. Members thus increasingly come to feel that they 'own' the emerging group consensus.

7   The group Mind Map acts as hard copy for the group memory. It also guarantees that at the end of the meeting each member of the group has a similar and comprehensive understanding of what has been achieved. (This again differs markedly from traditional approaches in which members of the group usually leave with an assumed understanding which is often later found to differ widely from the opinions of other members.)

8   The group Mind Map provides a powerful tool for each individual's self-development and acts as a relatively objective point of reference against which the individual can test and explore related ideas.

From this chapter and the earlier chapters on your own individual uniqueness, you will be drawn rapidly to the conclusion that the more individual you are, the more significant will be your contributions to both yourself and to the group. One particularly effective and enjoyable way to develop this uniqueness is to develop your own personal Mind Mapping style.

ONWORD

This chapter concludes your basic training in simple and more advanced Mind Mapping, both at individual and group level. The next division examines in detail the many exciting applications for your new-found skills. The division ends with intriguing new developments with Mind Mapping and computers, and a personal view by Tony Buzan of a Radiant Thinking and Mentally Literate future.

DIVISION 5
USES

In this division we explore the many practical ways in which you can use your newly acquired Mind Mapping skills: we begin with personal applications (self-analysis, problem-solving and keeping a Mind Map diary); this is followed by family study; then educational applications (thinking, teaching and Mind Mapping a book, lecture or video); and finally business and professional applications, including the new developments of computer Mind Maps and the prospect of a Radiant Thinking future. Some readers may wish to work through the whole division in sequence, others may prefer to consult the chapters that seem most relevant to their particular needs.

- Personal
    Self-analysis
    Problem-solving
    The Mind Map diary
- Family
    Family study and story-telling
- Educational
    Thinking
    Teaching
    Creating the Master Mind Map
- Business and Professional
    Meetings
    Presentations
    Management
    Computer Mind Mapping
- The Future
    Towards a Radiant Thinking and Mentally Literate World

SECTION A
Personal

CHAPTER 18

SELF-ANALYSIS

Preview
- Foreword
- Self-analysis using Mind Maps
- Reviewing the past and projecting future goals
- Helping others to analyse themselves
- Examples of self-analysis Mind Maps
- Benefits of self-analysis Mind Maps
- Onword

FOREWORD

This chapter investigates how Mind Maps can be used to give you a greater insight into yourself, your needs, desires and long-term aims. You will also learn how to help others analyse themselves, and get a chance to look at some fascinating examples of self-analysis Mind Maps.

SELF-ANALYSIS USING MIND MAPS

Whether you're weighing up the pros and cons of changing your job or trying to work out your long-term priorities, Mind Maps can be an enormous help in clarifying your thoughts and feelings. See Chapter 12 (page 123).

Because a Mind Map uses the full range of cortical skills it gives a comprehensive reflection of the self. Having seen this clear external image of yourself, you are less likely to suffer the unhappy consequences of making decisions that go against your nature and your real needs and desires.

It is helpful to begin with a 'complete picture' self-analysis Mind Map, which includes as many as possible of your major characteristics and personality traits. There are four major stages.

1 Preparation of your environment

Before you begin, you need to prepare your environment, following the recommendations given in Chapter 10 (pages 109–110). In such a sensitive area as self-analysis, it is particularly important that your materials should be of the highest quality and your environment as attractive, comfortable and mentally stimulating as possible. Caring for yourself will make your self-analysis more open, complete, profound and useful.

2 Quick-fire Mind Map burst

Draw a multi-coloured, three-dimensional central image which encapsulates either your physical or conceptual idea of yourself. Then do a quick-fire Mind Map burst, allowing a full and free flow of facts, thoughts and emotions. Working at speed will make it easier to express *all* your ideas, whereas attempting to be too neat and careful is likely to inhibit the spontaneous truthfulness needed for such an exercise.

3 Reconstruction and revision

Now select your major branches or Basic Ordering Ideas. Useful BOIs include:
- Personal history – past, present and future
- Strengths
- Weaknesses
- Likes
- Dislikes
- Long-term goals
- Family
- Friends
- Achievements
- Hobbies
- Emotions
- Work
- Home
- Responsibilities

(Continued on page 180)

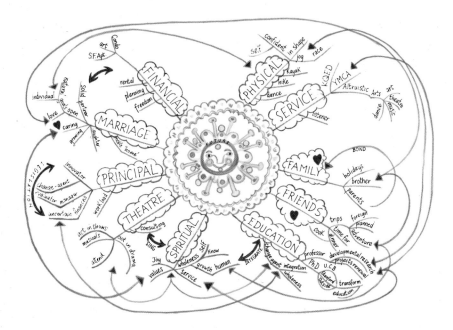

Mind Map by a female senior executive examining her belief systems, herself and her chosen directions for the future (see page 181).

Mind Map by a male chief executive of a multi-national organisation reconsidering his life and re-focusing upon his family (see page 181).

The last item, your emotional nature, is particularly important and all too often excluded. Colours, shapes, symbols and images are especially helpful in expressing this aspect of your personality in your Mind Map.

Other helpful BOIs are concerned with the directions your life is currently taking or that you might wish it to take in the future. These BOIs can also form the main branches of your Mind Map.

- Learning
- Knowledge
- Business
- Health
- Travel
- Leisure
- Culture
- Ambitions
- Problems

Having completed your quick-fire Mind Map burst and having selected your major branches, you should create a larger, more artistic and more considered version. This final Mind Map is the external mirror of your internal state.

4 Decision-making

Looking at your final Mind Map, you can make decisions and plan your future actions by using the methods described in Chapter 12 (pages 125–9).

REVIEWING THE PAST AND PROJECTING FUTURE GOALS

An annual personal review of past achievements and projection of future goals is extremely useful in ordering and planning your life, and the Mind Map is the ideal tool for both these tasks.

Having assessed the past year's achievements in Mind Map form, you can use the same Mind Map as the basis for another Mind Map describing your plan of action for the coming year. In this way you can use the next year to build on strengths and priorities, and perhaps choose to spend less time and energy on areas which have proved less productive or satisfying in the past.

As the years go by, these annual Mind Maps form an on-going record, revealing trends and patterns over your whole lifetime and giving you major insights into yourself and the path your life is taking.

PREVIOUS PAGE: *Natural Architecture Plate 20*

As well as annual Mind Maps, we recommend that you do self-analysis Mind Maps at the beginning and end of any important phase in your life, whether you are changing job or house, or beginning or ending a relationship or course of study.

HELPING OTHERS TO ANALYSE THEMSELVES

You may wish to help friends or colleagues analyse themselves, perhaps someone who has never done a Mind Map before. In such cases you can follow the same four stages described earlier (pages 177–8), the only difference being that, rather than analysing yourself, you become a scribe for someone else.

Your friends or colleagues can describe their central images while you draw them. They can then dictate all the thoughts, feelings and ideas that come to mind, while you write them down as a quick-fire Mind Map burst. You will probably need to help them find suitable Basic Ordering Ideas. You can then draw a comprehensive Mind Map incorporating everything that they have said, after which the analysis can be done either in private or, where appropriate, together.

EXAMPLES OF SELF-ANALYSIS MIND MAPS

The example on the bottom of page 178 is a Mind Map by a chief executive in a multinational corporation who originally wished to analyse his life in relation to his business activities. However, as the Mind Map increasingly revealed his feelings, it began to reflect all the major elements in his life.

These included family, business, sporting activities, learning and general self-development, and his interest in Eastern philosophies and practices.

He subsequently explained that, before the Mind Mapping self-analysis, he had assumed his business to be his prime concern. But, through Mind Mapping, he realised that his family was the true foundation of his life. As a result he transformed his relationship with his wife, children and other relatives, and adjusted his schedule to reflect his true priorities.

Predictably enough, his health and his mental state improved enormously, his family became much closer and more loving, and his business improved dramatically as it began to reflect his new positive outlook.

The example on the top of page 178 was created by a female executive who was considering a change of career and personal direction. She did the Mind Map in order to see who she was and what her belief systems were. Initially she suffered from relatively low self-esteem. However, by the time she had completed her self-analysis, she was as radiant as the Mind Map itself.

BENEFITS OF SELF-ANALYSIS MIND MAPS

1 They provide a comparatively and increasingly objective perspective on the self.

2 By utilising all the cortical skills, they give a full and realistic picture of the individual.

3 They provide both macroscopic and microscopic views of the individual, encompassing broad trends as well as small but nonetheless relevant details.

4 They make future planning easier and more accurate by putting it in the context of the individual's present state.

5 They act as a permanent record, thus allowing the Mind Mapper to gain a truer perspective over the long term.

6 They can be used to help others analyse themselves.

7 By using colours, images and codes, they make it easier to express emotions and incorporate them in self-analysis.

ONWORD

Having used Mind Maps for general self-analysis, the next chapter focuses on how you can use them to help solve specific personal problems.

CHAPTER 19

PROBLEM-SOLVING

Preview
- Foreword
- Personal problem-solving using Mind Maps
- Interpersonal problem-solving using Mind Maps
- The stages of interpersonal problem-solving
- Benefits of interpersonal problem-solving Mind Maps
- Onword

FOREWORD

In this chapter you will find out how to use Mind Maps both to solve personal problems and to resolve difficulties in your relationships with others. Many of the skills you have already acquired – such as self-analysis and decision-making – play a part in problem-solving.

PERSONAL PROBLEM-SOLVING USING MIND MAPS

This process is almost identical to self-analysis except that the focus is on a specific personality trait or characteristic that may be causing you concern.

For example, let's imagine that your problem is excessive shyness. You begin with a central image (perhaps a picture of you hiding your face behind your hands?), then do a quick-fire Mind Map burst, releasing all the thoughts and emotions triggered by the idea of shyness.

In the first reconstruction and revision, your Basic Ordering Ideas might include: the situations in which you feel shy; the emotions which make up your shyness; the physical reactions you experience; the verbal and physical behaviour that results; the background to your shyness (when it first started and how it developed); and the possible root causes.

Having comprehensively defined, analysed and incubated the problem, you need to do a second reconstruction and revision. In this second Mind Map you should look at each element of the problem and work out a specific plan of action to solve it. Implementing these various actions should then enable you to resolve the problem in its entirety.

In some cases it turns out that you are mistaken about the real problem. If the same word or concept appears on several branches, the chances are that it is actually more fundamental to your problem than the one you have placed in the centre. In this situation you should simply start another Mind Map, with the new key concept as your central image, and continue as before.

INTERPERSONAL PROBLEM-SOLVING USING MIND MAPS

Close personal relationships often come to grievous ends because neither person fully understands or appreciates the point of view of the other. If emotions are running high, and there is no real communication, individuals find themselves in an increasingly destructive negative associational spiral.

For instance, if person A feels that he or she has been hurt by person B, person A is more likely to think negatively about person B. These negative thoughts increase the degree of hurt experienced by person A, which in turn triggers further negative thoughts about person B. The destructive spiral gains momentum until, to use a familiar phrase, the problem has been 'blown up out of all proportion'.

Eventually even positive events from the past are drawn into the destructive whirlpool and are seen in a negative light. For instance, the birthday present one partner gave the other is no longer seen as a sign of love. Instead they are accused of using it as a 'bribe' or a way of distracting from some misdemeanour.

By opening up clear channels of communication between individuals, Mind Mapping can help people avoid the negative associational spiral. In addition, the radiant, all-embracing structure of the Mind Map enables the participants to put their problem in a wider and more positive context. All this is confirmed by the fact that a number of marriages and close friendships have been saved through Mind Mapping.

An example of such a personal problem-solving Mind Map is that by Tessa Tok-Hart on page 186. Her Mind Map externalises the problems she had both experienced herself and noticed in others while communicating. The central image of the two faces joined by a thick line show the fundamental human elements concerned, those items on the right being immediate hindrances and those on the left helpers to the process.

The outer right hand arcs show the circumstantial factors which are frequent causes of conflict. The outer left hand arcs indicate characteristic qualities that can overcome conflict. The ears of the face on the positive side are open and listening, the ears on the right closed to any incoming information. The shortened thick arrows in the centre of the right hand side of the Mind Map indicate a complete blockage of communication. The large arrows on the outer arcs of the Mind Map show war, destruction, alienation and disunity on one side, and creativity, friendship, happiness and unity on the other.

THE STAGES OF INTERPERSONAL PROBLEM-SOLVING

For interpersonal problem-solving to succeed, it is essential that both individuals fully understand the theory and application of Mind Maps. Assuming this basic knowledge, there are three major stages in the process.

1 Preparation of your environment

As with self-analysis, it is important that your materials should be of the highest quality, and your environment as comfortable and supportive of the entire process as possible. As the process may take several hours, especially for a major problem, you need to plan activity and rest breaks, and light food, to ensure that the exercise does not end simply with analysis but reaches resolution.

2 Creation of the Mind Maps

At this stage, each individual does three large, separate Mind Maps: dislikes, likes and solutions.

In each of the three Mind Maps you should follow the usual procedure of first completing a quick-fire Mind Map burst, which should be followed by a more careful reconstruction in which you select your BOIs.

Dislikes

For up to 1 hour (or more if required) each participant does an exhaustive Mind Map on every negative aspect of the relationship to date. No matter how many positive elements there may be in the situation, the aim at this point is to give a full and objective description of the negative aspects.

It is essential that the participants do their Mind Maps in complete privacy and that no views or opinions are exchanged during the Mind Mapping process.

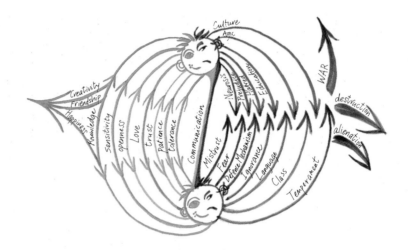

Mind Map by Tessa Tok-Hart on solving the problems of communication (see page 184).

After completion of the negative Mind Map, there should be a short break, during which conversation should be kept strictly to other matters.

Likes

An identical procedure is now followed to create a positive Mind Map, in which every past and presently satisfying aspect of the relationship is revealed. Once again, it is essential that no discussion takes place during the Mind Mapping process, the point being to have a formalised discussion after completion of all three Mind Maps.

Solutions

For this Mind Map, the individuals focus separately on resolution, working out plans of action to solve each aspect of the problem.

3   Formal discussion

At this stage each participant takes it in turn to give presentations (see Chapter 26, page 252), first on the negative Mind Maps, then on the positive ones, and finally on the solutions.

During the presentations, the listeners have new blank sheets of paper on which they Mind Map comprehensively and precisely everything that is being said about them. It is essential at this point that the listeners remain totally

Natural Architecture Plate 21

silent scribes. The only permissible comments are those made for the purpose of checking that they have understood the presenter's statements and for confirming that they can understand the others' point of view. It is particularly important to follow this rule during the exchange of negative Mind Maps, when some of the statements may be surprising, shocking or even traumatising.

The listeners need to remember that, based on the multi-ordinate nature of perception, whatever the presenters are saying *must be true from their perspective*. These statements must be absorbed and integrated by the listener if he or she is ever to understand why the problem has arisen and how it can be resolved.

It is also essential for all participants to tell 'the whole truth and nothing but the truth' from their perspectives, as holding anything back leaves festering incompletions.

The order of presentations should be as follows:

1   X presents negatives, while Y Mind Maps.

2   Short break.

3   Y presents negatives, while X Mind Maps.

4   Short break.

5   X presents positives, while Y Mind Maps.

6   Short break.

7   Y presents positives, while X Mind Maps.

8   Short break.

9   Y presents solutions, while X Mind Maps.

10 Short break.

11 X presents solutions, while Y Mind Maps.

12 Discussion. Agreement on solutions, and celebration!

It is best to exchange the negative aspects first because they are obviously the heart of the problem. The aim is definitely not to score points or to hurt each other, but to explain as fully as possible what is causing pain to one partner so that both may heal the wounds. Indeed, the very act of getting all the negative aspects out into the open in an atmosphere of objectivity and respect can frequently more or less resolve a problem which has been mainly caused by misunderstanding of the other person's point of view.

Following the negative with the positive will often produce as many positive surprises as there were negative shocks in the previous exercise. The positive aspects of the relationship give added impetus to the search for solutions, directing the individuals' energies into a mini-group brain which is instinctively drawn towards consensus. Immediately after the exchange of solutions, mutual areas of agreement should be identified and plans of action confirmed.

BENEFITS OF INTERPERSONAL PROBLEM-SOLVING MIND MAPS

1 Their structure guarantees openness on the part of the participants.

2 They give each participant a comprehensive view of the other's perspective.

3 They encourage honesty between the participants.

4 They place the problem within a much wider context, allowing a deeper understanding of its causes and a stronger impetus to resolve it.

5 They act as an on-going record of the relationship, and the positive and solution Mind Maps can be used as a source of strength and support as the relationship develops.

6 This method allows the individual not only to understand the other, but also to gain major insights into the self which lead to greater self-awareness and maturity.

7 As well as greater understanding, they result in a closer bond between partners, a less stressful relationship, and a greater respect for the unique viewpoints of others.

The process described in this chapter is made considerably easier once you have completed your objective self-analysis. In this context you will find that personal and interpersonal problem-solving becomes easier and more efficient, in most cases leading to an increasing individual and mutual delight.

ONWORD

In addition to self-analysis and problem-solving, Mind Maps can play many other useful roles in everyday life. In the next chapter we find out how to use a Mind Map diary – the Universal Personal Organiser!

CHAPTER 20

THE MIND MAP DIARY

Preview
- Foreword
- The principles of the Mind Map diary
- The yearly plan
- The monthly plan
- The daily plan
- The life-planning divisions
- Benefits of the Mind Map diary
- Onword

FOREWORD

Traditional diaries are the ultimate linear device, placing us firmly under the tyranny of time. In this chapter you will be introduced to a new, revolutionary Mind Mapper's diary which allows you to manage your time according to your needs and desires rather than the other way round. The Mind Mapper's diary can be used both as a planning diary and as a retrospective record of events, thoughts and feelings. The Mind Map diary alone offers the opportunity to synthesise these two traditional diary approaches.

THE PRINCIPLES OF THE MIND MAP DIARY

In the same way that Mind Mapping represents a large leap from standard linear note-taking, the Mind Map diary or Universal Personal Organiser (UPO) (see page 317) is far more efficient and effective than a standard diary.

As well as the cortical skills used in traditional diaries (words, numbers, lists, sequence and order), the Mind Map diary incorporates colour, imagery, symbols, codes, humour, daydreams, gestalt (wholeness), dimension, association and visual rhythm.

By giving you a true and full reflection of your brain, the Mind Map diary enables you to operate in all three spatial dimensions, as well as those of colour and time. The Mind Map diary thus becomes not only a *time*-management system but also a self and *life*-management system.

THE YEARLY PLAN

The yearly plan (or annoplan) should simply give you an overview of the major events in the year. It should be as positive as possible (in order to give you continuous supportive feedback), and it should contain no specific details, as these can all be shown in the monthly and daily plans.

You will need to make extensive use of colours, codes and images in your yearly plan, and you should establish your own colour codes to guarantee secrecy where necessary. This colour coding should be continued in your monthly and daily plans, to give consistency and immediacy in cross-referencing, planning and recall.

THE MONTHLY PLAN

The monthly Mind Map diary page is simply an expanded version of the single month from the yearly plan. Dates and days drop from the top left, while hours of the day range from top left to top right.

To keep the page and mind uncluttered, each day has no more than five meetings/events/tasks entered as coloured images, coloured codes or key words. Any additional details can be included on the daily plan.

The example on page 194 covers the month of August 1990 from my own diary, in which I have shown meetings, special events, goals and time spent on business trips to different countries.

With consistent colour coding, it is possible to get an instant overview of the whole of the coming year. Likewise, by laying out the previous year's plan alongside the 12 monthly plans, you can gain instant access to any period, with guaranteed recall.

Furthermore, these yearly and monthly plans provide the ideal basis for your annual review of the past and setting of future goals (see Chapter 18, pages 180–1). Cross-referencing, calculation and observation of overall trends all become much easier when you have an overview of the whole year.

THE DAILY PLAN

The daily Mind Map diary page is based on the 24-hour clock, the Mind Map as a planning and mnemonic device, and the fact that the human brain is a visionary, goal-oriented mechanism.

As with the yearly and monthly plans, as many Mind Mapping laws as possible are applied. Ideally, you will make two Mind Maps for each day: the first one to plan the day in advance; and the second to monitor its progression – this can also be used to recapture the day in retrospect.

The example on page 195 is the second day of August from my own monthly plan. In this daily plan the 24-hour clock in the upper left-hand corner gave me a true perspective on the amount of time in the day. The central image of the day's Mind Map was the book you are now reading. The smiling mouth, resembling Aladdin's lamp, indicated that I was dictating sections of the book and I was hoping that I would be inspired by the 'genie' of my imagination.

The day divided itself into five major branches, by far the largest being my work on the book. The walk and run, the massage and the physical training, were all intended to help me think about and physically prepare for the subsequent days on which I planned to work on the book. The evening was a celebration with a friend!

Like the yearly and monthly plans, these daily plans can be used to review any period in your life, either comprehensively or in-depth. A quick browse can thus bring back a whole week, month or year with glorious vividness.

THE LIFE-PLANNING DIVISIONS

Like other personal organisers, the Mind Map diary can also help you keep track of different aspects of your life. Once again, to keep the mind uncluttered, it's best to use only a few major Basic Ordering Ideas. The most useful are:
- Health and wellness
- Family and friends
- Creativity
- Wealth and work

In each of these divisions you can plan and Mind Map telephone calls, meetings, holidays, etc, and jot down creative ideas and things to remember.

BENEFITS OF THE MIND MAP DIARY

1 It provides both a macroscopic and a microscopic view of your life becoming, as it grows, a comprehensive life-management tool. It allows you to span future and past; to plan and record.

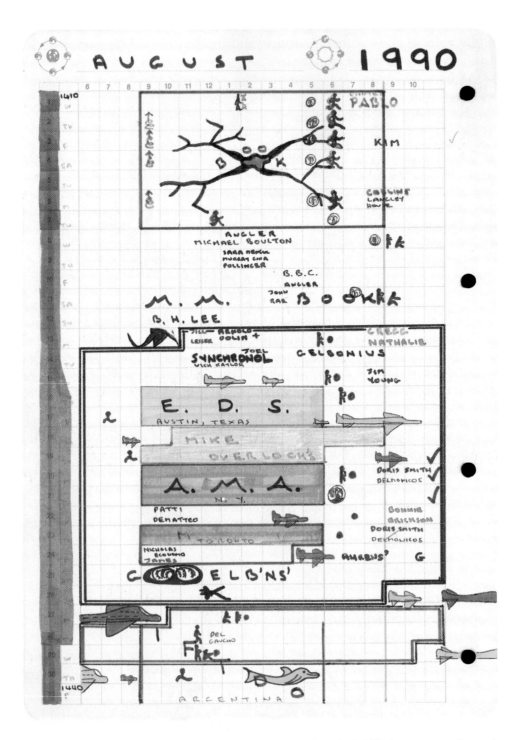

'Linear' page from Tony Buzan's diary showing use of all cortical skills for more creative and easily remembered diary keeping (see page 192).

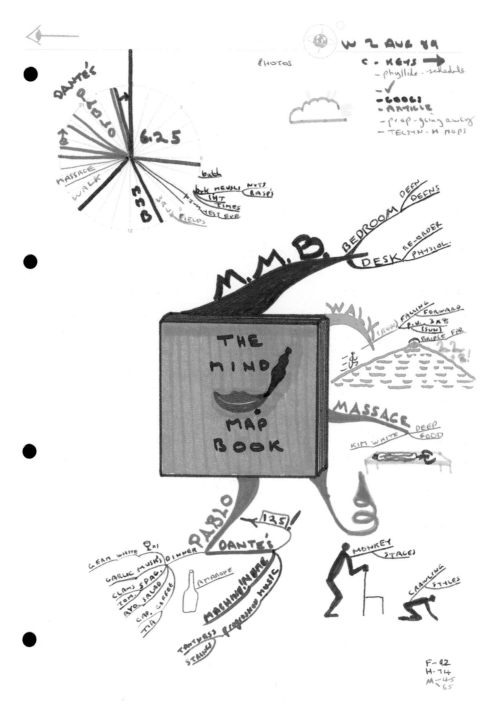

Mind Map from Tony Buzan's personal diary showing Mind Map of the day in which he began formally writing The Mind Map Book, *and symbolising the genie that came from ideas discussed in conversation (see pages 192–3).*

2   It is visually attractive, and becomes more attractive as the user's skill improves – the user eventually begins to create works of art.

3   The yearly, monthly and daily plans allow for instant review of year-long periods, with cross-referencing and observation of long-term trends.

4   The Mind Map diary puts every event in the context of your whole life.

5   The diary system is in itself a multi-dimensional mnemonic of multi-dimensional mnemonics! It thus provides a virtually complete externalised memory-core of your life.

6   It puts you in control of those areas of your life which are most important to you.

7   The system, by its design, encourages automatic self-development. It accomplishes this by allowing the brain to use more effectively the recently discovered TEFCAS model of learning. The TEFCAS model refers to the fact that the brain operates by *T*rial, after which there is an *E*vent, followed by *F*eedback, which is then *C*hecked by your brain and to which it *A*djusts towards its always and ultimate goal, *S*uccess.

8   Its use of image, colour-coding and the other Mind Mapping laws give you instant access to the information.

9   Because the Mind Map diary is visually stimulating and attractive, it encourages you to use it. This differs greatly from standard diaries which many people subconsciously reject – 'forgetting' to put things in their diaries, putting them in the wrong place, or feeling guilty about not using them at all.

10 Reviewing your diary becomes almost like 'going to the movies' of your life!

ONWORD

Mind Mapping not only enhances your powers of self-analysis, problem solving and personal organisation, it can also enrich your family life. The next section explores the many exciting ways in which you can use Mind Maps for family study and enjoyment.

SECTION B
Family

CHAPTER 21

FAMILY STUDY
AND STORY-TELLING

Preview
- Foreword
- Mind Map story-telling
- Group Mind Map Family Study
- The family Mind Mapping study day
- Benefits of family Mind Mapping
- Family Mind Mapping in practice
- Onword

FOREWORD

This chapter explores how you can apply the techniques described in Chapter 17 (page 165) to the family. Whether it's used for entertainment or study, family Mind Mapping is exciting, challenging – and fun. It can also strengthen and enhance your relationships with each other.

MIND MAP STORY-TELLING

First prepare your environment and materials: Mind Mapping paper spread out on the floor or tables and plenty of good-quality coloured pens. There are seven major stages in the story-telling process.

1   Thinking of an idea

Each member of the family does an individual brainstorm on ideas for a super-creative fairytale. The ideas might take the form of suggested titles (the more fantastic the better . . .) or perhaps central characters (animal, vegetable, extra-terrestrial or even human!).

Each person reads out his or her ideas and a vote is taken on which titles or characters to use for today's group story. It may be difficult to choose, but you can always keep the others and use them for another day's story-telling.

2   Individual brainstorming

Taking a new sheet of paper, everyone draws the chosen central image or character and spends about 20 minutes doing a quick-fire Mind Map burst of the first ideas that come to mind for making the story original, gripping and extraordinary.

3   Reconstruction and revision

Each family member now selects Basic Ordering Ideas, preferably including some or all of the following:

- Plots
- Characters
- Themes
- Settings
- Language level
- Colours
- Pictures
- Morals
- Feelings
- Outcomes

These form the major branches on the reconstructed and revised Mind Maps. Younger members may need a little help here from parents . . . Just explain that characters are 'the people in the story', plots are 'what happens in the story', and so on. These Mind Maps should be filled with images and colour, and should take between thirty or forty minutes to draw.

4   Incubation

By this time you'll all be ready for a break! Play games, rest, have a drink, and maybe a snack, and then spend about 30 minutes looking at and discussing each other's Mind Maps. This will probably be very amusing as well as surprising – people often find members of their family far more imaginative than they ever imagined! But remember that it's essential to be totally positive about everyone's ideas. Any criticism or discouragement at this stage will drastically reduce that individual's confidence and enjoyment.

5 Creating the first group Mind Map

Elect a scribe, or, alternatively, each member can take it in turns to draw part of the giant Mind Map. Begin with a multi-coloured, multi-dimensional central image, then select and combine the best Basic Ordering Ideas to make a complete outline for a story. Have as many concepts as you wish radiating out from each of the major branches.

6 Telling the story

Sitting in a circle round the completed Mind Map, each member takes it in turn to tell part of the story. The story can be passed on at any point but it should ideally be left slightly 'up in the air', leaving the next person to think of an imaginative, fantastic or witty continuation.

Each member should aim to make the story more bizarre and imaginative with every turn. This will encourage the group mind to use the Mind Map as a foundation on which to build a really inventive tower of fantasy.

It's a good idea to record this story-telling stage on tape.

7 Creating the second group Mind Map

After another short break, you can play back or re-tell the story, while creating a final and more beautiful Mind Map. This final Mind Map can be done either as a group exercise or individually. For the better stories, it is an especially good idea to transcribe the complete text, using a large type, and keeping to a maximum of ten lines per page. Opposite each page of type should be a blank page, and on each blank page a different member of the family can draw illustrations appropriate to the text. In this way the family creates a superb library of fairytale books and in the process of becoming authors also learns a large number of skills that can be transferred to the school situation. The Mind Maps and illustrations can be used as decorations for the walls in the children's bedrooms (indeed they often end up decorating the entire house!).

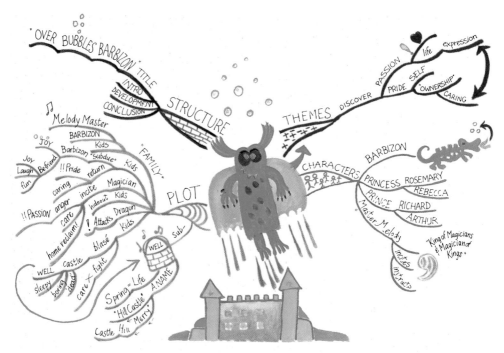

Fairy-tale Mind Map done by Donna Kim and her children (see pages 199–201).

GROUP MIND MAP FAMILY STUDY

The Mind Map Organic Study Technique (MMOST) – as described in Chapter 14 (pages 141–4) and Tony Buzan, *Use Your Head*, Chapter 9 – enables individuals to multiply the speed, comprehension, effectiveness and efficiency of their study by five to ten times. By applying the same techniques to family or group study, this improvement can itself be multiplied by the number of members of the group.

Briefly, MMOST consists of two main stages, preparation and application, and can be used for group study as follows:

1 Preparation

● As a group decide on the **amount** to be read in this study session, and ascertain the level of difficulty by very quickly scanning the text. The amount can range from a single chapter in a short study session, to a complete division in a longer study session, to a complete book in the family study day (see above). In the longer study sessions, family members can decide that each will study the same material and compare, or study different material and combine.

Natural Architecture Plate 23

- Decide on an appropriate amount of **time** for your study session, and divide it into chunks of an appropriate length to cover each section or division of text.
- As individual members, do a quick-fire Mind Map burst of all your **current knowledge** of the subject, raising your level of mental alertness and establishing associative 'grappling hooks' to take new information on board. This process also helps you identify areas of ignorance which will need special attention.
- Look at each other's Mind Maps, exchange ideas and create a Mind Map or Mind Maps of the group's existing knowledge.
- As individuals, Mind Map the **goals** and objectives of this study session. The Basic Ordering Ideas 'Who?', 'When?', 'Where?', 'Why?', 'What?', 'How?' and 'Which?' are particularly useful at this stage.
- Again, look at each other's Mind Maps, exchange ideas and create appropriate Mind Maps of the group's goals and objectives for the study session.
- Creating Mind Maps of your existing knowledge and your goals will sharpen the group's mental focus and increase your motivation and concentration.
- Individually and then as a group, Mind Map all the questions that need to be answered in this study session.

2 Application

- As individuals, take an **overview** of the text, looking at the table of contents, major headings, results, conclusions, important graphs or illustrations, and anything else which catches your eye.
- Try to identify the major elements in the text, discuss your impressions with other members of the group and create a preliminary group Mind Map, showing the basic structure of the text.
- Now move on to the **preview** stage, looking at the material not covered in the overview, particularly the beginnings and ends of paragraphs, sections and chapters, where the essential information tends to be concentrated.
- Again, discuss your impressions with the rest of the group, and start filling in some of the detail on the group Mind Map.
- Next comes the **inview**. In this stage you are at the filling-in stage of your mental jigsaw puzzle. Here you go back over the material, filling in the bulk of the material that you do not cover in the overview and preview. At this stage mark the difficulties and move on – they will be dealt with soon.
- Finally comes the **review**. During this stage you go back over the difficult bits and problem areas which you skipped in the earlier stages. During this stage you also look back over the text to answer any remaining questions, to

fulfil any remaining objectives, and to complete your ongoing personal Mind Map.

- Once more, group discussion afterwards will help resolve any 'problem areas', answer the tough questions, and fulfil the remaining objectives. You then individually or as a group put the finishing touches to your Mind Maps.
- Having completed this group study process, each individual has both a macro-understanding (an overall grasp) of the material and a micro-understanding (a more detailed knowledge of its content). The macro-understanding is contained in the large group Mind Maps and the major branches, whereas the micro-understanding is expressed in the detailed areas on the Mind Maps.

THE FAMILY MIND MAPPING STUDY DAY

The family study plan can be used by any family whose members wish to increase their knowledge, for academic purposes or for general interest. It has been designed to make studying as efficient and enjoyable as possible.

Using this type of study plan and well-organised Mind Map notes, the content of a whole book can be communicated to members of the group in from 30 minutes to one hour! The study day is designed to give each member over two hours of study time on an individual book. Thus in a family of four, four books can be read, Mind Mapped, understood and exchanged in a day!

The study plan has been described in detail in Tony Buzan, *Harnessing the ParaBrain*, Chapter 10, and the basic steps are summarised below. See Mind Map, page 239.

1 Start at about 10 am with some preparatory physical exercises (30 minutes). These exercises can take the form of games, stretching or aerobics and should be more for the purpose of warming up than strenuous exertion.

2 Quickly browse through the text to be studied (15 minutes).

3 Break – rest, play games, or relax in some other way (5–10 minutes).

4 Decide how much time you have available for study and breaks, and divide it into chunks to cover appropriate sections of material (10 minutes).

5 Mind Map your existing knowledge of the subject, your goals and objectives and the questions you want to answer (20 minutes).

6 Break (5–10 minutes).

7 Take a quick overview of your book, looking at the contents, major headings, and so on. Then put in the major branches on the group Mind Map (15 minutes).

8 Preview the book, looking at the material in more detail, and continue building your Mind Map (15 minutes).

9 Lunch break (1 hour).

10 This is the interview stage, during which you can discuss and resolve your problem areas with other members of the family (30 minutes).

11 Break (5–10 minutes).

12 Review the book, dealing with any outstanding problems or questions and filling in the final details on your Mind Map (30 minutes).

13 Break (5–10 minutes).

14 This is the exchange, during which family members present, from their own Mind Maps of the book, a complete summary of what has been learnt from the study text. (For details on giving presentations, see Chapter 26, page 252.)

Each presentation should take about 25 minutes, with a 5–10 minute break after the first two. While one member gives the presentation the other members

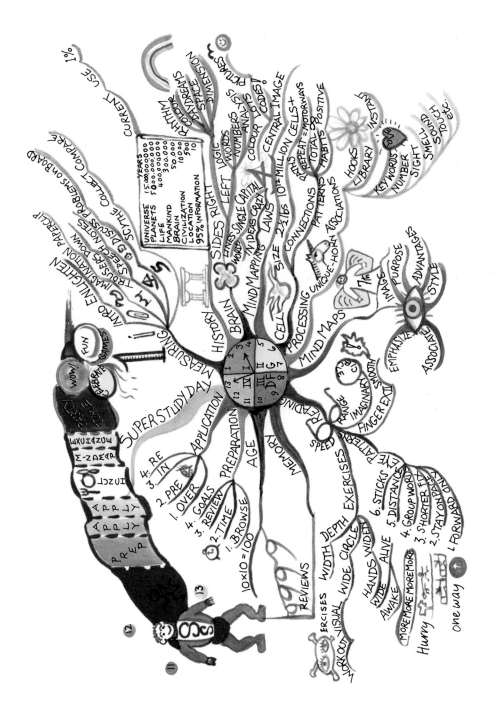

Mind Map of a complete study day completed by two mothers, Lynn Collins and Caro Ayre (see page 208).

act as scribes, making their own Mind Maps and attempting to gain an understanding at least equal to that of the presenter. With the benefit of hindsight, and the presenter's organisation and layout, you should all be able to refine and improve each other's and your own Mind Maps to the highest possible level. The Mind Map on page 207 is the result of a study day held outside in a garden in springtime Somerset, England. Two families, the Ayres and the Collinses, were studying books and information on developing family genius, and therefore were applying what they were learning to what they were learning! The final Mind Map of the study day was completed by the mothers, Lynn Collins and Caro Ayre. The central image represented the four quarters of their subjects of study, and each branch was cleverly numbered so that the number was also a picture representing the content of the branch. For example, the number three is incorporated into the shape of one half of the brain, as this branch deals with the left and right functions of the cortex (see Chapter 1, 'Modern Brain Research', page 32), while the number six is represented by a unicorn (unique-horn) – representing *uniqueness*! The Mind Map is filled with many other witty images for which the reader may enjoy searching!

15 Celebration – perfect your own method!

Some of the things done to celebrate include a night out at a cinema, theatre or sporting event, a special dinner, exchanging special 'awards' and buying a 'family' gift.

The day after this type of study day you may well find that you have an enhanced memory and understanding of the text studied. This is because dreaming or 'sleeping on it' has given the ideas a chance to integrate and realign themselves within your mind.

After this, regular reviews at the intervals recommended in Chapter 10 ('Rationale of the Mind Map recommendations', page 107) will enable you to maintain your recall and understanding of the text.

BENEFITS OF FAMILY MIND MAPPING

1 Family Mind Mapping offers all the benefits of group Mind Mapping

listed in Chapter 17 (pages 172–3).

2 By using Mind Maps for story-telling, the family's creativity is enhanced.

3 Individual study speed and effectiveness is multiplied by the number of family members.

4 Throughout the Mind Map study process, family members engage in conversation about the material they are studying, rather than studying in silence. Research has shown that active verbalising leads to more efficient processing and greater recall of information.

5 By using Mind Maps, rather than linear notes, knowledge is *enhanced* as it is communicated rather than debased and diffused.

6 Family members increase their ability to comprehend new areas of knowledge.

7 As a consequence, they enhance their ability to prepare for, and sit, examinations.

8 More importantly, their whole attitude to learning and examinations is transformed. Through family Mind Mapping, all family members can come to view study as a pleasure rather than a punishment.

9 Using the Mind Map as a means of helping and communicating with other family members can increase the motivation of all individuals to improve their thinking and Mind Mapping note-taking/making abilities.

10 Family Mind Mapping strengthens the family unit, as each member becomes involved in and supportive of the intellectual interests of the others, and shares a sense of satisfaction and increased motivation. The family becomes a family of friends.

FAMILY MIND MAPPING IN PRACTICE

Many families who have started holding regular study days have had their children go from bottom or near the bottom of the class to first, second or third place in all subjects. Likewise, the parents have found themselves excelling at work and in professional studies.

One Swedish family, with two parents and three children, enjoyed their study days so much that they held them regularly every weekend for six months. As the children did better and better at school, and as they told their friends about their exciting study days, word spread and the family ended up being almost besieged by neighbourhood children asking if they could join in!

ONWORD

In this chapter we have covered the main family applications of Mind Mapping and at the same time have seen how these can spill over into the educational area.

The next section expands on the educational advantages of Mind Maps in such specific tasks as writing essays, preparing for examinations, teaching, and taking notes from books, lectures and films.

SECTION C
Educational

CHAPTER 22

THINKING

Preview
- Foreword
- Mind Mapping for essays
- Mind Mapping for examinations
- Mind Mapping for projects and reports
- Examples of Mind Map projects
- Benefits of Mind Maps for presentations and writing tasks
- Onword

FOREWORD

This chapter covers three major thinking and note-making applications of Mind Maps – the preparation and writing of essays, examinations, and projects or reports.

MIND MAPPING FOR ESSAYS

Whereas note-*taking* from a book or lecture involves taking the essential elements from linear material to generate a Mind Map, note-*making* for an essay means first identifying the essential elements of the subject in a Mind Map and then using your Mind Map notes to build a linear structure.

- As always, you should begin your Mind Map with a central image representing the subject of your essay.

- You can then select appropriate Basic Ordering Ideas, as described in Chapter 9 (page 83) and Chapter 13 (page 132), as your major branches or principal sub-divisions. At this stage you should pay close attention to what the topic or question is asking you to do. The wording of essay topics usually suggests what the BOIs need to be.

- Let your mind range freely, adding items of information, or points you wish to make, wherever they seem most relevant on your Mind Map. There is no limit to the number of branches and sub-branches that can radiate outwards from your Basic Ordering Ideas. During this Mind Mapping stage you should use codes (colours, symbols, or both) to indicate cross-reference or association between different areas.

- Next, edit and re-order your Mind Map into a cohesive whole.

- Now sit down and write the first draft of your essay, using the Mind Map as a framework. A well-organised Mind Map should provide you with all the main sub-divisions of your essay, the key points to be mentioned in each, and the way those points relate to each other. At this stage you should write as quickly as possible, skipping over any areas that cause you special difficulty, especially particular words or grammatical structures. In this way you will create a much greater flow, and you can always return to the 'problem areas' later, much as you would when studying a book.

- If you come up against 'writer's block', doing another Mind Map will help you overcome it. In many cases just drawing the central image will get your mind going again, playing and freewheeling round the topic of your essay. If you get blocked once more, simply add new lines branching off from the key words and images you have so far generated, and your brain's natural gestalt or 'completing tendency' will fill in the blank spaces with new words and images. At the same time you should remind yourself of your brain's infinite capacity for association and allow *all* your thoughts to flow, especially the ones you may have been dismissing as 'absurd'. Such blocks will disappear as soon as you realise that they are actually created not by your brain's inability but by an underlying fear of failure and a misunderstanding of the way the brain works.

- Finally, review your Mind Map and put the finishing touches to your essay, adding cross-references, supporting your argument with more evidence or quotations, and modifying or expanding your conclusions where necessary.

It is worth mentioning that the Mind Maps we are discussing are meant to replace the voluminous linear notes that most students write before actually writing their essays. The Mind Map method uses a single Mind Map and a quick first draft in place of the standard twenty pages of notes and two or three drafts. It is also worth saying here that a word-processor is an excellent complement to a Mind Map in that it allows increased flexibility of drafting. Similarly, the Mind Maps Plus computer program (Chapter 28, page 274; and page 317) is a superb essay-writing companion.

School or university students, who take exams regularly, will find it very useful to write every essay to a strict time limit, as if it were an examination question. This approach is especially rewarding in highly competitive academic situations, where your brain needs constant training to excel under pressure-cooker examination conditions (see the Edward Hughes story in Tony Buzan, *Use Your Head*, Chapter 1).

Three of the Mind Maps on pages 214–15 are by Swedish school children, Karen Shmidt, Katarina Naiman and Thomas Enskog, and were done for essays on sports, Sweden, and computers, respectively.

As Katarina said when doing her Mind Map:

> 'The more I wrote and drew, the more things came to my mind – the more ideas I got, the more brave and original they were. I have realised that a Mind Map is never ending.
>
> 'Only some other person I respect, a stomach aching of hunger, or real thirst could make me stop building my Mind Maps!'

These Mind Maps, two in Swedish, further indicate the universality of the Mind Map language.

MIND MAPPING FOR EXAMINATIONS

Having taken Mind Map notes throughout your course of study, and having reviewed your Mind Maps at the recommended intervals, you should be more than ready for the examination. All you need to translate your excellent knowledge into excellent performance is the correct approach.

- The first step is to read the examination paper fully, selecting the questions you choose to answer, noting in mini-Mind Maps any thoughts that immediately spring to mind on reading the questions.
- Next, you have to decide in what order you are going to answer the questions, and how much time you will devote to each.
- Resisting the temptation to start answering the first question in detail straight away, do quick-fire Mind Map bursts on *all* the questions you intend to answer. By following this procedure, you enable your mind to explore, *throughout the examination,* the ramifications of all the questions regardless of the particular question you are answering at any given time.
- Now go back to your first question and do a Mind Map to act as the

Mind Map by Karen Schmidt on school sports (see page 213).

Mind Map by Katarina Naiman for a school project on Sweden (see page 213).

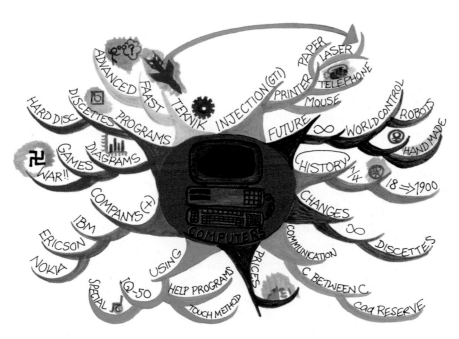

Mind Map by Thomas Enskog for a school project (see page 213).

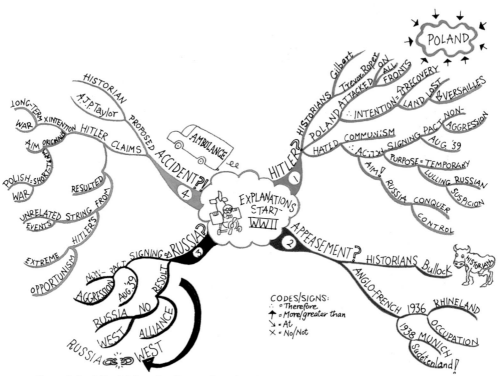

One of the Mind Maps by James Lee that helped him pass exams (see page 216).

framework for your answer. The central image corresponds to your introductory comments, while each of the major branches provides a major subheading or section of the essay. For each extension from your major branches, you should be able to write a paragraph or two.

• As you build up your answer you will find that you can begin to cross-refer throughout your knowledge structure, and can conclude by adding your own thoughts, associations and interpretations. Such an answer will demonstrate to the examiner a comprehensive knowledge, an ability to analyse, organise, integrate and cross-refer, and especially an ability to come up with your own creative and original ideas on the subject. In other words you will have achieved top marks!

The Mind Map on page 215 (bottom) is one of hundreds of Mind Maps by student James Lee. He prepared these Mind Maps to help him pass his senior and university entrance examinations. At the age of 15 James missed six months of schooling because of illness and was advised to go back a year in view of the fact that his O-level examinations loomed on the horizon. James persuaded his teachers to let him 'go for it' and started to Mind Map everything in sight! In just three months he did a year's work, and in ten examinations scored seven As and three Bs. The Mind Map on page 215 (bottom) is one that James did for History, outlining the main explanations given for the commencement of the Second World War.

MIND MAPPING FOR PROJECTS AND REPORTS

Writing a project or report, ranging from a few pages to the length of a doctoral thesis, can also be made much easier by using Mind Maps.

Such projects may involve extensive research and final presentation in written, graphic and oral form, but the approach is essentially the same as that used for essays and examinations.

As in any study task, the first step is deciding how much you plan to cover within a given time. These time/volume targets are just as important in long-term projects as in short-term ones.

Then, during the research phase, you can use Mind Maps to take notes from source material, to write up research results, to organise and integrate your ideas as they emerge, and to form the basis of your final written or oral presentation. (For more on giving presentations, see Chapter 26.)

Like a Mind Mapped essay or examination answer, projects and reports written in this way are likely to be much better structured, and more focused, creative and original, than those based on the laborious traditional methods of linear note-taking, drafting and re-drafting.

EXAMPLES OF MIND MAP PROJECTS

The Mind Map on page 219 summarises a project carried out by IBM and the British government's Youth Training Scheme. The aim was to give guidance on the most effective ways of teaching young people. This summary proved so useful that it was incorporated into the IBM/YTS Training Scheme Manual, as were a number of other Mind Maps.

Another example concerns a 13-year-old American schoolgirl called Lana Israel who has become a highly successful author with her book *Brain Power for Kids – How to Become an Instant Genius* co-written with Tony Buzan.

Lana's rise to fame started at Highland Oaks Middle School in Dade County, Florida, when she entered a school science project competition.

Having discovered Mind Mapping and become fascinated by it, Lana chose as her project an investigation of the effects of Mind Mapping on learning. She decided to run a series of experiments on recall and creativity, using her classmates as subjects. Like any good scientist, she divided her subjects into an experimental group and a control group, and carefully monitored the two sets of test results.

The group of students using Mind Maps showed a marked improvement in their results, and the precision and creativity of Lana's project won her first place in the county science fair. It also qualified her for the inter-state competition where she came second out of 42.

As a result, Amanda Morgan-Hagan, one of Lana's former teachers, invited her to the Eighth World Conference for Teachers of Gifted and Talented Students, to be held in Sydney, Australia. Said Amanda Morgan-Hagan: 'Lana showed me what she had done and I suddenly thought this would be marvellous for the conference, and a wonderful presentation for world educators to hear.'

Using Mind Maps as the basis of her presentation, Lana became an instant celebrity. She appeared on national television, gave numerous radio talks, and was interviewed by the leading daily newspapers. Her book *Brain Power for Kids* (see page 317) got hugh exposure, and she received hundreds of letters from people wanting to find out more. For an example of one of Lana's Mind Maps, see page 242.

What started out as a school science project has developed into Lana's life's work. In her words: 'Mind Mapping has helped me so much, I want to share that knowledge with other people. I want to change the face of education worldwide.' Indeed, John Sculley, head of Apple Computers, said he thinks that, through Mind Mapping, 'Lana will change the world'.

OVERLEAF: *Natural Architecture Plate 24*

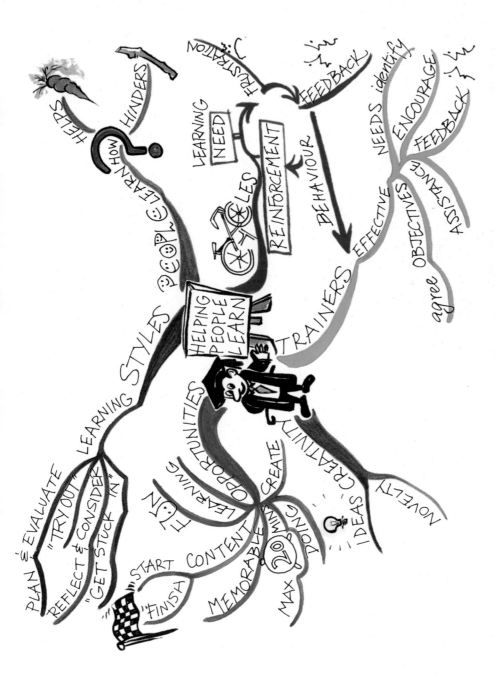

Mind Map by IBM Teaching Department for the 'Helping People Learn' initiative, in conjunction with the British Government (see page 217).

BENEFITS OF MIND MAPS FOR PRESENTATIONS AND WRITING TASKS

1   They eliminate the stress and unhappiness caused by disorganisation, fear of failure and 'writer's block'.

2   They free your associative 'grappling hooks' to take in new information and ideas, thus enhancing creativity and originality.

3   They enormously reduce the time needed for preparation, structuring and completion of the presentation or writing task.

4   They put you in continuous control of the analytical and creative process.

5   They result in a more focused, organised and integrated presentation, essay, project or report.

ONWORD

As demonstrated so clearly by the story of Lana Israel, the student who learns appropriately will naturally evolve into a good teacher. The next chapter explores the many ways in which Mind Mapping can help those involved in teaching others.

CHAPTER 23

TEACHING

Preview
- Foreword
- The developing brain
- Applications of Mind Maps in teaching
- Special Education
- Benefits of teaching with Mind Maps
- Onword

FOREWORD

This chapter sheds new light on the role of teachers and explores the many ways Mind Maps can be used to make teaching and learning more stimulating, enjoyable and effective.

The role of teachers

Teaching is arguably one of the most important professions in our society because teachers are responsible for that most treasured of all resources, the human intellect. Given that the brain operates synergetically building gigantic structures on the basis of knowledge it already possesses, the role of the teacher becomes even more important. If the knowledge base is false or weak then the more the student builds on it the more likely it is that the entire structure will eventually collapse. Sadly, in such cases, increasing effort results in ever more unsatisfactory performance.

OVERLEAF: *Natural Architecture Plate 25*

It is therefore essential that all teachers understand that the first lesson that must be taught to students is Mental Literacy, *Learning How to Learn* – even as they are taught the three Rs.

In order to accomplish this goal, the brain requires an appropriate tool. The Mind Map is that tool.

THE DEVELOPING BRAIN

When does the human brain first learn to Mind Map?

'When it is taught,' you might reply.

The correct answer is, 'The moment (and perhaps before) it is born!'

Consider the way a baby's brain develops, especially the way it learns language. One of the first words babies speak is 'Mama'. Why 'Mama'? Because 'Mama' is the centre of the Mind Map! From her radiate the main branches of love, food, warmth, protection, transport and education.

Thus the baby instinctively Mind Maps internally, from the moment it is born and throughout its life, building from each radiant centre, growing branches and networks of association that eventually develop into its adult body of knowledge.

The teacher needs to ensure that those intricate networks are constantly nurtured in order to ensure that they not only continue to grow throughout the student's life, but that they can also be used externally.

APPLICATIONS OF MIND MAPS IN TEACHING

Apart from familiarising his or her students with the theory and practice of Mind Mapping, the teacher can use Mind Maps in a number of practical ways to make teaching and learning easier and more enjoyable.

1 Preparing lecture notes

One of the most powerful ways to use Mind Maps is as lecture notes. Preparing a lecture in Mind Map form is much faster than writing it out and has the big advantage of allowing the lecturer and the student to keep an overview of the whole subject at all times. A Mind Mapped lecture is easy to update from year to year without becoming messy and its mnemonic qualities mean that a brief overview before the lecture quickly brings the topic right back into focus. Because the lecturer's own knowledge will evolve the same Mind Map will trigger quite different lectures if used from year to year. This avoids the tedium of stale lecture notes without requiring any extra work! It makes lecturing more fun and more interesting for both the lecturer and the students/audience.

As a framework for lecturing, a Mind Map enables the speaker to hold a perfect balance between a spontaneously spoken and fresh talk, on the one hand, and a clear and well-structured presentation on the other. It allows accurate time-keeping during the lecture or, if the time allowed changes for some reason, it allows the speaker to edit 'on the move' to adjust the talk to a greater or lesser length, as required. This editing function can also be very useful if some new information becomes available just before the lecture (a news story, a previous speaker).

The Mind Map on page 226 was done by Barry Buzan for a wide ranging lecture to a gathering of academics and foreign policy officials. The topic in the centre was fixed by the organisers of the conference and was therefore not reduced to a single word or a simple image. There are quite a few code words on the Mind Map that point to areas of knowledge or to the ideas of other authors that are familiar to the speaker. Note the long-line architecture, which provides an alternative way of laying out the primary and secondary branches. From this kind of Mind Map, a properly qualified lecturer could speak for ten minutes or ten hours. Any one of the main branches could itself be a lecture, so this could also be an outline for a course. It could be (and was) used as a university lecture. It could be (and in this case wasn't) used as a preparatory sketch for writing an article.

The Mind Map on Chemical Kinetics on page 227 (top) was prepared by Graham Wheeler, head of Chemistry at Herschel Grammar School in England. The Mind Map covers an entire section of a chemistry course for senior students preparing to go to university, and is used both by the teacher, to plan and guide his own lecturing, and by the students to help them follow the lectures.

Over the five-year period during which Graham Wheeler has taught A-level Chemistry with Mind Maps, he has had a 98 per cent pass rate. (See also Kastner, Chapter 27, 'Examples of management Mind Maps', pages 270–3.)

2 Yearly planning

The Mind Map can be used to give the teacher an overview of the whole year's study programme, showing the term divisions and the type of lessons to be given. (For instance, a geography teacher could get an idea of annual frequency of field trips and slide presentations in relation to standard lessons.)

3 Term planning

This is a sub-division of the yearly plan, and often takes the form of a smaller Mind Map expanding from a branch or branches on the yearly programme. The term plan might show which topics from the curriculum the teacher intends to cover and in roughly what order.

4 Daily planning

This takes a similar form to that of the daily Mind Map diary described in Chapter 20 (page 191), and would record the specific details of lessons, such as start and finish time, classroom, topic to be covered, and so on.

5 Lessons and presentations

Using a large blackboard, whiteboard, flip chart or an overhead projector, the teacher can draw, as the lesson progresses, the corresponding part of the Mind Map. This externalised reflection of the thought process will help clarify the structure of the lesson. It will also hold the students' interest and enhance their memory and understanding of the subject covered. 'Skeleton' Mind Maps can also be handed out for the student to complete or black and white photocopies can be provided for students to colour themselves.

6 Examinations

If the purpose of an examination is to test the students' knowledge and understanding rather than their writing ability, the Mind Map is the ideal solution. It can show the teacher at a glance whether or not the students have a general grasp of the subject, as well as their major strengths and weaknesses. The Mind Map also reveals those areas where the chain of association has, for some reason, gone awry. This approach gives the teacher a clear and objective idea of the student's state of knowledge, uncluttered by judgements about skills in other areas such as grammatical correctness, spelling ability and neatness of handwriting. In addition it saves a huge amount of time normally spent reading and marking piles of examination scripts!

This concept has been taken farther by Christine Hogan, Director of the School of Management, Curtin University of Technology in Perth, Australia. As co-ordinator of undergraduate Organisational Behaviour programmes Hogan introduced Mind Mapping to all staff and students. She says:

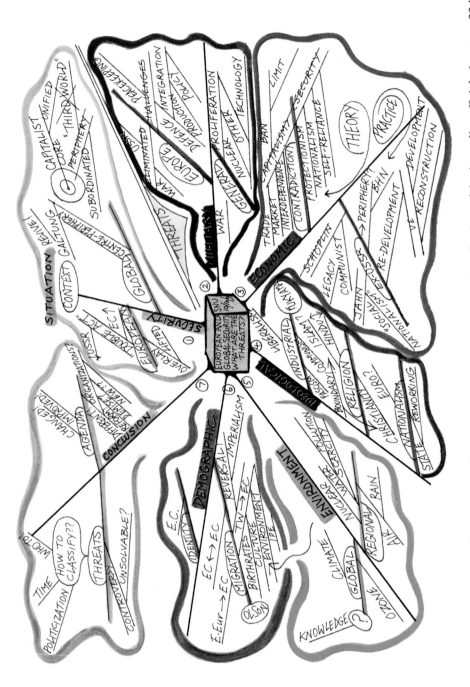

Mind Map by Professor Barry Buzan for a wide-ranging lecture to a gathering of academics and foreign policy officials (see page 224).

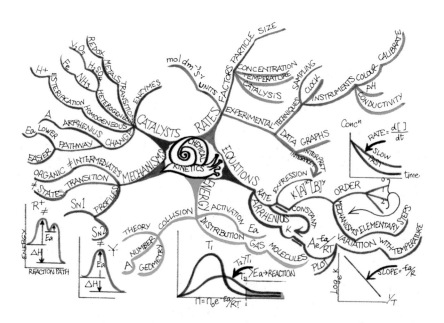

Mind Map on Chemical Kinetics by Graham Wheeler covering an entire section of a chemistry course (see page 224).

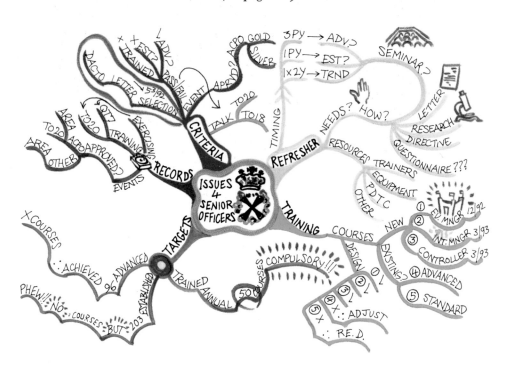

Mind Map by Superintendent Douglas Brand considering training (see page 229).

'We introduced it as an examination tool. At the beginning of the semester students were given a unit guide plus objectives for each week. On the opposite page they were encouraged to make a summary Mind Map. They were told that a Mind Map would appear on the exam and they would be given a choice of weekly topics, e.g.:

Choose either "motivation" or "leadership" and draw a Mind Map illustrating the basic theories/concept/models and your own ideas on the topic. Use a double page in your answer book.

We then developed a scheme in which we could grade students' Mind Maps:

Marking Scheme

a) Content:

Breadth (coverage of range of theories/concepts)	5
Depth (coverage of detail)	5

b) Covered own ideas   4

c) Used Mind Mapping strategies:

Colour	2
Symbol	2
Arrows	2

TOTAL   20

We believe that Mind Mapping is a strategy that can be used to encourage "deep" rather than "surface" learning. Biggs and Telfer (1987), and Marton and Slajo (1976) conducted research into deep and surface learning where "deep" is intrinsically motivated, where students try to understand the meaning to their work and understand the context of new ideas and concepts. 'Surface' learning tends to be externally motivated and leads to rote learning.

Watkins and Hattie (1985) indicate that surface approaches are most frequently used successfully at primary and secondary level and that few students find it necessary to modify their strategies at university level. Many of our students are being asked to change to deep learning in Mind Mapping where they are encouraged to see the whole picture and make connections between theories, concepts and their own ideas.'

7 Projects

Mind Maps are ideal for planning, monitoring and presenting projects. They encourage comprehensive and focused thinking in the early stages, enable both teacher and student to check on progress and observe the growing web of inter-related information, and provide an ideal framework for either written or oral presentations at the end.

The Mind Map can be especially useful in professional education. In the London Metropolitan Police Service (a body of 44,000 personnel) training is a growing and major concern. Superintendent Douglas Brand used a Mind Map (see page 227, bottom) to consider all residual issues concerning training after the Service had completed a general review. The Mind Map shows how both comprehensive considerations and intricate details can be incorporated on a single Mind Map. It also covers areas that those involved in training might find useful for themselves.

Another example shows how Mind Maps can be used to plan lessons in one of the fastest-growing areas of learning at the moment: language training. The Mind Map on page 230 was drawn as a lesson plan for a group of non-native English speakers by Charles La Fond, who runs a series of international language training schools. The pictures in the Mind Map are designed to stimulate the minds of the students to ask questions during the course of teaching, to encourage discussion and to indicate activity. This Mind Map provides a half-day's worth of learning and is also used as a review.

The companion Mind Map, on page 231, shows in even more detail how Mind Maps can be used specifically for the teaching of grammar. The Mind Map by Lars Soderberg, a Swedish master linguist and teacher, incorporates a comprehensive overview of the main elements of French grammar on a single page. In a single 'visual grasp' the Mind Map takes that which for many is considered difficult, if not impossible, and makes it clear and easily accessible.

SPECIAL EDUCATION

Mind Maps are particularly useful for helping those with learning disabilities. The Mind Map on page 231 was done by the author in conjunction with a nine-year-old boy we shall call 'Timmy'. Timmy suffered from fairly severe Cerebral Palsy, which meant that his motor functions were significantly impaired. He was considered by many to be ineducable and unintelligent.

When spending an afternoon with him surrounded by coloured crayons and blank notepaper, Tony first asked him to say who his family was. As notes were made Timmy watched intently, even correcting a fairly complicated spelling of his sister's name.

Timmy was then asked what his main interests were, and without hesitation he said, 'space and dinosaurs', so these were put down as major branches of the Mind Map. Timmy was asked what he liked about space. He said, 'the

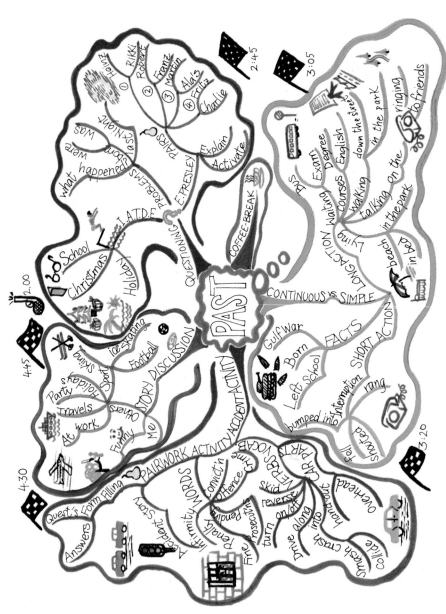

Mind Map of a language lesson for a group of non-native English-speakers by their teacher Charles La Fond (see page 229).

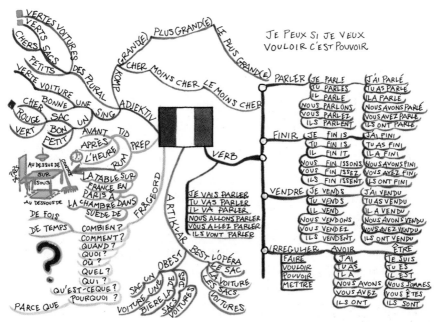

Lars Soderberg's Mind Map of an overview of French grammar (see page 229).

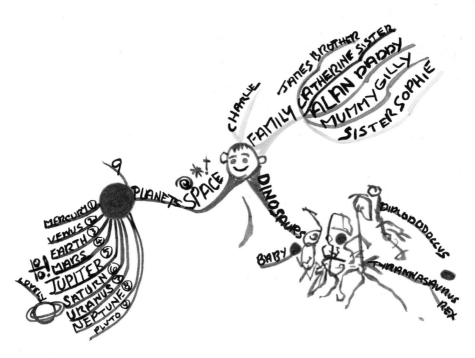

Mind Map by 'Timmy' with the help of Tony Buzan, demonstrating the abilities and knowledge of the 'learning disabled' (see page 229).

planets'. Timmy then concisely named the planets in their correct order showing that he not only had a far better grasp of our local solar system than 90 per cent of the population, but that his picture of it was clear. When Timmy got to the planet Saturn, he paused, looked straight into Tony's eyes and said, 'L-U-H-V-L-E-Y . . .'

When it came to discussing the dinosaurs, Timmy asked for the pencil and did a quick scribbled drawing. Knowing that such scribbles are never meaningless, Tony asked him to explain what it meant. Timmy explained that it was, fairly obviously, a diplodocus and a tyrannosaurus rex: father, mother and baby. Timmy's mind was as bright and clear as any good university student's, his only difficulty being between the wiring of his thought and his physical expression of it.

He asked to do his own Mind Map. He produced another 'scribble' and explained it as follows: the orange represented his body, which made him very happy. The black squiggle in the top section represented his brain, which made him very happy. The yellow squiggle represented those parts of his own body which did not work, which made him unhappy. He paused for a moment and finally added a dark squiggle covering the bottom of the Mind Map, which he said represented how he was going to use his thinking to help make his body work better.

In this and many other such cases, the Mind Map frees the 'learning disabled' brain from semantic restrictions which often increase the disability if there is one, and may even create one where, in the beginning, there was not.

BENEFITS OF TEACHING WITH MIND MAPS

1 They automatically inspire interest in the students, thus making them more receptive and co-operative in the classroom.

2 They make lessons and presentations more spontaneous, creative and enjoyable, both for the teacher and the students.

3 Rather than remaining relatively rigid as the years go by, the teacher's notes are flexible and adaptable. In these times of rapid change and development, the teacher needs to be able to alter and add to teaching notes quickly and easily.

4 Because Mind Maps present only relevant material in a clear and memorable form, the students tend to get better marks in examinations.

5 Unlike linear text, Mind Maps show not just the facts but the *relationships between those facts*, thus giving the students a deeper understanding of the subject.

6 The physical volume of lecture notes is dramatically reduced.

7 Mind Maps are especially useful for children with 'learning difficulties', particularly dyslexia. By freeing the child of the 'tyranny of semantics', which often accounts for 90 per cent of the difficulty, the Mind Map allows the child a far more natural, complete and accelerated self-expression.

ONWORD

Having discussed ways of using Mind Maps in educational writing tasks and teaching, we still need to look at their applications in one of the most important learning activities, note-taking. The next chapter goes into detail about how best to use Mind Maps when taking notes from a book, lecture, video, computer or film.

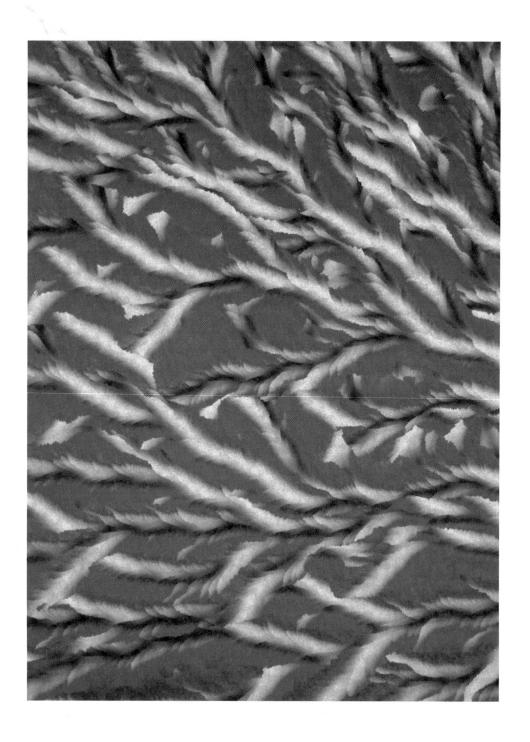

Natural Architecture Plate 26

CHAPTER 24

CREATING THE MASTER MIND MAP

Preview
- Foreword
- Mind Mapping a book
- Mind Mapping from lectures/videos/computers/films
- Reviewing your Mind Map notes
- Creating a Master Mind Map
- Benefits of Mind Map notes and the Master Mind Map
- Onword

FOREWORD
We have already seen (in Chapter 3, page 43) the appalling intellectual quagmire created by traditional linear methods of note-taking, and the many advantages offered by Mind Map notes. In this chapter the Mind Mapping technique is related specifically to reading books, attending lectures, and acquiring a large body of integrated knowledge.

MIND MAPPING A BOOK
To recap briefly, the technique of Mind Mapping a book falls into two parts – preparation and application. Within these divisions there are eight stages. For ease of reference, the stages are summarised below, with recommended time limits. A complete summary Mind Map by Vanda North of the MMOST technique, incorporating a study-day plan, is on page 239.

Preparation

1 Browse – create the central image of the Mind Map (10 minutes)

2 Setting time and amount targets (5 minutes)

3 Mind Mapping existing knowledge on the subject (10 minutes)

4 Defining and Mind Mapping goals (5 minutes)

Application (times dependent on material studied)

5 Overview – add main Mind Map branches

6 Preview – first and second levels

7 Inview – fill in the Mind Map details

8 Review – complete the Mind Map

Preparation

1 Browse (10 minutes)

Before you start reading the book in detail, it is essential to gain a quick overview. The best way is to look at the front and back cover and the list of contents, and flick through the pages a few times, getting the general 'feel' of the book.

Then take a large blank sheet or Mind Map pad and draw a central image that summarises the subject or title. If there is a particularly striking or colourful image on the cover or inside the book, feel free to use it. If you are also reasonably sure of the main branches that are going to radiate from the centre, you can add these at the same time. They will often correspond to the major divisions or chapters of the book, or your specific objectives in reading it.

By starting your Mind Map at this early stage, you are giving your brain a central focus and the basic architecture within which it can integrate all the information gained from studying the book.

2   Setting time and amount targets (5 minutes)

In view of your study objectives, the book's content and level of difficulty, and the amount of knowledge you already have, decide on the amount of time you will devote to the entire task, and the amount you will cover in each study period.

3   Mind Map of existing knowledge on the subject (10 minutes)

Now 'turn away' from the book and your previous Mind Map, take a new sheet of paper, and *as fast as you can* do a quick-fire Mind Map burst on everything you already know about the topic you are about to study. This will include whatever information you have gained from your initial browse through the book, plus any general knowledge or specific items of information you may have picked up during your whole life that relate to the topic in any way.

Most people are delighted and surprised to find that they actually know a lot more about the topic than they had previously thought. This exercise is also especially valuable because it brings appropriate associations or 'grappling hooks' to the surface of your brain and sets it moving in the direction of the topic you are studying. It also enables you to identify areas of strength and weakness in your knowledge, indicating which aspects you need to supplement.

4   Defining and Mind Mapping Goals (5 minutes)

At this stage you can either add to the existing knowledge Mind Map you have just completed, using a different-coloured pen, or you can take a new blank sheet and do another quick-fire Mind Map burst on your goals in reading the book. These goals may take the form of specific questions to which you wish to find the answers, areas of knowledge you wish to find out more about, or perhaps skills you wish to acquire.

Mind Mapping your goals in this way greatly increases the probability of your eye/brain system registering any information it comes across that seems relevant to those goals. In effect, the Mind Map of your goals acts as an 'appetite' that naturally motivates your search. In the same way as a person who has not eaten for several days will become obsessed with food, good preparatory Mind Maps increase your 'hunger' for knowledge.

Application (times dependent on material studied)

5–8 Overview, Preview, Inview, Review

Having completed your preparation, you are ready to start the four levels of reading – overview, preview, inview and review – which take you ever deeper into the content of the book. For details of these stages see Chapter 21 ('Group Mind Map family study', pages 204–5).

At this point you can either: Mind Map the book as you read; or mark the book while reading and complete your Mind Map afterwards. These approaches are both equally valid – the one you adopt is entirely a matter of personal choice and may depend on whether the book is yours.

• Mind Mapping while you read is like having an ongoing 'conversation' with the author, reflecting the developing pattern of knowledge as the book progresses. The growing Mind Map also enables you to keep checking your level of understanding and adjusting the focus of your information-gathering.

• Mind Mapping afterwards means that you produce your Mind Map only once you have gained a complete understanding of the book's content, and the way each part relates to the others. Your Mind Map will therefore be more comprehensive and focused and less likely to require revision.

Whichever method you choose, it is important to remember that Mind Mapping a book is a two-way process. The aim is not simply to duplicate the author's thoughts in Mind Map form. Rather, it is a question of organising and integrating his or her thoughts in the context of your own knowledge, understanding, interpretation and specific goals. Your Mind Map should there-fore ideally include your own comments, thoughts and creative realisations arising from what you have read. Using different colours or codes will enable you to distinguish your own contributions from those of the author.

MIND MAPPING FROM LECTURES/VIDEOS/ COMPUTERS/FILMS

This is very similar to Mind Mapping a book, except that you are often subject to the linear progression of the lecture or presentation and do not have the luxury of being able to refer to different parts of the material at will.

For this reason, it is especially important to get an overview of the topic as quickly as possible. Before the lecture, video or film begins, you should draw your central image and as many of the main branches as you can. (Most good lecturers are pleased to help anyone who shows an interest in their subject and

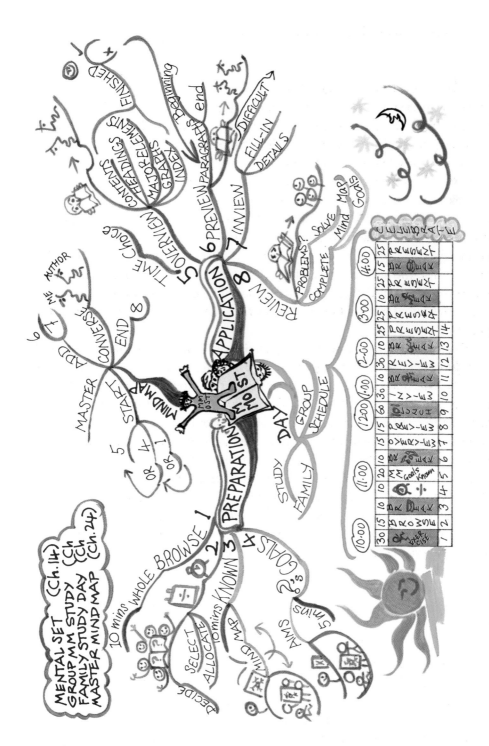

Mind Map by Vanda North summarising the entire MMOST technique (see page 235 and Chapter 21, page 199).

will be happy to give you a preview of the lecture showing the main areas they plan to cover.)

Again, before the lecture, video, or film begins and if circumstances permit, you can do a quick-fire two-minute Mind Map burst of your existing knowledge on the subject, in order to prepare your brain to take in new information.

As time progresses, you can fill in the information and ideas on your original Mind Map wherever they seem most relevant, adjusting your basic structure if necessary. As with Mind Mapping a book, you should always include your own comments and contributions in response to those of the lecturer.

Don't worry if the information you are receiving becomes disorganised and your Mind Map notes appear 'messy'. As we have already seen, so-called 'neat' linear note-taking is actually a far less efficient means of communicating information to the brain.

Lana Israel, the girl mentioned in Chapter 22, page 217, obviously uses Mind Maps as a standard part of her school life. Her Mind Map on page 242 is a combination of note-taking, and essay and exam preparation. As Lana said:

> 'This Mind Map is taken straight from my history notes. My teacher usually lectures every day and naturally I Mind Map his lectures. This Mind Map deals with America's earliest political parties and their stands. The central image illustrates the split in politics which lead to the formation of two separate parties. Just by glancing at my image, I am made aware of the theme of the Map and general characteristics of the parties. Democrats being more common men and Federalists more concerned with aristocracy. The use of pictures in Mind Mapped notes is wonderful for chunking down concepts, recalling information and making history fun. The equivalent of this Map, linearly, is at least two to three pages of linear notes – studying three pages rather than one is certainly not fun. Furthermore, this Map can be reviewed in under a minute, saving time and enabling one to remember more as key words are strongly linked. The use of Mind Mapping adds so much more to study: fun, uniqueness, creativity, stronger recall, organisation while subtracting tedious hours of cramming, review and revising. At the same time Mind Maps have helped me get As in History – "A" Definite Advantage!'

REVIEWING YOUR MIND MAP NOTES

Having completed your Mind Map notes, you should review them regularly in order to maintain your understanding and recall of what you have learnt. The natural rhythms of your memory are discussed in detail in Tony Buzan's *Use*

Your Memory, Chapter 11, and *Use Your Head*, Chapter 5. The essential points are summarised here.

For a 1-hour period of study the optimum intervals and time limits for review after the study are as follows:

- After 10 minutes – take a 10-minute review
- After 24 hours – take a 2–4 minute review
- After a week – take a 2-minute review
- After a month – take a 2-minute review
- After six months – take a 2-minute review
- After a year – take a 2-minute review

The information will then be stored in the long-term memory.

Rather than just looking at your original Mind Map for each review, it is best to start by doing another quick-fire Mind Map burst of what you remember. This will show what you are able to recall *without any assistance*. You can then check against your original Mind Map, adjusting any discrepancies and strengthening any areas of weak recall.

CREATING A MASTER MIND MAP

If you are involved in a long-term course of study it is a good idea to keep a giant Master Mind Map reflecting the major sub-divisions, themes, theories, personalities and events in that subject. Every time you read a book or go to a lecture, you can record any major new insight on your Master Mind Map, thus creating an external mirror-image of your growing network of internal knowledge. In Chapter 27, page 271, a multiple-purpose Master Mind Map outlines their uses in handling a management emergency!

The Mind Map on page 243 on bird classification and 'orders' by Brian Heller, a devoted amateur ornithologist and senior executive with IBM, is an excellent example of such an external mirror-image. On a single page, Brian has managed to summarise a life-time of knowledge.

Those who have done this notice a surprising and rewarding trend. After a reasonable length of time, the boundaries of the Mind Map begin to edge into other subjects and disciplines. Thus the periphery of a Master Mind Map on psychology begins to touch on neurophysiology, mathematics, philosophy, astronomy, geography, meteorology, ecology, and so on.

This does not mean that your knowledge structure is disintegrating and moving too far from the point. It actually means that your knowledge is becoming so deep and extensive that it is beginning to relate to other areas of knowledge. This is the stage of intellectual development familiar to the great thinkers of history where all disciplines are found to relate to all others. It is also the stage at which your Master Mind Map helps you to contribute to the continuing expansion of human knowledge.

BENEFITS OF MIND MAP NOTES AND THE MASTER MIND MAP

1 They enable you to keep the whole knowledge 'picture' in view at all times, thus giving you a more balanced and comprehensive understanding of the subject in its entirety.

2 They take up far less space than linear notes. Between 10 and 1,000 pages of text can be summarised on one large Mind Map page.

3 They give your brain a central focus and structure within which to integrate your knowledge of any subject.

Mind Map by Lana Israel in preparation for a history exam (see pages 219 and 240).

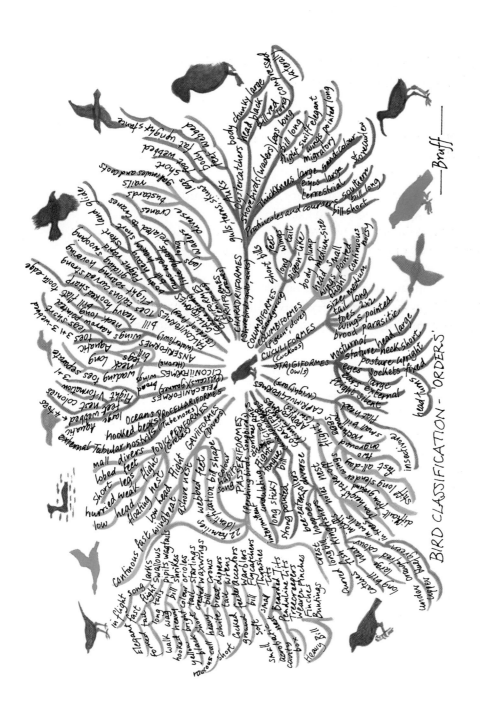

Master Mind Map by Brian Heller of IBM summarising a life-time study of birds (see page 241).

4   They increase your brain's 'hunger' for knowledge.

5   They allow you to relate your own thoughts and ideas to those expressed in books, lectures or presentations.

6   They are far more effective and efficient for review purposes.

7   They enhance your memory and understanding of books, lectures and presentations, enabling you to excel in any course of study.

ONWORD

Having completed their formal education, many people find employment in business or in one of the professions. The next few chapters show how you can use Mind Mapping to make your working life easier, more enjoyable and more productive.

SECTION D
Business and Professional

CHAPTER 25

MEETINGS

FOREWORD

At meetings everyone should ideally be both a presenter and a member of the audience. Using Mind Maps results in active participation, both at individual and group level, and active participation is the key to a truly stimulating and productive meeting.

MIND MAPPING AS INDIVIDUALS

Using the techniques already described in Chapter 14 (page 139) and Chapter 24 (page 235), individuals can create their own Mind Maps throughout the meeting.

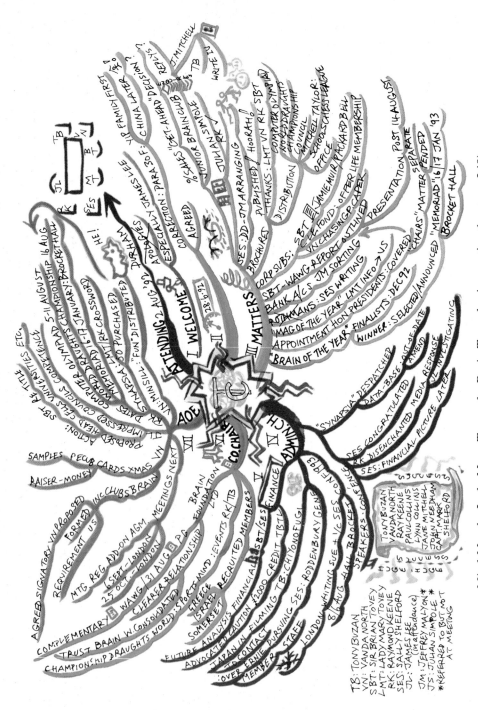

Mind Map by Lady Mary Tovey of a Brain Trust charity meeting (see page 248).

The subject of the meeting provides the central image, and the major items on the agenda correspond to the main branches. As the meeting progresses, you can add ideas and information wherever they seem most relevant. Alternatively, you may wish to have a mini-Mind Map for each speaker. As long as these are all on the same large sheet of paper, it will be quite easy to indicate cross-references as themes and trends begin to emerge.

Once again, there is no need to worry if your Mind Map notes look 'messy'. They are simply reflecting the confused state of communication at that particular time, and can always be clarified and redirected later on.

The Mind Map on page 246 was made by Lady Mary Tovey at a four-hour meeting of the Executive Council of The Brain Trust charity. The central image depicted the central theme of the meeting, and the Mind Map itself covered the equivalent of eight pages of standard minutes. The particular useful technique that Lady Mary used on the Mind Map was the recording of the positions of the people at the board table throughout the meeting – an extra and very helpful mnemonic aid.

The Mind Map on page 251 is another example of a multi-lingual Mind Map incorporating Japanese and English. The Mind Map was done by a senior executive of IBM Japan and was made as an on-going record of meetings both professional and social over a three-day period in Barcelona, Spain. This Mind Map also served as the basis for a presentation upon the return of the executive to his local business centre in Japan.

MIND MAPPING AS A GROUP

As well as individual Mind Maps, it is advisable to have a Master Mind Map on a large board, screen or chart that is visible to all. In this way the elected scribe can register every contribution and place it within the overall structure of the meeting.

This avoids the all-too-common problem of good or brilliant ideas being discarded, or never emerging, because the traditional methods of structuring meetings and recording minutes counteract the growth of natural group communication.

A group Mind Map can incorporate both brain storming and planning. A Mind Map was created to summarise a meeting between Chess Grandmaster Raymond Keene, OBE, Annette Keene, Vanda North and Tony Buzan. The meeting concerned the use of Simpson's-in-the-Strand as an international centre for Mind Sports and also as the venue for a series of other events

PREVIOUS PAGE: *Natural Architecture Plate 27*

including the World Draughts (Checkers) Championships, the World Memory Championships, various Chess Championships, the launching of books and a massive Mental Olympic Games.

Location, finance and marketing were all considered in depth. As a result of the meeting six new Mind Sports events were established.

A particular advantage of using Mind Maps in meetings is that the Mind Map gives a clearer and more balanced picture of the true content of the meeting. Research shows that in traditional meetings preference is given either to those who speak first, last, loudest, with particular accents, with a higher level of vocabulary, or with a greater position of authority. The Mind Map cuts through this informational prejudice, gives a more objective and integrated view which allows everyone to be heard and encourages balanced participation and increased teamwork.

CHAIRING A MEETING WITH A MIND MAP

Mind Maps are particularly useful for chairing meetings. The chairperson has the agenda on a basic Mind Map and can use this fundamental frame to add thoughts, guide discussions, and record the basic outline of what will eventually be the minutes of the meeting. Colour coding can be used to indicate action, ideas, question marks, and important areas. Chairing a meeting this way allows the person in the chair to be much like a captain of a starship guiding it safely through the clusters and galaxies of ideas.

A variation on this theme is to have an official Mind Map-minuter, sitting next to the chairman, in order to enable the chairman to participate on many levels at the same time, while keeping a constant overview of the developing thrust of the meeting.

One individual who used this Mind Mapping approach with particular success was Fidelity's Bruce Johnstone. In a January issue of *Money* magazine, the feature article on Johnstone explained how he had ground out average annual returns of 21 per cent over the past ten years and had become 'America's Best Income Investor'. The article states:

> '*Several books in his office mark him as a man determined to make the most of his mind: such titles as* The Brain User's Guide *and* Use Both Sides of Your Brain. *One fruit of his studies is the Mind Map, a note-taking diagram that marshalls key words and ideas on a single page. At fortnightly staff meetings, often with thirty or so analysts and fund managers on hand, Johnstone sits at one end of the conference table diagraming the discussion, while Peter Lynch, mastermind of Fidelity Magellan, the*

nation's best growth fund, rations each speaker to three minutes with an egg-timer. At one session last November, for example, Johnstone drew a green branch on which he wrote "AT&T – maybe – deregulated". Branching off, in purple, was another line labelled "flexibility – raise – rates" and another marked "B translation: buy AT&T!" After the meeting Johnstone ordered 20,000 shares at 25 dollars. In two weeks the price went to 27 dollars!'

BENEFITS OF MIND MAPS FOR MEETINGS

1 They ensure that every member understands the viewpoints of the other members.

2 They place all contributions in context.

3 Including *all* individual contributions on the Mind Map increases energy, enthusiasm and co-operation within the group.

4 Each member of the group has a complete record of the meeting, thus ensuring that everyone understands and remembers exactly what has been decided.

5 Because Mind Maps are such an efficient means of communication, Mind Map meetings usually take about one-fifth of the time taken by traditional meetings.

6 They increase the probability of stated goals being reached.

ONWORD

As we have seen, most meetings also involve presentations. The next chapter focuses on using Mind Maps to enhance your skill in presenting ideas and

Multi-lingual Mind Map of a meeting over three days in Spain (see page 248).

CHAPTER 26

PRESENTATIONS

FOREWORD

Presentations – on a one-to-one basis, in small or large groups, on radio or television – are a vital part of business life. Yet many people are terrified of public speaking, ranking their fear of making speeches above their fear of spiders, snakes, diseases, war and even death! This chapter looks at how Mind Maps can help in overcoming fear thereby enabling you to prepare and present your information and ideas clearly, interestingly and effectively. There are also some amusing examples of how *not* to give speeches and presentations!

USING MIND MAPS TO PREPARE A PRESENTATION

Business is actually far more closely related to education than is commonly realised. In both environments, communication is central. And any act of communication involves imparting and receiving information; in other words, teaching and learning.

So preparing business presentations is almost identical to preparing examination or essay Mind Maps (see Chapter 22, page 211). It also bears many similarities to self-analysis and problem solving Mind Mapping (see Chapters 18, page 176, and 19, page 183).

- Having drawn your central image, the first step is to do a quick-fire Mind Map burst of any ideas that come to mind which are in any way connected to the topic you have chosen.
- Look again at your quick-fire Mind Map, organise your main branches and sub-branches, and fill in any other key words that come to mind. As each key word will take up at least 1 minute of your presentation, it's a good idea to restrict your Mind Map to a *maximum* of 50 key words and images for a 1-hour speech.
- Look at your Mind Map again and pare it down even further, getting rid of all extraneous material. At this stage you should also put in codes to indicate where you wish to insert slides, videos, particular cross-references, examples, and so on.
- Now consider the order in which you wish to present your main branches and number them accordingly.
- Finally, allocate an appropriate length of time to each branch, and then just follow your own instructions!

MIND MAPPING VERSUS LINEAR PREPARATION
There are several disadvantages to linear methods of preparing speeches:

1 Because speakers have to keep referring to written notes, they lose eye contact with the audience.

2 Having to 'hold on' to the notes makes it impossible to reinforce major points with physical gestures.

3 Written English is very different from spoken English. 'Grammatically correct' written language is inappropriate for a spoken presentation, and will almost certainly induce extreme boredom in the audience. A Mind Map gives the presenter a perfect balance between the spontaneity of natural talk and the structure of worked-out ideas. This powerful combination is the key to effective (and confident) presentation.

4 A pre-prepared speech is always 'out of date'. It does not allow the speaker to adjust to the audience's immediate needs or to adapt the speech in response to points made by other speakers.

5   After about 20 minutes, the attention of the people in the first 30 rows tends to be less on the content of the speech than on how many pages are left!

6   Being totally dependent on any inflexible form has inherent dangers.

7   Because the speaker is chained to his notes it is difficult to adjust the presentation so that it finishes within the allocated time.

Here are a couple of true stories to illustrate these points.

Our first presenter had to make a speech at a three-day design conference in Washington DC, USA. The conference was attended by 2300 delegates and our man was number 72 out of 75 speakers. He had to give his prepared speech from behind a podium and he was allotted the 'graveyard shift' – the slot that starts immediately after lunch.

He was not a trained speaker, and as he approached the end of his 45-minute presentation most of the audience were dozing off. They all awoke at the screamed conclusion of his speech, which was, 'Oh my God! The last page has gone!' The last page had indeed disappeared. And in that moment of sheer terror he had not the faintest idea what was on it!

Our second presenter was an admiral who was known for his ability to make even the most boring prepared speeches sound interesting. He could read a speech in much the same way as an audio-typist transcribes it – perfectly but without any knowledge of its content.

He was asked to give a speech to some senior naval officials and, as he was short of time, he asked his aide to prepare a one-hour speech for him. He gave his presentation but began to suspect something was amiss when, after an hour, he found that he still had about the same number of pages to go.

Finally the truth dawned – he had been given two copies of the same speech. But the real horror was that the copies were ordered page 1, page 1, page 2, page 2, page 3, page 3, and so on. Because of his senior rank, no one had dared point out that perhaps this was carrying the mnemonic value of repetition a bit too far! A Mind Map would have saved him the embarrassment.

GIVING A MIND MAPPED PRESENTATION

In contrast to linear notes, a Mind Map gives the speaker freedom and flexibility

OPPOSITE: *Natural Architecture Plate 28*

as well as order and precision.

If the audience has particular needs or questions that arise, either before or during the speech, you can immediately link them into the Mind Map. Equally, if the time available for your presentation suddenly expands or shrinks, you can edit quickly and easily. The flexibility of a Mind Map allows you to monitor your progress easily and to accelerate or expand your presentation accordingly. Exactly timed performances are impressive in themselves as well courteous to other speakers and the audience.

Likewise, if the previous speaker has made similar points but with more knowledge or force than you, then you can quickly add to or alter your Mind Map, highlighting these points for agreement and thus form the 'brilliant him, brilliant me' association!

On the other hand, if the previous speaker has made misinformed or illogical comments, these can also be linked into your Mind Map and then expanded in your presentation in order to encourage subsequent discussion and debate.

To hold the audience's interest and ensure that they follow the pattern of thought, you can build up a Mind Map as the speech progresses, introducing it as a 'simple little map of ideas'.

EXAMPLE OF A MIND MAPPED PRESENTATION

The Mind Map on page 258 forms the basis of a presentation on the predictions of John Naisbitt, the futurist. The central image is a picture of Naisbitt and the arrow from the top of his head represents his vision of the future, from 1990 to the year 2000. The ten numbered branches correspond to the ten major areas of change predicted by Naisbitt over this time span.

In summary, Naisbitt predicts that the economy will become information-based and global; that the world will experience another renaissance in the arts, literature and spirituality; that the major cities will decline as centres of commerce; that socialism in the form of state welfare will disappear; that English will become the global language; that the media will become electronic, interlinked and global; that the major business area will shift from the Atlantic to the Pacific Rim; that politics will become individual and entrepreneurial; that growth in all areas will be seen as infinite; and that trade will be free. As a result of these changes, the overall trend will be towards a general lessening of war and conflict. All these changes can be seen in the context of Naisbitt's first set of megatrends, shown in the box in the top left-hand area of the Mind Map.

This Mind Map forms the basis of a discussion, lasting from a day to a week, of the future of the planet. It was made by Tony Buzan, using the techniques described in Chapters 14 (page 139), 16 (page 153) and 24 (page 235), during a two-day seminar held in Stockholm in 1987. At this seminar John Naisbitt presented his ideas to a group consisting of government, business, professional and educational leaders.

The second Mind Map (page 259 top) was prepared by Tony Buzan, Dean of the Young Presidents' Organisation Faculty, as a welcoming speech given to an international body of professors and dignitaries (who were lecturing aboard the QE2). The Mind Map served as both the basis for the opening speech and also as a review for the participating Faculty.

The third Mind Map (page 259 bottom) is by Raymond Keene, OBE, Grandmaster in Chess, Chess Correspondent for *The Times* and *Spectator*, and the most prolific author on chess and thinking in the history of the field. The Mind Map was in preparation for a lecture Raymond Keene gave in Spanish on Spanish TV (Television España for the programme *En Jaque*). The Mind Map was on the great sixteenth century Spanish chess player and writer Ruy Lopez and the intellectual and political influences of his time. As Keene says:

> *'The virtue of a Mind Map when preparing a speech or writing an article is two-fold: the writer is constantly stimulated by the branching trees of ideas to new and more daring thoughts; while at the same time the key words and images ensure that in the verbiage of speaking and writing, no major point is overlooked.*
>
> *The Mind Map is particularly useful in this context. Without turning or shuffling any pages, it is possible to inform the audience in advance about the structure and key points. Because you are always operating from one sheet, you can tell your audience what you plan to say, you can say it with confidence and then you can recap to demonstrate you have proved your point. With linear notes, the danger is ending simply where the notes stop, in essence a random moment, often determined by chronology rather than meaning.*
>
> *Assuming that the lecturer has complete command of his or her subject, the key words act as a catalyst for enthusiasm and ex tempore ideas instead of a dry recitation of facts often determined by dates (i.e. lecture starts at the beginning of subject's life and finishes at the end) rather than significant content. If the lecturer does not have perfect grasp of the subject, linear notes simply make it worse. Whether writing an article or giving a verbal lecture, the Mind Map acts like a steering wheel to navigate through the main oceans of the presentation.'*

Keene wrote this as part of an article for *The Times*; and it was based on the Mind Map he used for his presentation on Spanish Television.

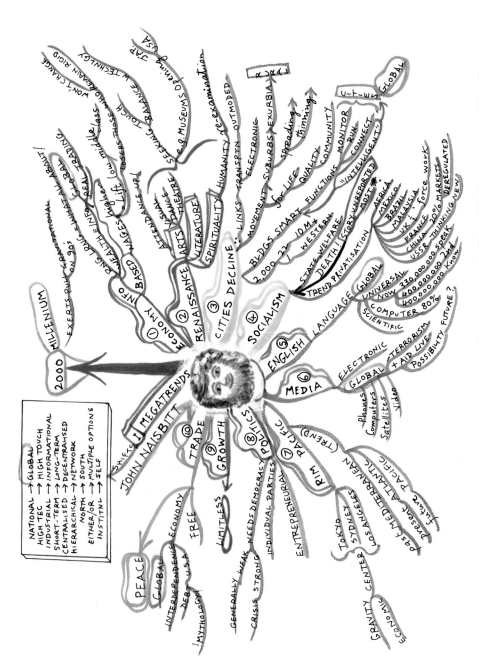

Mind Map by Tony Buzan of a two-day lecture/400 page book by John Naisbitt (see pages 256–7).

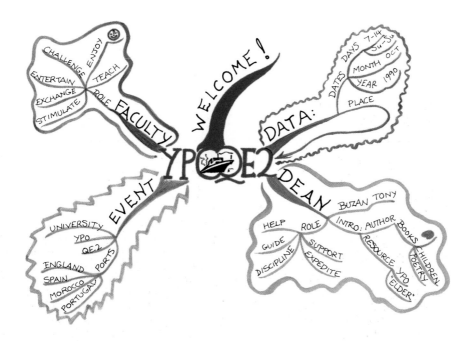

Mind Map by Tony Buzan for welcoming speech (see page 257).

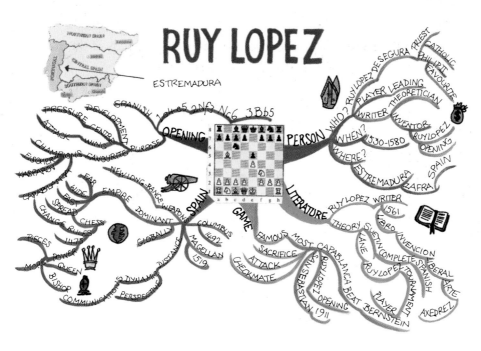

Mind Map by Raymond Keene OBE in preparation for a lecture given on Spanish television (see page 257).

Mind Maps have proved so useful in presentations, that neuro-psychologist and author Michael J. Gelb has written an entire book, *Present Yourself,* based on Radiant Thinking and the Mind Map approach. Not surprisingly, to present the book he devised a complete Mind Map.

BENEFITS OF MIND MAPS FOR PRESENTATIONS

1   They increase eye contact with the audience.

2   They give you freedom of movement.

3   They increase involvement, both for the speaker and the audience.

4   They utilise a greater range of cortical skills.

5   They enable you to adapt your presentation to the needs of the audience and to time it precisely.

6   They make it easier to alter or expand on key points.

7   They result in a more memorable, effective and enjoyable performance for both the speakers and the audience.

8   They give you the freedom to be yourself.

ONWORD

Having explored the specific applications of Mind Mapping for meetings and presentations, the next chapter broadens the focus to look at the way Mind Maps can be used to enhance communication and increase efficiency in many other management situations.

CHAPTER 27

MANAGEMENT

FOREWORD

Management with Mind Maps is a book in itself, and, on many levels, it is the book you have almost finished reading! This chapter shows how all the previously described Mind Map applications can be brought together in a management context to increase efficiency, productivity and enjoyment.

USING MIND MAPS FOR MANAGEMENT

Mind Maps can be used by every individual in a business or professional organisation in any situation where linear notes would normally be taken.

To begin with, the day can be planned using a Mind Map diary (see Chapter 20, page 191). Subsequently, telephone calls, meetings, counselling sessions and interviews can all be Mind Mapped, to ensure that the participants have a full and accurate grasp of what has been discussed and agreed.

By using Mind Maps in their training courses, companies like EDS, Digital Computers and British Petroleum have already found that they can make huge savings – in some cases as much as 80 per cent! In fact Dr Mike Stanley, Project Leader at the Boeing Aircraft Corporation in Seattle, reduced an aircraft design manual to a 25 foot long Mind Map which won him awards within the company (see Chapter 17, 'Examples of group Mind Maps in action', pages 170–71). Stanley says:

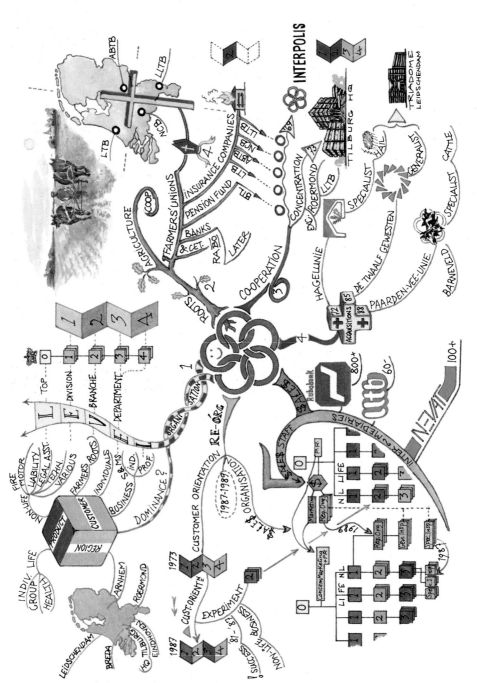

Mind Map by Jan Pieter Six of Interpolis (see page 264).

Natural Architecture Plate 29

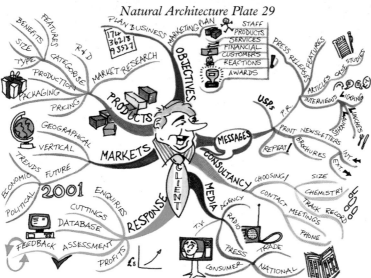

Mind Map by Nigel Temple, founder of Temple Marketing in Britain, used as the basis for discovering the marketing needs of each customer (see page 267).

'The use of Mind Mapping is an integral part of my Quality Improvement programme here at Boeing. This programme has provided savings of over $10 million this year for my organisation (ten times our goal). We have developed a unique application of Mind Mapping techniques to identify Quality Improvement projects here at Boeing. Within one month's time, over 500 projects were identified which represent millions of dollars of potential cost savings.'

In addition to increasing the speed and efficiency of learning, Mind Maps overcome the usual memory loss curve, whereby 80 per cent of what is learnt is forgotten within 24 hours. Reviewing Mind Maps at the intervals recommended in Chapter 24 ('Reviewing your Mind Map notes', pages 240–41) ensures that what is learnt is both 'held' and utilised by the brain. In general, the skills previously covered – making choices; organising your own and other people's ideas; individual and group creativity; analysis; defining and solving problems; setting time and amount targets; and especially memory and communication – are essential to successful management.

EXAMPLES OF MANAGEMENT MIND MAPS

1 Management Structure

Mind Maps can be used to structure an organisation, act as a stabilising vision for the organisation, and explain the organisation to others. The Mind Map on page 262 is by Mr Jan Pieter H. Six, Vice-President of Interpolis, a Dutch insurance company. In structuring and explaining his organisation he considered: organisation; roots; co-operation; acquisitions; sales; and reorganisation.

Organisation

The organisational development will be looked upon from two points of view: level of command (top, division, branch or department) and dominance in the organisational structure of product (life/non-life), customer (farmers/individuals/business) or region.

Roots

Interpolis is rooted in the Catholic agricultural cooperatives. The farmers are organised into four Catholic farmers' unions, one in each diocese. These unions have created their own cooperative institutions like banks, a pension fund and insurance companies, originally mutual fire insurance companies.

Cooperation

In 1969 the pension fund and the four insurance companies merged into Interpolis. Four years later the five companies were concentrated in Tilburg. The organisational structure was heavily determined by product.

Acquisitions

In 1972, Interpolis acquired specialist hail insurer Hagelunie, followed in 1985 by general insurer De Twaalf Gewesten. Both companies have a joint office called Triadome. Specialist cattle insurer Paarden-Vee-Unie is Interpolis' latest acquisition.

Sales

Interpolis sells its products through intermediaries. Three distribution channels can be distinguished: the 800+ Rabobanks, the 60 LLTB-agents and 100+ NEVAT-agents.

Until recent years the sales staff consisted of a marketing department and five regional sales organisations, each with its general and specialist inspectors.

Reorganisation

Reorganisation brought many changes between 1987 and 1989. In 1987 the specialist inspectors were detached from Sales, transformed into several specialist corps and added to three branches.

2 Marketing

The Mind Map is a major tool in marketing. Temple Marketing in Britain uses a 'Marketing Matrix Mind Map' (MMMM) to plan the marketing needs of every customer.

The Mind Map on page 263 is by Nigel Temple, President and Chief Executive Officer of Temple Marketing, and forms the basis of their marketing plan with every client.

The Mind Map considers: the range of products the client wishes to market; the business and marketing objectives of the client; the prime messages the

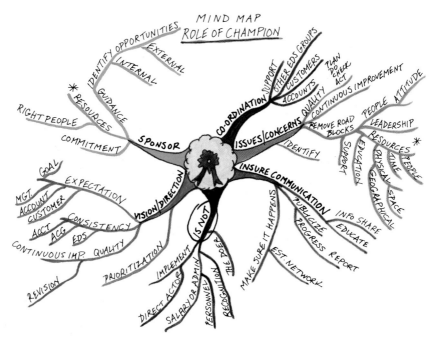

Completed EDS 'Championship' Mind Map (see pages 266–7).

client wishes to get across to the public and the medium by which they wish to do so; the nature and structure of the consultancy agreements; the use of various media and the inclusion or exclusion of them in the overall marketing plan; the nature of the response desired and the means for monitoring that response; and the target markets in the near, mid and long-term future. As the Temple group says:

> 'We use Mind Mapping to improve our account planning and issue-management process on all levels. In brain-storming sessions, for example, we find Mind Mapping to be a powerful tool for recording the creative output in a more logical order.'

3 Leadership

Electronic Data Systems (EDS), the information systems conglomerate, makes the teaching of Mental Literacy among its employees a prime corporate goal.

One main feature of this campaign is the development of leadership capabilities. To accomplish this it was essential to establish a complete understanding of what individual project goals were and to establish the purpose of the leader or 'champion' for the many and various projects.

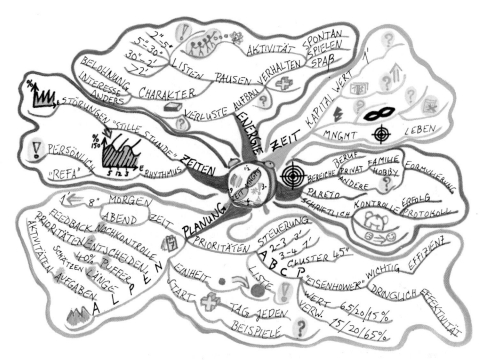

Mind Map by Thomas H. Schaper of the Association International Management in Germany, on incorporating effective use of time management in life (see below).

To identify the role of the champion in each project group, the entire group was handed a blank Mind Map (see page 268), which they then, as a group, filled in. As Jim Messerschmitt and Tony Messina, the Directors of the projects and originators of the Mind Maps, said:

> 'It worked especially well, took a very short period of time, and everyone had a complete understanding of what we were trying to accomplish and what the purpose of their champion leader was.'

An example of a completed leadership/champion Mind Map can be seen opposite.

4 Time Management

As discussed in Chapter 20 the Mind Map is especially useful for time management. The Mind Map above was done by Thomas H. Schaper of the Association International Management in Göttingen, Germany.

Schaper's Mind Map deals with his instructions to other managers on the effective use of their time in the management of their lives. The Mind Map

MIND MAP
ROLE OF CHAMPION

'Championship' Mind Map used by Jim Messerschmitt and Tony Messina, Director of Leadership Project at EDS. This is the first stage (see page 267).

focuses on target areas: the nature of planning (incorporating a German mnemonic 'ALPEN' for the prime steps in personal time management); the nature of biological rhythms; and the maximisation of energy by the appropriate management of one's time.

As often happens with Mind Maps, Schaper has found his to serve multiple purposes. It helped him streamline his own time and self-management and enabled him to guide his colleagues. Mind Maps became a focal point of interest, making him an expert in the field and someone who others approached for guidance.

5 Accountancy – Practice Development

Mind Maps are becoming an increasingly valuable currency in the accounting field. Award-winning students in the English Institute of Chartered Accountants use them to prepare for examinations, tax advisers in such prestigious companies as Price Waterhouse use them for solving problems and advising clients, and as can be seen from the Mind Map by Brian Lee (page 270), founding partner of B.H. Lee & Company, Accountants, Auditors & Taxation Consultants, Mind Maps are being used in the development and expansion of practices.

Lee had three major points on his Mind Map: dangers; practice development; and expansion. He describes the Mind Map in the following way:

'Dangers

The major danger is the overuse of resources by over-committing and over-extending. It is essential to consider what dangers might exist to the career structures of Partners and staff when expanding, what pressures would be felt on income, spending and reinvestment plans and how much energy might be misplaced, diverted or prove to be too limited.

Practice Development

Not only do we need to develop, we need to consolidate. There is no point in obtaining new customers if at the same time you lose old ones. It is also important to realise that development applies to staff as well as clients.

Development can be achieved by marketing, advertising, referrals and in particular, from existing clients. This can all be aided by holding budget meetings, emphasising other services and seminars and holding special events.

Expansion

Expansion needs to be defined. It revolves around a number of initial questions. Who is expanding: Partners, Associates, customers, staff? When is the expansion to take place? Over what period? Where are you aiming to expand, i.e. the place, catchment area? Are you intending to do so by joint venture, purchasing other business, co-operating with others or forming other partnerships? Also, how do you identify opportunities in each of those areas and what might persuade somebody to join in such an expansion plan, i.e. them being able to retire, take holidays, have on-hand help, expand a business empire, or lessen responsibility and at the same time actually make more money! What are the costs involved in such expansion: capital costs, resource costs and costs against normal rate of income?

Care should be exercised in using methods to achieve expansion and identify opportunities. What are the reasons? Where is the money coming from? Will it make a profit? Is it secure? Does it give the status that everybody requires? External and internal along with other areas of knowledge exist and should be used in pursuit of the answers to these questions.'

Lee summarises:

'Accountancy traditionally works within a very logical and sometimes restricted framework. Mind Mapping takes thought far beyond these boundaries.'

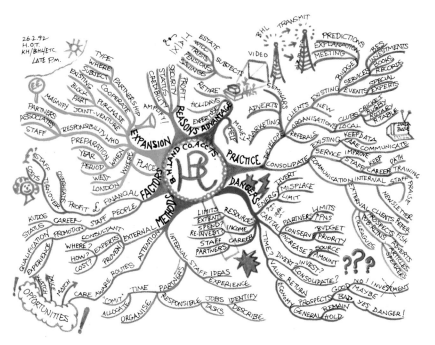

Mind Map by B. H. Lee of B. H. Lee & Company, Accountants, on the development, dangers, and expansion of a business practice (see pages 268–9).

6 *Multiple Uses-in-One*

Jean-Luc Kastner, a Senior Manager in Hewlett Packard Medical Products Group Europe, was confronted with a problem. His company manufactures a computer system that is able to monitor and analyse the rhythms of the heart, detecting malfunctions early enough to alert the attending physician in order to take proper corrective actions. They run a four-day 'Cardiac Arrhythmia Training Course' taught by specialised trainers.

One day the staff member in charge of this application training reported ill and was going to be absent for two months. Kastner, as 'the boss' and as the only person with enough background information to even consider running the course, was obliged to fill in for his employee. The emergency required that he organise and supplement his existing knowledge and teach the course.

The 'Cardiac Arrhythmia Training' is a course intended to provide HP application support engineers with in-depth knowledge of:
- *the human heart physiology*
- *the main rhythm problems and their consequence*
- *computer algorithm works*
- *arrhythmia system operation.*

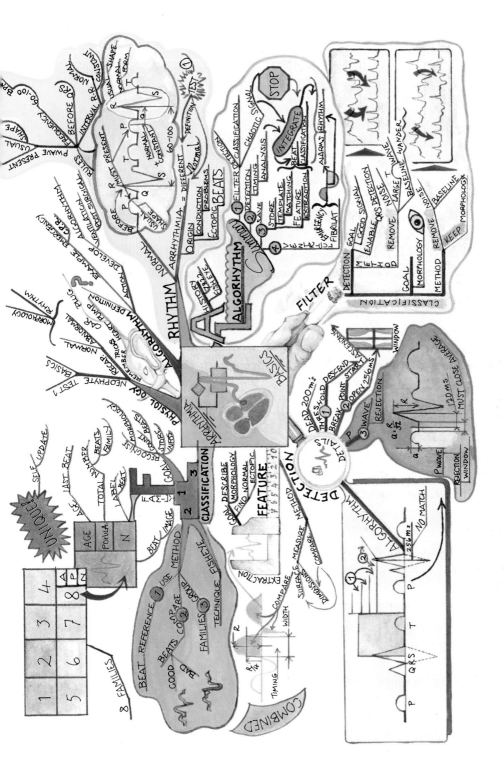

Jean-Luc Kastner's Mind Map of a four-day training course (see pages 270–3).

In addition trainees must be able to:
- *train the end user (a nurse or a doctor)*
- *explain some of the features that may lead the device into difficult situations (The computer is still not as good as a cardiologist!)*

Using the Mind Map Teaching Method

This training course seemed to be an ideal case for testing teaching by Mind Maps on a very difficult subject.

I developed the course within five days by Mind Mapping the existing material, with the following goals:

a) *To have all students pass successfully the graduation tests at the end of the 4 days.*
b) *To have all students build their own reference manuals.*
c) *To not use overhead projections (unless a copy of a medical record).*
d) *To improve the recall factor after one month by 100% (it was often well below 40%).*
e) *To have both teacher and students enjoy the experience.*

Structure

The training was structured using the Master Mind Map as a 'road map'. Each branch represented one major topic, and for each branch I developed a detailed Mind Map designed in order to be reproduced on a flip chart. Every second hour a major break was taken.

The Course

At the beginning of the course the trainees were instructed to leave all personal writing materials outside the room. They were confronted with tables that had only A3 blank sheets of paper and a wide variety of coloured pens.

The trainees were introduced to Mind Maps. For the 4 days to come they were requested to copy from the flip chart whatever Mind Map notes the teacher made.

The course was organised in sections of 40 minutes, with 10 minute breaks. During these breaks trainees had access to computer-aided training tools that simulated patient electro-cardiograms (ECGs). They tested their knowledge as the course progressed.

When one branch of the Master Mind Map was completed the trainees were asked to develop their own Master Mind Maps. For this purpose a gigantic sheet of paper was posted on the wall and the group as a whole participated in building the Master Mind Map [see page 271].

At the end of the day, the students were asked to copy the Master Mind Map on their own documents and to review and file the documents of the day.

On the next morning one of the students reviewed the Master Mind Map of the previous day with the group. The next activity then started.

At the end of the course and before the final test the group reviewed the Master

Mind Map and discussed it in detail.

The final 2-hour examination (required for graduation) was then taken.

Results

We have run the course based on the outline described. (Twelve students, from England, France, Germany, Italy and Ireland attended.) All twelve graduated with 18 out of 20 – the best grade ever.

I conducted an informal survey after one month and the recall factor was well above 70%. In fact out of 10 questions asked, they could answer, on average, nine of them!

Course feedback was excellent, the students judged the method to be more successful, more useful and more fun than the old slide-show-based course. Some students even commented that the pace of the Mind Map-based course was much better adapted to trainees whose English knowledge was not perfect. This demonstrates the success of Mind Map-based training.

The Mind Map-based course has been run in the meantime 4 times by different trainers with comparable results.

Mind Map teaching is definitely the teaching tool of the 90s.

BENEFITS OF MIND MAPS FOR MANAGEMENT

1 They result in better management and organisation, leading to a happier, more motivated workforce. This in turn means fewer working days lost through illness and a better public image for the company.

2 They improve communication between members of staff.

3 They make training more efficient and effective.

4 They can make marketing and promotion more focused, leading to improved sales.

ONWORD

The computer Mind Map has only very recently been achieved. The next chapter explains how computer technology interacts with human technology.

CHAPTER 28

COMPUTER MIND MAPPING

Preview
- Foreword
- Creating and editing a Computer Mind Map
- Managing complexity
- Sharing
- Adding intelligence
- Transferring knowledge
- Transformations – looking at things differently
- Team working
- Delivering results
- The future of Computer Mind Maps
- Onword

FOREWORD

Computer Mind Mapping software now provides new, exciting capabilities for the Mind Mapper which were once a future vision. Admittedly computers cannot yet fully compete with the infinite visual variety, portability and 'minimum tool requirements' of traditional Mind Mapping techniques (using just paper and coloured pens) but the gap is reducing fast! 'Digital ink' is already here which allows you to input data simply by writing on your computer screen.

The new software offers significant improvements in personal productivity in the areas of:
- automatic Mind Map generation
- editing
- analyzing
- creating different views

Natural Architecture Plate 30

- navigating
- linking to information sources
- generating new Mind Maps from existing information
- sharing Mind Maps
- converting Mind Maps into reports, presentations and plans

Computer Aided Thinking® (CAT) has finally arrived.

This chapter introduces you to Computer Mind Mapping and features examples from MindGenius®, a productivity and thinking tool that has been developed by Gael Limited, a strategic partner of The Buzan Group.

CREATING AND EDITING A COMPUTER MIND MAP

Creating a Computer Mind Map is simple. First, you are prompted to enter the key word which will be the focus for your new Mind Map. Once this key word – your central image – is entered, the computer automatically draws, colours and positions your central Mind Map image in the middle of your screen.

Then you simply type the titles of your main themes/branches (Bois) and hit the 'Return' key. Branches are then automatically entered and structured. You just think, type and 'Return' and your Mind Map grows before your very eyes! You don't have to worry about the precise structure and the correct placement of ideas. The Mind Map grows following your thought sequence, and radiates as your ideas flow. You are left free to be creative!

Computer Mind Mapping provides an excellent separation of the creative and editing parts of your thinking process. You free flow ideas without being distracted by the computer. When you have completed your free-flow ideas you can go back to your Mind Map and add colour and images to make it memorable and interesting.

Branches can be repositioned, recoloured, images added, copied, moved and the complete structure re-organised as required – all via simple mouse click operations. Each branch property (shape, font, colour, connection type) can be individually changed or you can apply pre-customised styles.

Computer Mind Maps can be developed over an extended period of time and, you won't ever need to redraw your Mind Map as computer Mind Maps 'flex' and re-structure automatically to accommodate any new ideas and insights that you have derived from further deliberation or from new experiences and understanding.

MANAGING COMPLEXITY

Computer Mind Maps of *enormous* complexity can now be developed. Your Mind Map is no longer limited by the size of paper that you use – it is only limited by your imagination and that is infinite!

An essential feature of Computer Mind Mapping is therefore the ability to explore and navigate through the complexity of the Mind Maps. You need to know where you are, always remain in control, have the ability to view specific areas but in context of the overall Mind Map. Normal zoom, scroll, and pan capabilities are not the answer.

Instead, Mind Map Explorer navigation functions provide a structured outline of the hierarchy of your Mind Map, similar to a work breakdown structure. When you click on a branch element of the Mind Map Explorer outline, a new Mind Map is automatically redrawn from the selected branch and its sub-branches, with the selected branch promoted to be the central focus of the new Mind Map.

This allows you to take a helicopter view of your Mind Map, exploring vertically and horizontally within the Mind Map hierarchy without getting lost. The Mind Map Explorer feature (combined with branch expand and collapse options), allows you to see as much or as little detail of the Mind Map as you require. This means, in effect, that you are no longer constrained by the size of your computer screen and you do not need to have your Mind Map spread over a number of pages or files.

SHARING

It is important that knowledge is shared and what better way than to be able to make your Mind Maps quickly available to other people? You can do this in a number of ways:

Printing

If you want to provide hard copy Mind Maps then 'Print' options allow you to print out your Mind Maps in a variety of formats (single/multiple pages, colour, Map or Text Outline/Map and Text Outline).

E-mail

A simple 'Send' function attaches your Mind Map to an e-mail, which you can address to your intended recipients.

Viewer

You can bundle up your map with a proprietary 'Viewer' application that

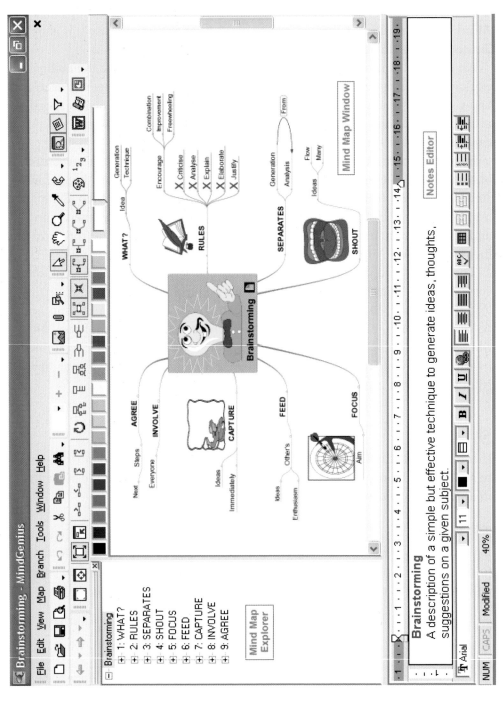

A Mind Map being created on screen using MindGenius® software (see pages 274–289).

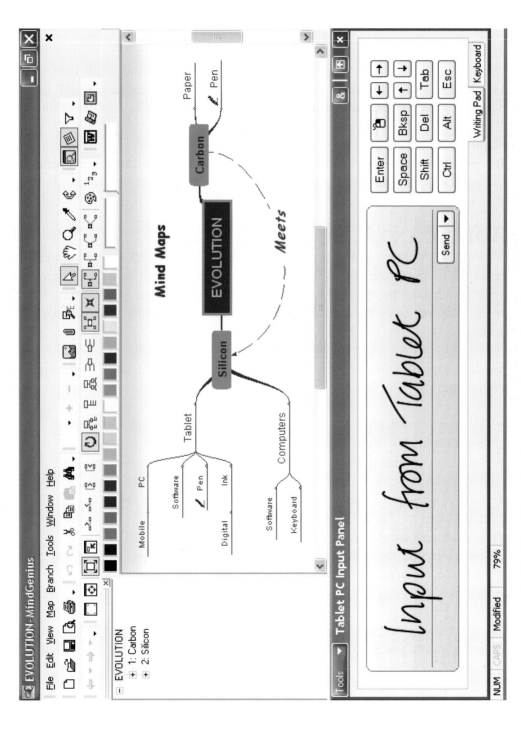

A Mind Map being created on screen using 'Digital Ink' technology (see page 288).

allows people to view and navigate your Computer Mind Map.

HTML

'Save As HTML' options allow you to convert your Mind Map into an HTML file, which can then be placed on the web for others to view. All the Map Explorer navigation features are included.

Adobe

It is possible to save your Mind Map as an 'Adobe PDF' file and share it using the open *de facto* standard for electronic document distribution worldwide.

ADDING INTELLIGENCE

Now Mind Mappers can harness the power of modern PCs and perform tasks once only imagined. You can add attributes to each branch bringing your Mind Map to life and enabling you to improve your productivity by being able to carry out a wide range of additional tasks (see following sections).

You can add the following attributes to branches within your Computer Mind Map:

- Categories (multiple) – key words to differentiate and add meaning to each branch
- Resources (multiple) – associate named people/resources with a given branch
- Actions and dates – designate a branch as an action and assign an action date
- Attachments (multiple) – link the branch to electronic files that your computer can access
- Mental Connections – create links across the Mind Map hierarchy structure

These attributes add intelligence to your Computer Mind Map and allow you to question and analyse the Mind Map to gain an improved understanding.

TRANSFERRING KNOWLEDGE

The single word-per-branch rule is intended to introduce ambiguity to open up new avenues of thought. However, when you provide your Mind Map to others, they may not understand what you mean by certain branches. You can add notes to each branch of your Mind Map using a 'Note Editor' window with full word processing capability. The content of the note can be as much, or as little as you need to ensure that the reader understands the messages you are aiming to get across. The addition of notes to branches provides powerful approaches to enable effective pre-writing and summarizing.

Mind Maps can now be used to collate information or to gain understanding from a wide variety of sources. These sources are often in the form of electronic files and you can now link multiple electronic files to each branch, regardless of whether your information sources are on your computer, an intranet or the internet If your computer can access the information then you can launch into the information directly from the branch in your Computer Mind Map. Your Mind Map can therefore become a structured, visual front-end for your knowledge sources and a knowledge base that can be shared with others.

TRANSFORMATIONS – LOOKING AT THINGS DIFFERENTLY

When struggling with a task, we are often asked to take a step back in order to take a different view. Why? Because it helps you with breakthrough thinking and coming up with novel, innovative ideas. Computer Mind Maps encourage you to do this.

The underlying structure of Mind Maps (sequence and hierarchy) is very similar to other visual methodologies that have been developed to tackle specific types of tasks. At the click of a mouse button you can transform your Mind Map into the following diagrams:

- Outlines (lists in a structured format)
- Affinity Diagrams (post-brainstorming grouping technique)
- Organograms
- Funnel Diagrams
- Input Trees (useful for Cause and Effect analysis – identify the true cause of your problem)
- Output Trees (useful for Solution and Effect analysis – try out your solutions before you implement them. It is the cheapest way to identify and resolve potential problems)

You have instant access to a variety of proven techniques and you don't have to redraw a single Mind Map!

Natural Architecture Plate 31

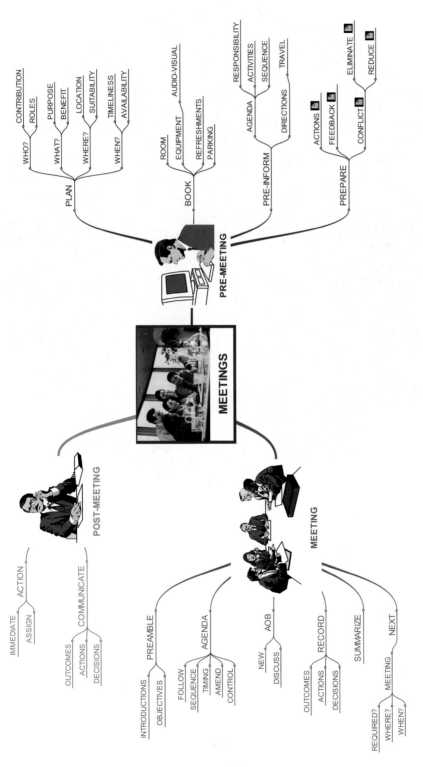

An example of how a computer-generated mind map can be used to great effect in a business environment.

You can build queries that allow you to question and analyze your Computer Mind Map and gain more meaningful insights into its contents. You can then filter your Mind Map to see only the branches that meet the filter criteria that you set and you can then generate new maps from the filtered output.. You sort the wheat from the chaff.

You see what you need to see. You can filter on the branch attributes and gain answers to such questions as: What actions do I have to do today? What branches are specifically relevant to me? Which of the branches listed have been identified as high priority activities? Do any of the branches listed refer to brainstorming? You can look at your Mind Map from different perspectives – in essence you have changed the central focus of your Mind Map. Instead of one Mind Map, you have a subset of Mind Maps, which show you different facets of your original Mind Map and provides an invaluable stimulus for breakthrough thinking.

TEAM WORKING

Groups of people stimulate and inspire each other to create ideas by thinking together, feeding off their diverse experiences and harnessing their collective imaginative brain power. So how do you form a 'creative huddle' around a Mind Map? It's easy to do with Computer Mind Maps.

Computer Mind Maps provide you with the capability of group collaboration. People in different locations can work together on the same Mind Map. Participants log onto a session and can then provide input and comment. As information is added to the Computer Mind Map the participants are able to see the changes being implemented in real time and comment accordingly. Global Mind Map generation – great for corporate/government creativity!

Whilst many Mind Maps are generated by individuals, each often works as part of a team or organizational structure. The Mind Map content may have to go through an approval cycle, or you may have the beginnings of an idea and want others to flesh it out. You can perform review and comment activities using Computer Mind Maps. The Mind Map is distributed electronically to the targeted recipients with a request for action. Each contributor's additions to the map are coded with special identifying attributes so that when the maps are returned to the originator their input can be automatically extracted and merged into one Mind Map.

It saves time, you see the big picture and it is considerably reduces the time it takes to gain agreement/consensus.

DELIVERING RESULTS

Now for the WOW factor! For years business has been waiting for a 'global language tool' and now it is here! Business decisions are based on reports, proposals, presentations and project plans. CAT software bridges that gap. At the click of a button, your Computer Mind Maps are transformed into Word® documents, or PowerPoint® presentations, or MS Project® plans. By adding attributes to branches, there is a commonality of structures that allows your Computer Mind Maps to be transformed into these key deliverables.

Map Branches	Word®	PowerPoint®	MS Project®
Map key theme	Document Title	Presentation title	Plan title
Parent Branches	Paragraph Title	Slide titles	Summary tasks
Sub-branches	Sub-paragraph title	Bullet points	Activities
Branch Notes	Paragraph text	Lecture notes	Activity notes
Resources	-	-	Resource needed
Action dates	-	-	Activity dates

So for the times when your colleagues, managers or clients expect a document, presentation, project plan or action you don't need to put in mountains of additional work – the software does the work for you. This is an immensely powerful benefit and positions Mind Mapping where it is most beneficial, as the creative front-end of the vast wide variety of tasks that business and professional people are required to perform.

You can also export branches that are action points as tasks to MS Outlook®, e-mailing the task to the person responsible for the action and inserting the action in your own task list so that, via MS Outlook®, you can progress such actions to a timely completion.

In many cases, if the information already exists, you don't have to create Mind Maps from scratch. You can create Computer Mind Maps from Word® documents, PowerPoint® presentations and MS Project® plans. A great time saver!

THE FUTURE OF COMPUTER MIND MAPS

Computer Mind Maps have finally arrived. Through them, Mind Mapping will realize its true potential in the modern electronic world and is already

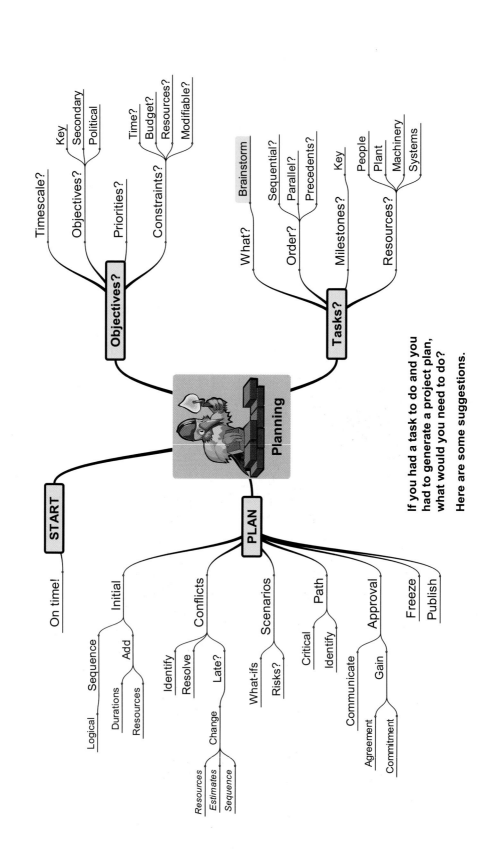

Planning

START

On time!

Initial
Logical   Sequence
Durations
Add
Resources

Conflicts
Identify
Resolve
Late?
Change
Resources
Estimates
Sequence

Scenarios
What-ifs
Risks?

Path
Critical
Identify

Approval
Communicate
Gain
Agreement
Commitment

Freeze
Publish

PLAN

Objectives?

Timescale?

Objectives?
Key
Secondary
Political

Priorities?

Constraints?
Time?
Budget?
Resources?
Modifiable?

Tasks?

What?
Brainstorm

Order?
Sequential?
Parallel?
Precedents?

Milestones?
Key

Resources?
People
Plant
Machinery
Systems

If you had a task to do and you had to generate a project plan, what would you need to do?

Here are some suggestions.

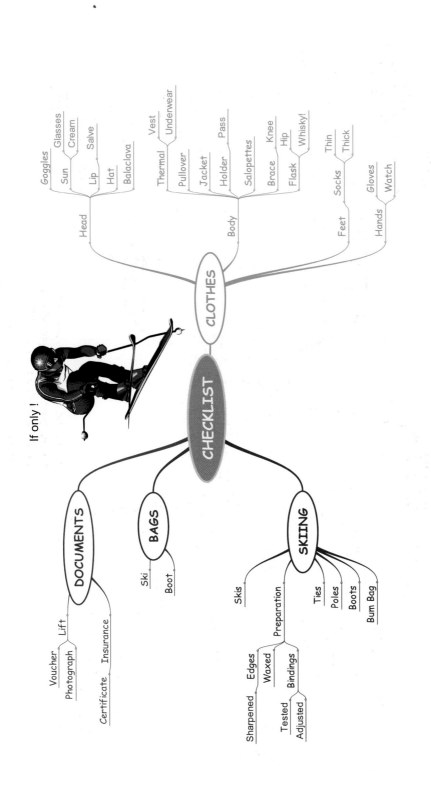

If only !

CHECKLIST

CLOTHES

Head
- Goggles
- Sun — Glasses
- Cream
- Lip — Salve
- Hat
- Balaclava

Body
- Thermal — Vest
- Underwear
- Pullover
- Jacket
- Holder — Pass
- Salopettes
- Brace — Knee
- Hip
- Flask — Whisky!

Feet
- Thin
- Socks — Thick

Hands
- Gloves
- Watch

DOCUMENTS
- Voucher — Lift
- Photograph
- Certificate — Insurance

BAGS
- Ski
- Boot

SKIING
- Skis
- Preparation
  - Sharpened — Edges
  - Waxed
  - Tested — Bindings
  - Adjusted
- Ties
- Poles
- Boots
- Bum Bag

becoming the technique of choice in the workplace. Technology also continues its relentless progress. So how might technology influence the progression of Mind Mapping in the future?

Firstly, there's some magical technology already with us that gives a strong indication of the future of Computer Mind Maps. It revolves around the concept of 'digital ink'. Tablet PCs are available that allow users to input data with a digital pen directly onto their computer screens, just as if they were writing on a piece of paper. Powerful handwriting recognition software converts the ink to standard text, or you can continue to use the handwritten text. CAT software accepts and handles ink input – now you can hand-write your Computer Mind Maps!

From this it is obvious that the natural progression will be to handwrite your Mind Maps directly into your PC and then use the PC based version for your analysis and delivery activities.

How else will technology impact the world of Computer Mind Maps? PC technology is continuing to make rapid progress in the realms of ultra-light-weight notebooks, ever more powerful low-voltage processors, higher power capability batteries, built-in wireless capability and the increasing deployment of wireless cells, and improved docking and undocking capabilities. The way is clear to provide everything you would expect in a mobile PC. Computer Mind Maps will go truly mobile! You will be able to generate Mind Maps on the move and transmit your Mind Maps (and any resulting reports, presentations, actions and plans) immediately to the intended recipients.

Computer Mind Maps are already making make major inroads into the language of business. Some companies (such as Mind Genius/Gael) have already moved most of their business work onto a Mind Map-only environment. This will introduce a new, more visual way of working in the businesses of the future. It encourages people to think something through before developing any level of detail, lets them develop content, review it and gain consensus as they go and ensures that all parties anticipate and address the impact of changes on others and the organisation at the earliest possible time.

Looking further out? 3-D Mind Maps/spatial models of Mind Maps will be created where cross-hierarchical connections are portals into other layers of Mind Maps and avenues of thought – virtual Mind Map walkthroughs!

Computer Mind Mapping clearly has an exiting future ahead of it. Freedom of thinking combined with the ever-increasing power of computing will undoubtedly ensure that Computer Mind Maps will be, and continue to be, the technique of choice for individuals and companies seeking to unleash themselves and their organisations to achieve their key objectives and company or life visions.

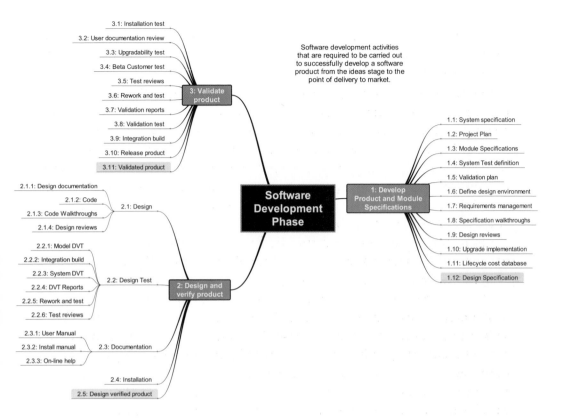

The advantages of computer-generated Mind Maps are clearly demonstrated here in this effective and sophisticated map.

ONWORD

With the growth in tandem of machine and human intelligence, what is our most likely and possible future? In the final chapter Tony Buzan gives a personal perspective on a predicted Intelligence Revolution, the rise of Brain Stars, and the prospect of mentally literate individuals working towards a mentally literate society and a Radiant Thinking radiant future.

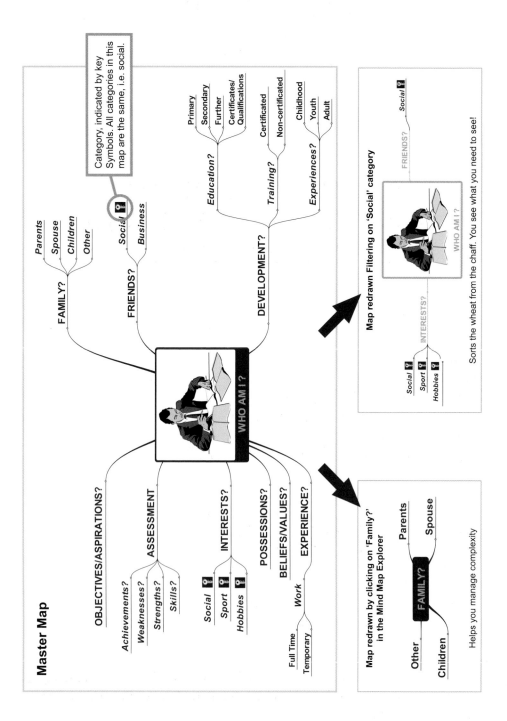

Master Map

OBJECTIVES/ASPIRATIONS?

FAMILY?
- Parents
- Spouse
- Children
- Other

FRIENDS?
- Social
- Business

Category, indicated by key Symbols. All categories in this map are the same, i.e. social.

DEVELOPMENT?

Education?
- Primary
- Secondary
- Further
- Certificates/ Qualifications

Training?
- Certificated
- Non-certificated

Experiences?
- Childhood
- Youth
- Adult

ASSESSMENT
- Achievements?
- Weaknesses?
- Strengths?
- Skills?

INTERESTS?
- Social
- Sport
- Hobbies

POSSESSIONS?

BELIEFS/VALUES?

EXPERIENCE?
- Full Time
- Temporary
- Work

WHO AM I ?

Map redrawn Filtering on 'Social' category

FRIENDS? — Social

WHO AM I ?

INTERESTS?
- Social
- Sport
- Hobbies

Sorts the wheat from the chaff. You see what you need to see!

Map redrawn by clicking on 'Family?' in the Mind Map Explorer

FAMILY?
- Parents
- Spouse
- Children
- Other

Helps you manage complexity

An example of a Mind Map that has been 'filtered', thus enabling the creator/user to focus on specific branches (see page 284).

SECTION E
The Future

CHAPTER 29

TOWARDS A RADIANT THINKING AND MENTALLY LITERATE WORLD

Preview
- Foreword
- The Intelligence Revolution
    The brain information explosion
    Brain Stars
    The Mind Sports Olympiad/World Memory
        Championships
- Mental Literacy
    1 The Mentally Literate individual
    2 The Mentally Literate family
    3 The Mentally Literate organisation
    4 The Mentally Literate society
    5 A Mentally Literate civilisation
- Radiant Thinking – Radiant Future

FOREWORD

The last chapter of *The Mind Map Book* looks at the startlingly encouraging current trends in the field of thinking and the brain, and the rise of new heroes and heroines – the Brain Stars.

This chapter explores the implications of Radiant Thinking and Mind Mapping for our future, and examines the possibilities of a Mentally Literate world from the perspectives of the individual, families, organisations, societies and a global civilisation.

THE INTELLIGENCE REVOLUTION

As *The Mind Map Book* goes to press, the world stands on the brink of a major revolution: the discovery that intelligence can understand its own nature, and in so doing can enhance and nurture itself. Simultaneously, we are realising that our main asset is our Intellectual Capital.

National Olympic squads are currently devoting as much as 50 per cent of their training time to the development of mental strength and stamina, while the top US information technology companies alone spend hundreds of millions of dollars on developing the Mental Literacy skills of their employees.

The brain information explosion

In 1992 alone, interest in our brain power exploded into the popular domain, as an increasing number of national and international newspapers and magazines ran major feature articles on the workings of the brain.

- *Fortune* magazine splashed 'Brain Power' across its cover, claiming that 'intellectual capital' was becoming society's most valuable asset.
- *Omni* magazine (twice) featured 'The Brain and Ageing' and a 'Brain Diet'.
- *Stern* in Germany wrote on 'The Development of Mental Fitness'.
- *Synapsia* magazine featured 'The Development of a Global Brain'.
- *Newsweek* explored how science was opening new windows on the mind and featured Mental Literacy in an article that generated a record response.
- *Time* magazine discussed drugs and the brain.
- *US News* produced a special double issue featuring creative thinking and another issue headlining the relationship between mind and body.
- *The New Scientist* produced a cover illustration featuring twenty brains!
- *The Times* newspaper in England investigated the neuro-scientific revolution.
- *The Wall Street Journal* popularised research into the brain cell.
- The September 1992 issue of *Scientific American* was totally devoted to 'Mind and Brain', featuring memory and learning.

Coinciding with this accelerating media coverage, we are seeing a new breed of superstar emerging on the international stage – the Brain Star.

Brain Stars

The twentieth century started with film stars, and rapidly moved on to singing stars, rock stars, pop stars and sports stars. The twenty-first, the Century of the Brain, has already begun with Brain Stars who demonstrate the principle of a healthy mind in a healthy body. Gary Kasparov, the athletic and dynamic World Chess Champion, has millions of children around the world pinning posters of him on the walls of their rooms and dreaming of becoming international chess Grandmasters and champions.

Similarly, the charming young Hungarian girl Judit Polgar, the youngest ever chess Grandmaster, is becoming a cult figure. Dominic O'Brien, the first, six-time and reigning World Memory Champion, who uses Memory Mind Maps to help him recall record-breaking amounts of data, now regularly appears on international television. And there is Raymond Keene, game master and world record holder for books written on games and thinking (100+!). Through his Mind Maps, articles, books and television presentations (see Chapter 26, pages 257, 259) he has built up a following of 180,000 people who stay up until 1 a.m. to watch his programmes. Other members of this growing 'Charge of the Bright Brigade' include Carl Sagan, famous astronomer and leader of the billion-dollar-plus search for extraterrestrial intelligence; Omar Sharif, whose brilliance as a bridge player is now outshining his career as an actor; Edward De Bono, who travels around the world speaking to vast audiences about lateral thinking; Bobby Fischer, the weight-lifting American chess genius who resurrected the game in the public's consciousness, and who recently returned at the age of 50 to beat Boris Spassky; and Stephen Hawking, the Cambridge physicist, whose book *A Brief History of Time* has, to date, been on the bestseller lists for longer than any other book in the history of publishing. These Brain Stars and mental athletes were recently joined by the extraordinary polymath and Professor of mathematics, 65-year-old Dr Marion Tinsley, the World Draughts/Checkers Champion. Tinsley, disproving all the myths about age and mental abilities, has been the world Number One since 1954, during which time he has lost only seven games. He recently beat the world's new Number Two player, Chinook, a computer programme. Stating that he was using only a small part of his brain's Radiant Thinking abilities, Tinsley crushed a computer that could calculate three million moves a minute, and which had a database of over 27 billion positions!

Paralleling this trend is the growing popularity of intellectual quiz programmes such as *Brain of Britain* and *Mastermind*, and the establishment of prizes such as the Brain Trust's 'Brain of the Year', most recently awarded to Gary Kasparov for mental games, Chiyonofuji for physical exploits, and Gene Roddenberry for his work in engineering media.

The Mind Sports Olympiad/World Memory Championships

According to a recent survey, over 100 million people play Trivial Pursuit and Monopoly, while 200 million play Scrabble and do crosswords. As many as 60 million play bridge, 250 million play draughts/checkers, and over 300 million play chess. As the Mind Map was creating its own revolution, a concurrent revolution in global Mind Sports was taking place. In 1997 the First Mind Sports Olympiad was held in London, attracting over 3,000 entrants from 50 countries. As the century turned, four Olympiads had been held (over 30,000 entrants from over 74 countries)! The Olympiads feature board, card and computer games, and all the major mental skills including Memory, Creative Thinking, Speed Reading, Intelligence and Mind Mapping.

MENTAL LITERACY

All these trends reflect the increasing international drive towards Mental Literacy, defined thus:

> Standard and numerical literacy involve an understanding of the alphabets of letters and numbers and their infinite permutations and combinations. Mental Literacy is an understanding of the alphabets of the biological and behavioural aspects of your brain, including especially the cortex, the brain cell, learning, memory and creativity.

The Mind Map Book, with its emphasis on the radiant biological and conceptual architecture of the brain, is an introduction to Mental Literacy, a concept which we hope will have profoundly positive effects on the individual, the family, the organisation, societies and civilisation in general.

1 *The Mentally Literate individual*

In our historically 'mentally illiterate state', the mind of the individual is imprisoned in a relatively small conceptual framework, without the use of even the most primary Mental Literacy tools with which to help expand this conceptual framework. Even traditionally 'well-educated' and literate individuals are significantly restricted by the fact that they are able to use only a fraction of the biological and conceptual thinking tools which are available.

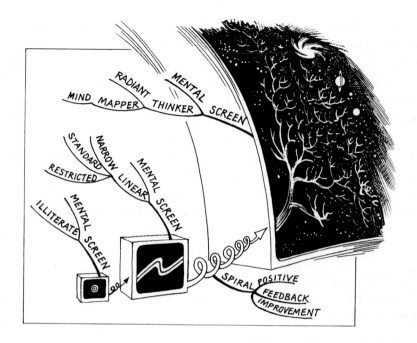

Illustration showing relative sizes of the 'mental screens' of the illiterate, linear and radiantly thinking minds. The radiant thinker's automatic self-enhancing feedback loop allows the screen the possibility of becoming infinitely large (see below).

Cognitive amplification

The Mentally Literate human is capable of turning on the radiant synergetic thinking engines, and creating conceptual frameworks and new paradigms of limitless possibility. The illustration above shows the 'mental screens' of the illiterate, the linear, and the Radiant Thinking mind. It can be seen that this last screen, by the nature of the intellectual machinery which drives it, continues to grow with an infinite possibility for size and dimension. It is the Radiant Thinker's automatic self-enhancing feedback loop which allows this massive intellectual freedom, and which reflects the inherent ability of each individual's brain – a formidable powerhouse, compact, efficient and beautiful, with potentially limitless horizons.

Applying Radiant Thinking principles to the brain enables you to range more freely among the major intellectual activities of making choices, remembering and creative thinking. Knowing the architecture of your thinking allows you to make choices and decisions using not only your conscious mental processes, but also your paraconscious – those vast continents, planets, galaxies and mental universes waiting to be explored by those who are Mentally Literate.

The Mentally Literate individual is also able to see the vital powerhouses of memory and creative thinking for what they really are: virtually identical mental processes that simply occupy different places in time. Memory is the re-*creation* in the present, of the past. Creativity is the projection, from the present, into the future, of a similar mental construct. The conscious development of memory or creativity through Mind Maps automatically increases the strength of both.

The most effective way for the individual to develop Mental Literacy skills, and to amplify the cognitive screen, is to follow the Radiant Thinking guidelines outlined in Chapter 10 (page 91). The guidelines are a training ground for the development of mental skills such as those used by the 'Great Brains' (see Chapter 2, page 39, and the Addenda, 'Notes by the Great Brains' Quiz, pages 302–312). Indeed Leonardo da Vinci, arguably the greatest all-round user of mental abilities, devised a four-part formula for the development of a fully functioning, Mentally Literate brain that reflects these guidelines perfectly.

Leonardo da Vinci's Principles for the Development of a Mentally Literate Mind

1 *Study the science of art.*
2 *Study the art of science.*
3 *Develop your senses – especially learn how to see.*
4 *Realise that everything connects to everything else.*

In modern Mind Mapping terms, da Vinci was saying to the individual:

'*Develop all your cortical skills, develop the entire range of your brain's receiving mechanisms, and realise that your brain operates synergetically and is an infinite and radiant association machine in a radiant universe.*'

By applying the Mind Map guiding principles and da Vinci's laws, the brain can develop its own individual expressions, exploring undreamed of domains. As Professor Petr Anokhin continued, after the quote in Chapter 1, page 31:

'*There is no human being alive or who has ever lived who has even remotely explored the full potential of the brain. We therefore accept no restrictive limitations on the potential of the human brain – it is* infinite!'

---

2 *The Mentally Literate family*

In a Mentally Literate family, the emphasis will be on growth, communication, learning, creativity and love, in a context in which each family member realises and cherishes the miraculous, radiant and indescribably complex individuals who are the other members of that same family. As John Rader Platt has said:

> *'If this property of complexity could somehow be transformed into visible brightness so that it would stand forth more clearly to our senses, the biological world would become a walking field of light compared to the physical world. The sun with its great eruptions would fade to a pale simplicity compared to a rose bush, an earthworm would be a beacon, a dog would be a city of light, and human beings would stand out like blazing suns of complexity, flashing bursts of meaning to each other through the dull night of the physical world between. We would hurt each other's eyes. Look at the haloed heads of your rare and complex companions.*
>
> *Is it not so?'*

It is so.

3 *The Mentally Literate organisation*

In the future, we hope the Mentally Literate organisation, whether it be a club, a school, a university or a business, will be seen in the context of an extended family, guided by the same principles, understandings and visions.

We have already, in the early 1990s, begun to see the first dramatic signs. The Brain Trust, an international charity for all those who wish to learn how to use their brains, has established Use Your Head 'cells' in ten different countries, and publishes a magazine called Use Your Head/*Synapsia*, the international Use Your Head Club Journal.

In schools, a growing number of teachers and students are becoming involved in Mental Literacy, and at Eton, the famous English public school, the school's Brain Club has, in its first year, 300 members! (See page 298.)

Meanwhile, students at Durham University, led by James Lee, have formed a club devoted to the promotion of Mental Literacy, and established a network throughout the entire English university system.

In the business world too, the trend towards Mental Literacy is accelerating. In addition to the numerous examples given in Chapters 25 (page 245), 26 (page 252) and 27 (page 261), both professional business writers and thinkers are reaching the same conclusions. Peter Drucker, in his book *Innovation and Entrepreneurship*, predicted that 'the manager of the future will simply be a

Mind Map by Jonathan Montagu of Eton College, outlining seminar weekend (see page 297).

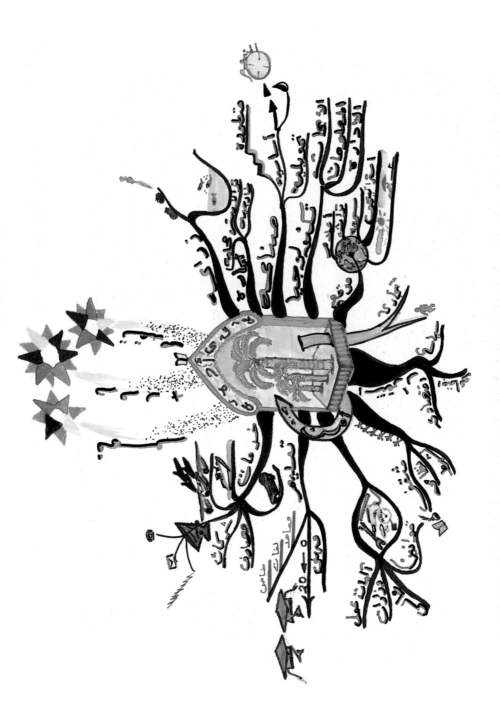

Mind Map by Sheikh Talib outlining a plan for a Mentally Literate society (see pages 300–301).

learning guide', while John Naisbitt, in *Megatrends 2000*, summarised ten trends for the human race as it approaches the millennium by identifying the metatrend underlying all the megatrends: *'Learning how to learn is what it's all about'*. See Chapter 26 (Mind Map, page 258).

Almost identically, Alvin Toffler (the author of *Future Shock*) in his new book *Power Shift* says, 'The illiterate of the future will no longer be the individual who cannot read. It will be the person who does not know how to learn how to learn.'

4   *The Mentally Literate society*

With increasing numbers of Mentally Literate individuals, families and organisations, we will soon see the dawning of Mentally Literate societies.

Realising the importance of this trend and its implications, the United States Senate recently declared the 1990s the 'Decade of the Brain', stating:

'Resolved by the Senate and House of Representatives of The United States of America in Congress assembled, that the decade beginning January 1, 1990, hereby is designated the "Decade of the Brain", and the President of The United States is authorised and requested to issue a proclamation calling upon all public officials and the people of The United States to observe such decade with appropriate programs and activities.'

This initiative has already had considerable effect. Apart from encouraging further research and exploration into the brain, companies such as EDS have initiated 'Education Outreach' programmes promoting Mental Literacy. We have also seen the launch of the Education 2000 programme, searching for new ways of understanding the brain's ability to learn, establishing life-long learning programmes throughout the country, and researching the future needs of schools. In addition an intellectual climate has been created in which the brain increasingly features on radio and television programmes and in the general media.

Societies are considering both the general impetus of the 'Decade of the Brain', as well as such specific initiatives as that of the Venezuelans in creating a 'Minister for the Development of Human Intelligence'.

The Mind Map on page 299, done by Sheikh Talib the Arabian philosopher and thinker, outlines a plan for the development of a Mentally Literate society. Demonstrating its pan-linguistic nature, the Mind Map covers the stabilising roots of education, economy and politics, and includes the other major factors of agriculture, services, operating mechanisms, industry, communication and marketing.

On the right-hand side of the Map, 'Information Technology' is emphasised because it is becoming more and more important in the way modern societies communicate and conduct business. On the left-hand side of the Map, the 'Education' branch shows two eyes with hats on them facing each other.

As Sheikh Talib says:

'This is a strong depiction for the need to educate the educators. This task has been neglected by many countries who fail to see the enormous importance of it. A good plan can only be successful if modifications can be applied at any stage. Therefore, the plan should be flexible and dynamic; it must be alive.'

One of the interesting things about this particular Mind Map is that, during the early stages, a young waitress took a quick look at it, and when asked what she thought she saw, replied: 'It's a picture about making a better world.' She did not read the Arabic language, nor did she know beforehand what the subject was. This is a clear and vivid example of the success of the Mind Map as a basic communication tool, and of the importance of the application of research on how a human brain works.

5 *A Mentally Literate civilisation*

From the development of a literate society it is only a single step to the development of a Mentally Literate civilisation. Indeed, at the dawn of the 21st century, The Brain Trust Charity took that step, by proclaiming the 21st century to be the Century of the Brain and the third millennium to be the Millennium of the Mind. If you wish to find out more about this initiative, and to join others of similar mind, search for the virtual petition on *www.msoworld.com*. With the explosion of Radiant Thinking through the computer, satellite and media networks, we are taking the first steps towards a global information structure that begins to mimic that of an embryonic brain. It thus becomes increasingly possible to envision a planet in which communication and understanding become faster and more complex while simultaneously becoming more accessible and understandable. We are beginning to move towards the realisation of the philosopher Olaf Stapledon's vision, in *Star Maker,* of a global brain some four million years hence:

'In the true racial experience the system of radiation which embraces the whole planet, and includes the million million brains of the race, becomes the physical basis of a racial self. The individual discovers himself to be embodied in all the

bodies of the race. He savours in a single intuition all bodily contacts, including the mutual embraces of all lovers. Through the myriad feet of all men and women he enfolds his world in a single grasp. He sees with all eyes, and comprehends in a single vision all visual fields. Thus he perceives at once and as a continuous, variegated sphere, the whole surface of the planet.

But not only so.

He now stands above the group-minds as they above the individuals. He watches them as one might study the living cells of his own brain; but also with the aloof interest of one observing an ant hill; and yet again as one enthralled by the strange and diverse ways of his fellow-men; yet chiefly as the artist who has no thought but for his vision and its embodiment.

In the racial mode a human apprehends all things astronomically. Through all eyes and all the observatories, he beholds his voyaging world, and peers outward into space. Regarding the solar system simultaneously from both limbs of his world, he perceives the planets and the sun stereoscopically, as though in binocular vision. Further, his perceived "now" embraces not a moment but a vast age.'

Is it possible for us to even *begin* to approach such a Mentally Literate future? *The Mind Map Book* suggests that it is.

RADIANT THINKING – RADIANT FUTURE

In order to examine the possibilities, it is necessary to return momentarily from the cosmos to the cortex, and to search for Rader Platt's beacons of hope in the welter of discouraging news about economics, pollution and the general global state. If we are to achieve a complete understanding of our current situation, and a more realistic interpretation of our future, it is necessary to look very closely at the single factor which most dramatically affects all future possibilities. This crucial factor is *not* the general environment, nor is it the theories of economics or psychology, nor even the 'basic aggressiveness of mankind', nor the 'irreversible tide of history'. The main, almost blindingly obvious factor is that which has been the subject of *The Mind Map Book*, and which in large part records, controls and directs the rest of the equation: the Radiant Thinking human brain.

In our increasing understanding of this incredibly complex and mysterious organ, in our increasing understanding of the family of mankind – ourselves and our radiant fellow humans – and in our increasing understanding of the inter-connectedness and relativity of all things, lies our hope for the future.

IT CAN BE SO.

SO BE IT!

ADDENDA

NOTES BY THE GREAT BRAINS QUIZ

The addenda features 17 notes by great thinkers from the fields of politics, the military, architecture, art, poetry, science and literature.

They show that it is natural for an advanced intelligence to use a greater than average range of cortical skills. They are included here, for your information and entertainment, in the form of a quiz. It is suggested that you leaf through them, attempting to identify which great thinker made which note. At the time of going to press, the highest score on this quiz was 7 out of 17!

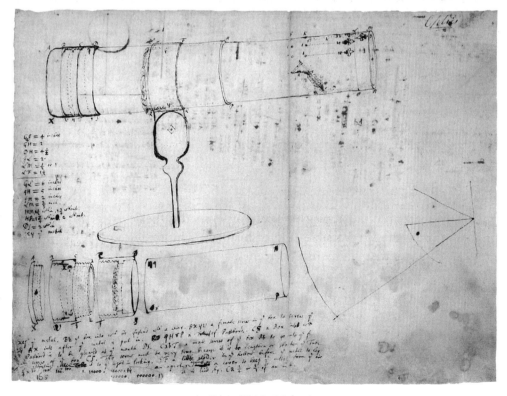

Great Brain Note A

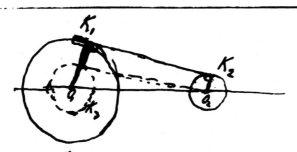

The radius of K_3 is the difference $r_3 = r_1 - r_2$.

The tangent $O_2 \rightarrow K_3$ is $\parallel$ to the tangent on K_1 and K_2 and can be easily constructed. This gives the solution.

A. E.

Great Brain Note B

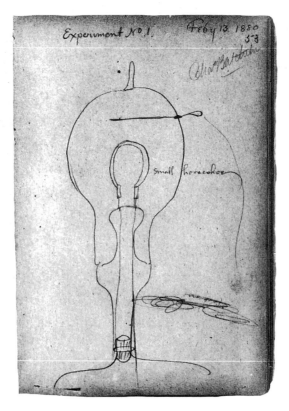

Great Brain Note C

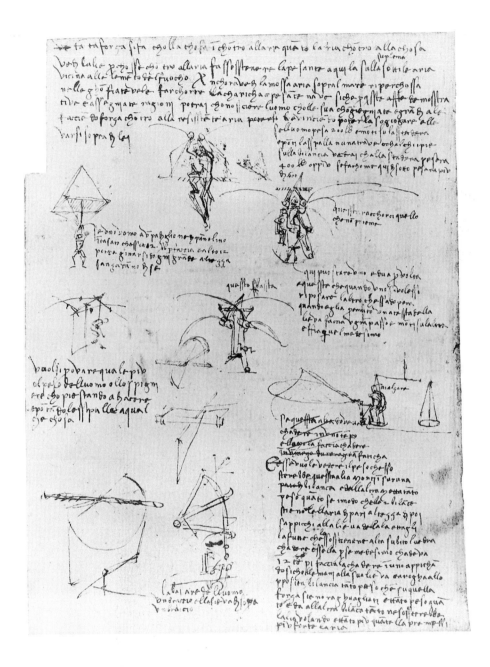

Great Brain Note D

In the annexed designe of this experiment

ABC represents the Prism set endwise to light, close by the hole F of the window EG. Its verticall angle ACB may conveniently be about 60 degrees. MN designes the lens. Its breadth 2½ or 3 inches. ST one of the straight lines in wch difform rays may be conceived to flow successively from the Sun. TP & TR two of those rays unequally refracted, which the Lens makes to converge towards Q, & after decussation to diverge again. And HI the paper at divers distances on which the colours are projected: which in Q constitute whitenesse, but are red & yellow in R, r, & ρ; & blew & purple in P, p, & π.

If you proceed further to try the impossibility of changing any uncompounded colour wch I have asserted in the 3d & 13th propositions; 'tis requisite that the Room be made very dark, least any scattering light mixing wth the colour disturb & allay it & render it compound contrary to the designe of the experiment. 'Tis also requisite that there be a further separation of the colours then after the manner above described can be made by the refraction of one single Prism; & how to make such further separations will scarce be difficult to them that consider the discovered laws of refraction. But if tryall shall be made wth colours not throughly seperated, there must be allowed changes proportionable

Great Brain Note E

Great Brain Note F

Great Brain Note G

Great Brain Note H

Great Brain Note I

Great Brain Note J

Great Brain Note K

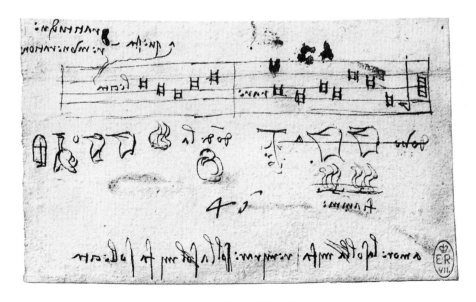

Great Brain Note L

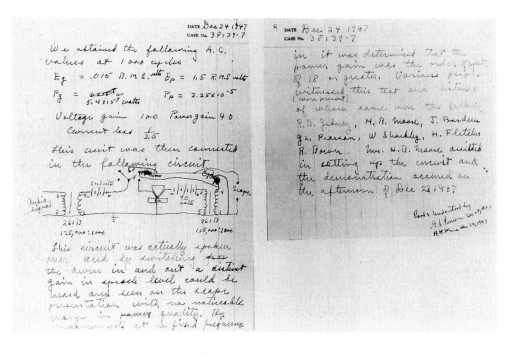

Great Brain Note M

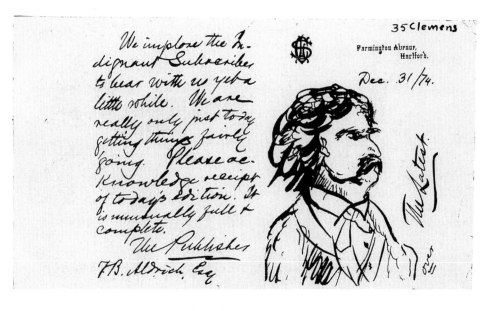

Great Brain Note N

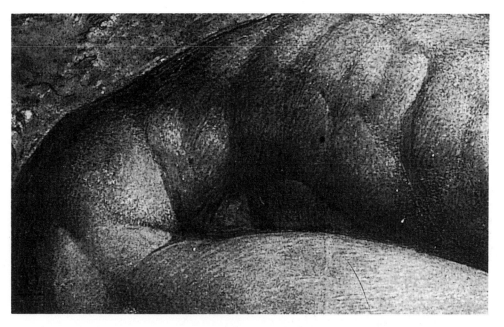

Great Brain Note O

Great Brain Note P

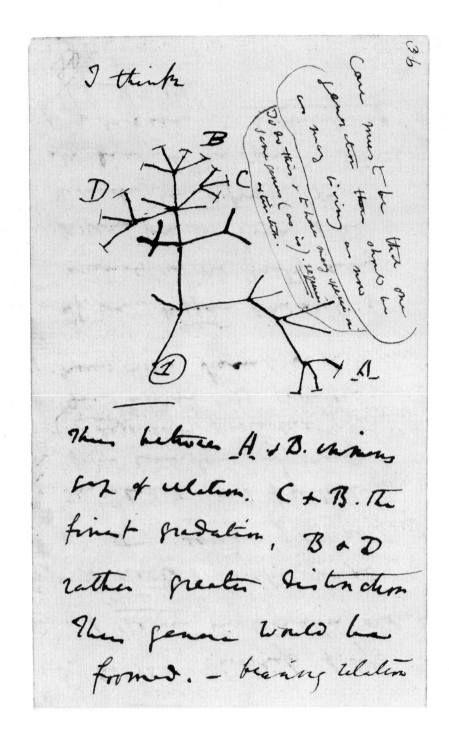

Great Brain Note Q

ANSWERS TO NATURAL ARCHITECTURE PLATES QUIZ

ANSWERS TO GREAT BRAINS QUIZ

ALSO BY TONY BUZAN

BOOKS

Buzan Bites:
Mind Mapping
Speed Reading
Brilliant Memory

The Mind Set:
Use Your Head
Use Your Memory
Master Your Memory
The Speed Reading Book
The Mind Map® Book
THE ILLUSTRATED MIND MAP BOOK
Embracing Change

Other titles:
How to Mind Map
The Ultimate Thinking Tool that will change your life.

The Power of Social Intelligence
10 ways to tap into your social genius.

The Power of Verbal Intelligence
10 ways to tap into your verbal genius.

Head Strong
Use your brain to help you to improve your physical fitness.

The Power of Creative Intelligence
10 ways to tap into your creative genius.

The Power of Spiritual Intelligence
10 ways to tap into your spiritual genius.

Head First!
10 ways to tap into your natural genius.

Mind Maps for Kids
The shortcut to major success at school.

BOOKS WITH OTHER AUTHORS
Lessons from the Art of Juggling
By Michael J. Gelb and Tony Buzan
Juggling is a delightful metaphor for living and learning. In *Lessons from the Art of Juggling*, you'll discover the secrets of transforming failure and mastering the art of relaxed concentration. Learn to juggle and learn to learn.

Get Ahead
By Vanda North with Tony Buzan
A practical, easy and inviting introduction to Tony Buzan's Mind Mapping. How to apply it to your life to 'Get Ahead' quicker.

Brain Power for Kids
By Lana Israel with Tony Buzan
Lana, the 1994 Brain Trust Brain of the year, explains how to make schoolwork easier by using the Mind Map originated by Tony Buzan. She explains how to Mind Map and apply mind mapping to reports, essays, research and note-taking to increase your brain power.

AUDIO TAPES

Buzan on the Brain
Buzan on Memory
Buzan on Radiant Thinking & Creativity
Buzan on Mind Mapping®
Buzan on Reading
Buzan on Success
Buzan on Mind and Body

In the Buzan on ... audio series, Tony Buzan is questioned by Vanda North on a range of relevant topics.

Each audio is 45 minutes of fast-paced Buzan wisdom, ending with ten Action Points for improvement in that specific area.

VIDEO TAPES

If At First ...
(One video of 25 minutes with booklet)
Many organisations say they encourage risk-taking and making mistakes. Many individuals say they embrace it. But it is not simple to cast aside an anxiety we've carried since our first year at school. In *If At First ...*, Tony Buzan helps us to bring those deep feelings to the surface. He helps us look at fear of failure as an event on our learning curve. The film gives rise to group discussions that shift people's attitudes and stimulate the free flow of ideas. It encourages all of us to give our very best.

Mindpower
(2 videos of 25 minutes each)
Mind Mapping applications for today's business. In the BBC's new technologically superb video-led course, Tony Buzan teaches you how to use Mind Maps to clarify your thinking and make better use of your mental resources. Includes one trainer workbook and participant workbooks. Additional participant workbooks are available in packs of five.

Developing Family Genius (4 tapes of 70 minutes each)

A complete, entertaining and highly participative course for the entire family or individual, where Tony Buzan introduces you to the wonders of the human brain. Learn how to learn: think; remember; read fast with comprehension; study effectively and easliy take and pass exams. Covers state-of-the-art information on the brain.

Get Ahead (60 minutes with booklet)
In this fun-to-watch video, Tony introduces Lana Israel, a sixteen year old student. Lana takes students on a step-by-step demonstration of how to apply Mind Mapping to improve study, revise for exams and enhance memory.

OTHER PRODUCTS

Mind Maps® Plus Software Programme
The new computer thinking tool may be used on any PC compatible with VGA running DOS. The first Mind Map computer programme doubles creativity, allows flexible and instantaneous manifestation of ideas and logs levels of thought. Can translate to linear for the non-Mind Map Literate.

Mind Map® Pads/Kits
Each printing of a Mind Map pad is frontispieced with a limited edition Mind Map. Collect them all! The kit contains an A3 and A4 pad, a packet of felt-tipped pens and highlighters.

Body and Soul Poster
Master Mind Map style poster, a limited edition poster depicting, in a surrealist manner, all the principles of Radiant Thinking. This beautiful picture is called *Body and Soul* and each numbered copy is signed by the Swedish artist, Ulf Ekberg. (Size 85 × 67 cms.)

SEM[3]
User-friendly laminated chart of the Self-enhancing Master Memory Matrix to enable the *Master Your Memory* reader to memorise up to 10 000 items with ease.

The Universal Personal Organiser (UPO)
This unique approach to self/time-management is a diary system, based on the techniques created and taught by Tony Buzan and the Buzan Centres. The Universal Personal Organiser is a living system that grows with you, and gives a comprehensive picture of your life, your desires, and your business and family functions.

The Mind Map Map
Unfolded, this simple introduction to Mind Maps offers a 'How To' and 'Question and Answer' on one side and a beautiful multi-coloured Mind Map on 'Mind Mapping' on the other.

TRAINING COURSES IN MENTAL LITERACY AND RADIANT THINKING

Full range of Radiant Thinking skills for study, work and life includes courses prepared for:
- Individuals from five years of age upwards
- Families of any size
- Clubs, organisations, committees,
- People of *any* intellectual level of ability
- Learners from beginner to advanced levels, especially 'Learning Disabled'.
- Corporations of any size, including the board and directors, managers, and all staff.

There are Five Radiant Thinking Training Programmes

Radiant Thinking
This foundation course allows you tap the full creative potential of your brain. Application of the Mind Map® process to a range of life and business needs, i.e. problem solving; studying; communication and planning; including creative thinking and memory.

Radiant Remembering
Practical application of the memory principles, to all the major systems for remembering data, lists, names and faces and anything else!

Radiant Reading
Practical application of information about the eye and brain to manage all kinds of reading material with speed, efficiency, comprehension and appreciation. Climb over that stack of information. Make informed decisions.

Radiant Speaking
Three leaders in the field give step-by-step practical applications for effective speaking with confidence and enjoyment under any circumstances.

Radiant Selling
BrainSell from one-brain-to-another the way in which you would want to be sold. A new revolution in selling techniques.

RADIANT THINKING TRAINING PROGRAMME FORMATS

Open Introductory Radiant Thinking Programmes
Usually conducted over a weekend, and covering Mind Mapping®, Radiant Thinking, Reading and Memory.

Open Radiant Thinking programmes

One day, including a course book, focusing on either Radiant Thinking (Mind Maps®), Remembering, Reading, Speaking or Selling.

Company Radiant Thinking

Radiant Thinking Courses are specially customised to be applicable immediately for groups of ten (+) in any one or more of the Radiant Thinking Programmes. The five courses are created to stand alone, to be combined with each other or existing company courses.

Radiant Thinking Instructor Programmes

In-depth training, licensing you to teach the Radiant Thinking Programmes. Pre-course preparation prior to a full week of training. Competency based. Certification through to full diploma.

For full information on:
- Training courses in the new Radiant Thinking / remembering / reading / speaking / selling programmes, or
- Products to learn how to learn

Contact:

The Buzan Centres Limited

54 Parkstone Road, Bournemouth, Dorset BH15 2PG, U.K.

Telephone: +44 (0)1202-674676

FAX: +44 (0)1202-674776

buzan@buzancentres.com
www.Mind-Map.com

The Buzan Centres USA Inc.,

PO Box 4, Palm Beach, Florida 33480, U.S.A.

Telephone: +1 (561) 881-0188

BIBLIOGRAPHY

Aiken, E.G., Thomas, G.S., and **Shennum, W.A.** 'Memory for a lecture: Effects of notes, lecture rate, and information density.' *Journal of Educational Psychology* **67** (3), 439–44, 1975.

Anderson, J.R. *Cognitive Psychology and Its Implications.* Second edition. New York: W.H. Freeman & Co., 1985.

Anderson, J.R. 'Retrieval of propositional information from long-term memory.' *Cognitive Psychology* **6**, 451–74, 1974.

Anokhin, P.K. 'The Forming of natural and artificial intelligence'. *Impact of Science on Society, Vol. XXIII* **3**, 1973.

Ashcraft, M.H. *Human memory and cognition.* Glenview, Illinois: Scott, Foresman & Co., 1989.

Atkinson, Richard C., and **Shiffrin, Richard M.** 'The Control of Short-term Memory'. *Scientific American*, August 1971.

Baddeley, Alan D. *The Psychology of Memory.* New York: Harper & Row. 1976.

Bever, T. and **Chiarello, R.** 'Cerebral dominance in musicians and non-musicians.' *Science* **185**, 137–9, 1974.

Bloch, Michael. 'Improving Mental Performance' biographical notes. Los Angeles: Tel/Syn 1990.

Borges, Jorge Luis. *Fictions* (especially 'Funes, the Memorious'). London: Weidenfeld & Nicolson, 1962.

Bourne, L.E., Jr., Dominowski, R.L., Loftus, E.F., and **Healy, A.F.** *Cognitive Processes.* Englewood Cliffs, NJ: Prentice-Hall Inc., 1986.

Bower, G.H., and **Hilgard, E.R.** *Theories of Learning.* Englewood Cliffs, NJ: Prentice-Hall Inc., 1981.

Bower, G.H., Clark, M.C., Lesgold, A.M., and **Winzenz, D.** 'Hierarchical retrieval schemes in recall of categorized word lists.' *Journal of Verbal Learning and Verbal Behavior* **8**, 323–43, 1969.

Breznitz, Z. 'Reducing the gap in reading performance between Israeli lower- and middle-class first-grade pupils,' *Journal of Psychology* **121** (5), 491–501, 1988.

Brown, Mark. *Memory Matters.* Newton Abbot: David & Charles, 1977.

Brown, R., and **McNeil, D.** 'The "Tip-of-the-Tongue" Phenomenon'. *Journal of Verbal Learning and Verbal Behavior* **5**, 325–37.

Bugelski, B.R., Kidd, E., and **Segmen, J.** 'Image as a mediator in one-trial paired-associate learning,' *Journal of Experimental Psychology* **76**, 69–73, 1968.

Buzan, Tony. The Mind Set. Incorporates a smaller format edition of *The Mind Map Book*, plus revised and updated editions of *Use Your Head, Use Your Memory, Master Your Memory* and *The Speed Reading Book*. All revised editions published by BBC Worldwide, London, 2000.

Head First!, The Power of Creative Intelligence, The Power of Spiritual Intelligence, The Power of Social Intelligence, The Power of Verbal Intelligence, Head Strong, How to Mind Map, Mind Maps for Kids. All London: Harper Collins, 2003

Buzan, Tony. WH Smith GCSE Revision Guides (60).

Carew, T.J., Hawkins, R.D., and **Kandel, E.R.** 'Differential classical conditioning of a defensive withdrawal reflex in Aplysia Californica,' *Science* **219**, 397–400, 1983.

Catron, R.M., and **Wingenbach, N.** 'Developing the potential of the gifted reader.' *Theory into Practice,* **25** (2), 134–140, 1986.

Cooper, L.A., and **Shepard, R.N.** 'Chronometric studies of the rotation of mental images. In Chase, W.G. (Ed.) *Visual Information Processing.* New York: Academic Press, 1973.

Daehler, M.W., and **Bukatko, D.** *Cognitive Development.* New York: Alfred A. Knopf, 1985.

Domjan, M. and **Burkhard, B.** *The Principles of Learning and Behavior.* Monterey, Cal.: Brooks/Cole Publishing Co., 1982.

Dryden, Gordon and **Vos, Jeanette** (Ed.). *The Learning Revolution.* California; Jalmar Press, 1993.

Edwards, B. *Drawing on the Right Side of the Brain.* Los Angeles: J. P. Tarcher, 1979.

Eich, J., Weingartner, H., Stillman, R.C., and **Gillin, J.C.** 'State-dependent accessibility of retrieval cues in the retention of a categorized list.' *Journal of Verbal Learning and Verbal Behaviour* **14**, 408–17, 1975.

Erickson, T.C. 'Spread of epileptic discharge,' *Archives of Neurology and Psychiatry* **43**, 429–452, 1940.

Fantino, E., and **Logan, C.A.** *The Experimental Analysis of Behavior: A Biological Perspective.* San Francisco; W.H. Freeman & Co., 1979.

Frase, L.T., and **Schwartz, B.J.** 'Effect of question production and answering on prose recall,' *Journal of Educational Psychology* **67** (5), 628–35, 1975.

Freidman, A., and **Polson, M.** 'Hemispheres as independent resource systems: Limited-capacity processing and cerebral specialisation,' *Journal of Experimental Psychology: Human Perception and Performance* **7**, 1031–58, 1981.

Gawain, S. *Creative Visualization.* Toronto: Bantam Books, 1978.

Gazzaniga, M. 'Right hemisphere language following brair. bisection: A 20-year perspective.' *American Psychologist* **38** (5), 525–37, 1983.

Gazzaniga, M. *Mind Matters.* Boston: Houghton Mifflin Co., 1988.

Gazzaniga, M. *The Social Brain.* New York: Basic Books Inc., 1985.

Gazzaniga, M. and **DeDoux, J.E.** *The Integrated Mind.* New York: Plenum Press, 1978.

Gelb, Michael J., *How to Think Like Leonardo da Vinci.* Delacorte Press, 1998.

Gelb, Michael and **Buzan, Tony.** *Lessons from the Art of Juggling.* USA; Crown Harmony 1994.

Glass, A.L., and **Holyoak, K.J.** *Cognition.* New York: Random House, 1986.

Godden, D.R., and **Baddeley, A.D.** 'Context-dependent memory in two natural environments: On land and under water,' *British Journal of Psychology* **66**, 325–31, 1975.

Good, T.L., and **Brophy, J.E.** *Educational Psychology.* New York: Holt, Rinehart and Winston, 1980.

Greene, R.L. 'A common basis for recency effects in immediate and delayed recall,' *Journal of Experimental Psychology: Learning, Memory and Cognition* **12** (3), 413–18, 1986.

Greenfield, Susan. *Brainpower: Working out the Human.* Element Books, 2000.

Greenfield, Susan. *Human Brain: A Guided Tour.* Phoenix, 2000.

Grof, S. *Beyond the Brain: Birth, Death, and Transcendence in Psychotherapy.* New York: State University of New York Press, 1985.

Haber, Ralph N. 'How We Remember What We See'. *Scientific American,* 105, May 1970.

Halpern, D.F. *Thought and Knowledge: An Introduction to Critical Thinking.* Hillsdale, NJ: Erlbaum, 1984.

Hampton-Turner, C. *Maps of the Mind.* New York: Collier Books, 1981.

Hearst, E. *The First Century of Experimental Psychology.* Hillsdale, NJ: Lawrence Erlbaum Associates, 1979.

Hellige, J. 'Interhemispheric interaction: Models, paradigms and recent findings. In D. Ottoson (Ed.) *Duality and unity of the brain: Unified functioning and specialization of the hemispheres.* London: Macmillan Press Ltd., 1987.

Hirst, W. 'Improving Memory.' In M. Gazzaniga (Ed.) *Perspectives in memory research.* Cambridge, Mass.: The MIT Press, 1988.

Hooper, J., and **Teresi, D.** *The Three-pound Universe.* New York: Dell Publishing Co. Inc., 1986.

Howe, M.J.A. 'Using Students' Notes to Examine the Role of the Individual Learner in Acquiring Meaningful Subject Matter.' *Journal of Educational Research* **64**, 61–3.

Hunt, E., and **Love, T.** 'How Good Can Memory Be?' in A.W. Melton and E. Martin (Eds.) *Coding Processes in Human Memory.* Washington DC: Winston/Wiley, 1972.

Hunter, I.M.L. 'An exceptional memory.' *British Journal of Psychology* **68**, 155–64, 1977.

Kandel, E.R., and **Schwartz, J.H.** 'Molecular biology of learning: Modulation of transmitter release.' *Science* **218**, 433–43, 1982.

Keyes, Daniel. *The Minds of Billy Milligan.* New York: Random House, 1981.

Kimble, D.P. *Biological Psychology.* New York: Holt, Rinehart and Winston Inc., 1988.

Kinsbourne, M., and **Cook, J.** 'Generalized and lateralized effects of concurrent verbalization on a unimanual skill,' *Quarterly Journal of Experimental Psychology* **23**, 341–5, 1971.

Korn, E.R. 'The use of altered states of consciousness and imagery in physical and pain rehabilitation,' *Journal of Mental Imagery* **7** (1), 25–34, 1983.

Kosslyn, S.M. *Ghosts in the Mind's Machine.* New York: W.W. Norton & Co., 1983.

Kosslyn, S.M. 'Imagery in Learning.' In M. Gazzaniga (Ed.) *Perspectives in Memory Research.* Cambridge, Mass.: The MIT Press, 1988.

Kosslyn, S.M., Ball, R.M., and **Reiser, B.J.** 'Visual images preserve metric spatial information: Evidence from studies of image scanning,' *Journal of Experimental Psychology: Human Perception and Performance* **4**, 47–60, 1978.

LaBerge, S. *Lucid Dreaming.* New York; Ballantine Books, 1985.

LaPorte, R.E., and **Nath, R.** 'Role of performance goals in prose learning.' *Journal of Educational Psychology,* **68**, 260–4, 1976.

Leeds, R., Wedner, E., and **Bloch, B.** *What to say when: A guide to more effective communication.* Dubuque, Iowa: Wm. C. Brown Co. Publishers, 1988.

Loftus, E.F. *Eyewitness Testimony.* Cambridge, Mass.: Harvard University Press, 1979.

Loftus, E.F., and **Zanni. G.** 'Eyewitness testimony: The influence of wording of a question.' *Bulletin of the Psychonomic Society* **5**, 86–8, 1975.

Luria, A.R. *The Mind of a Mnemonist.* London: Jonathan Cape, 1969.

Madigan, S.A. 'Interserial repetition and coding processes in free recall.' *Journal of Verbal Learning and Verbal Behavior* **8**, 828–35, 1969.

Matlin, W.M. *Cognition.* New York: Holt, Rinehart & Winston Inc., 1989.

Mayer, R.E. *Thinking, problem solving, cognition.* New York: W.H. Freeman & Co., 1983.

Mendak, P.A. 'Reading and the Art of Guessing.' *Reading World* **22** (4), 346–51, May 1983.

Miller, G.A. 'The magical number seven, plus or minus two: Some limits on our capacity for processing information.' *Psychological Review* **63**, 81–97, 1956.

Miller, W.H. *Reading Diagnosis Kit.* West Nyack, NY: The Centre for Applied Research in Education, 1978.

Neisser, U. *Memory Observed: Remembering in Natural Contexts.* San Francisco: W.H. Freeman & Co., 1982.

Nelson, T.O. 'Savings and forgetting from long-term memory.' *Journal of Verbal Learning and Verbal Behavior* **10**, 568–76, 1971.

North, Vanda. *Get Ahead.* Buzan Centres Limited.

Ornstein, R. *The Psychology of Consciousness.* New York: Harcourt Brace Jovanovich, 1977.

Paivio, A. 'Effects of imagery instructions and concreteness of memory pegs in a mnemonic system,' *Proceedings of the 76th Annual Convention of the American Psychological Association,* 77–8, 1968.

Paivio, A. *Imagery and Verbal Processes.* New York: Holt, Rinehart & Winston Inc., 1971.

Penfield, W., and **Perot, P.** 'The Brain's Record of Auditory and Visual Experience: A Final Summary and Discussion.' *Brain* **86**, 595–702.

Penfield, W., and **Roberts, L.** *Speech and Brain-Mechanisms.* Princeton, NJ: Princeton University Press, 1959.

Penry, J. *Looking at Faces and Remembering Them: A Guide to Facial Identification.* London: Elek Books, 1971.

Recht, D.R. and **Leslie, L.** 'Effect of prior knowledge on good and poor readers' memory of text.' *Journal of Educational Psychology* **80** (1), 16–20, 1988.

Reid, G. 'Accelerated learning: Technical training can be fun.' *Training and Development Journal* **39** (9), 24–7, 1985.

Reystak, R.M. *The Mind.* Toronto: Bantam Books, 1988.

Rickards, J.P., and **DiVesta, F.J.** *Journal of Educational Psychology* **66** (3), 354–62, 1974.

Robertson-Tchabo, E.A., Hausman, C.P., and **Arenberg, D.** 'A classical mnemonic for older learners: A trip that works!' In K.W. Schaie and J. Geiwitz (Eds.) *Adult development and aging.* Boston: Little, Brown & Co., 1982.

Robinson, A.D. 'What you see is what you get.' *Training and Development Journal* **38** (5), 34–9, 1984.

Rogers, T.B., Kuiper, N.A., and **Kirker, W.S.** 'Self-reference and the encoding of personal information.' *Journal of Personality and Social Psychology* **35**, 677–88, 1977.

Rosenfield, I. *The Invention of Memory: A New View of the Brain.* New York: Basic Books Inc., 1988.

Rossi, E.L. *The Psychobiology of Mind-Body Healing: New Concepts of Therapeutic Hypnosis.* New York: W.W. Norton & Co., 1986.

Ruger, H.A., and **Bussenius, C.E.** *Memory.* New York: Teachers College Press, 1913.

Russell, Peter. *The Brain Book.* London: Routledge & Kegan Paul, 1979.

Schachter, S., and **Singer, J.E.** 'Cognitive, social and physiological determinants of emotional state.' *Psychological Review* **69**, 377–99. 1962.

Schaie, K.W., and **Geiwitz, J.** *Adult Development and Aging.* Boston: Little, Brown & Co., 1982.

Siegel, B.S. *Love, Medicine and Miracles.* New York: Harper & Row, 1986.

Skinner, B.F. *The Behavior of Organisms: An Experimental Analysis.* New York: Appleton-Century-Crofts, 1938.

Snyder, S.H. *Drugs and the Brain.* New York: W.H. Freeman & Co., 1986.

Sperling, G.A. 'The information available in brief visual presentation.' *Psychological Monographs* 74, Whole No. 498, 1960.

Sperry, R.W. 'Hemispheric deconnection and unity in conscious awareness.' *Scientific American* 23, 723–33, 1968.

Springer, S., and **Deutch, G.** *Left Brain, Right Brain.* New York: W.H. Freeman & Co., 1985.

Standing, Lionel. 'Learning 10,000 Pictures.' *Quarterly Journal of Experimental Psychology* 25, 207–22.

Stratton, George M. 'The Mnemonic Feat of the "Shass Pollak",' *Physiological Review* 24, 244–7.

Suzuki, S. *Nurtured by love: a new approach to education.* New York: Exposition Press, 1969.

Tart, C.T. *Altered States of Consciousness.* New York: John Wiley & Sons Inc., 1969.

Thomas, E.J. 'The Variation of Memory with Time for Information Appearing During a Lecture.' *Studies in Adult Education,* 57–62, April 1972.

Toffler, A. *Power Shift: knowledge, wealth and violence in the twenty first century.* London: Bantam Books, 1992.

Tulving, E. 'The Effects of Presentation and Recall of Materials in Free-Recall Learning.' *Journal of Verbal Learning and Verbal Behaviour* 6, 175–84.

Van Wagenen, W., and **Herren, R.** 'Surgical division of commissural pathways in the corpus calloseum.' *Archives of Neurology and Psychiatry* 44, 740–59, 1940.

von Restorff, H. 'Über die Wirkung von Bereichsbildungen im Spurenfeld.' *Psychologische Forschung* 18, 299–342.

Wagner, D. 'Memories of Morocco: the influence of age, schooling and environment on memory.' *Cognitive Psychology* 10, 1–28, 1978.

Walsh, D.A. 'Age difference in learning and memory.' In D.S. Woodruff and J.E. Birren (Eds.) *Aging: Scientific perspectives and Social Issues.* Monterey, Cal.: Brooks/Cole Publishing Co., 1975.

Warren, R.M., and **Warren, R.P.** 'Auditory illusions and confusions.' *Scientific American* 223, 30–6, 1970.

Wolford, G. 'Function of distinct associations for paired-associate performance,' *Psychological Review* 73, 303–13, 1971.

Yates, F.A. *The Art of Memory.* London: Routledge & Kegan Paul, 1966.

Zaidel, E. 'A response to Gazzaniga: Language in the right hemisphere: Convergent perspectives.' *American Psychologist* 38 (5), 542–6, 1983.

INDEX